REVELATION'S
Predictions
FOR A
New Millennium

MARK A. FINLEY
Speaker/Director
It Is Written Television

HART BOOKS
A MINISTRY OF HART RESEARCH CENTER
FALLBROOK, CALIFORNIA

Edited by Herbert E. Douglass, Th.D.
Page Design and Composition by
Linda Anderson McDonald
Cover art direction and design by Ed Guthero
Cover illustration by Darrell Tank
Body text set in 10.5/13 Times New Roman

ISBN: 1-878046-55-1

Contents

This book is a an adaptation
of Mark Finley's sermons
presented in his
international satellite seminar,
Revelation of Hope.

For more information
about the It Is Written Television Ministry,
and to receive a broadcast schedule,
please call (800) 253-3000.
or visit us at the web at www.iiw.org.

1
REVELATION'S PREDICTIONS FOR THE NEW MILLENNIUM

The new millennium has dawned. Millions of people are developing a new interest in prophecy. They are asking, "What on earth will happen next?" They wonder, "Where in the world are we headed?" They are fascinated with the future. They are curious about the uncertainty of world events now unfolding. They are desperately looking for answers. According to a recent Newsweek magazine poll, forty percent of all Americans (that's over 120 million people in the United States alone) believe the world will end in a dramatic, cataclysmic battle called Armageddon, between Jesus and the Antichrist.

For the last 30 years, interest in the future has been dramatically growing. In the 1970s the best selling book of the decade was Hal Lindsey's *The Late Great Planet Earth,* with 28 million copies sold by 1990. More recently, a series of novels titled, *Left Behind,* by Tim LaHaye and Jerry Jenkins, including two published in 1999, have sold nine million copies. These novels use the book of Revelation as their base.

Movie producers have jumped on board this prophetic end-time train roaring into the future. The smash-hit film, *The Omega Code,* grossed 2.4 million in its opening weekend. The last days have become popular entertainment.

Over 239 web sites are multiplying end-time scenarios.

The November 1, 1999 edition of *Newsweek* magazine's front cover shouted the words, "Prophecy—what the Bible says about the end of the world."

It is not only Christians who are concerned about end events.

♦ Jews believe that the world will be ushered into a final sequence of events which will ultimately liberate Israel from the bondage of its oppressors. They are convinced the Messiah will come in glory to defeat all their foes and establish the kingdom of God with Jerusalem at the center of this new kingdom.

♦ The Moslems also are looking for an apocalyptic end of the world. They believe the Battle of Armageddon will soon take place followed by the last conflict. In their view, Jesus and Imin, one of Mohammed's descendants, will fight against the Antichrist.

Bernard McGinn, a specialist at the University of Chicago Divinity School says, "Over the past 30 years more scholarship has been devoted to apocalypticism (last-day events) than in the last 300."

The tempo is picking up. Interest in the future is at an all-time high. People are desperate for answers. They are anxious for some word about the future. Unfortunately, millions are searching in all the wrong places. Millions are turning to so-called psychics to discover answers to their questions regarding the future.

See what one psychic seer predicted would occur early in 1999. Nostradomus, who many believe was the world's greatest seer, wrote from France 500 years ago in the 16th century. He made hundreds of predictions.

"Clashes among racial, ethnic and nationalist groups in Eastern Europe climax with the use of nuclear weapons. Millions are not only feared dead—they are dead. What used to be considered European civilization is an increasingly distant memory."

Obviously, this prediction simply did not occur. It utterly failed.

Here is a prophecy from Edgar Cayce, called "the sleeping prophet," who died in 1945:

"There will be a major financial crash in January of 2000. Vicious ice and electrical storms will rake the United States and Western Europe killing a million or more senior citizens and other innocent people who lost their homes or incomes in the January crash."

Another psychic prophecy which utterly failed.

Here's a predication from another reputed futurist, Janice Seymour:

"Terrorists will attack New York City with Sarin, the deadliest nerve gas known to man. So many citizens are already dead (by April, 2000) from violence and disease that a death toll is never established."

Another failed predication.

Read the next two so-called prophecies.

"The earth's magnetic poles show signs of becoming unstable, suggesting the beginning of a polar shift that will literally knock the planet on its ear, turning north to south and east to west in a matter of days" *(Great Pyramid Prophecy)*.

"The hole in earth's ozone layer quadruples in size exposing virtually the entire southern hemisphere to lethal levels of ultraviolet radiation and sparking the mass migration north of more than a billion people" *(An Ancient Mayan Prophecy).*

All of these prophecies were supposedly to occur early in the year 2000. They all have a common thread: Destruction is on the way. Disaster is just around the corner. Disease and death will walk hand in hand through our streets.

Is there any hope for tomorrow? How can we face the future with greater confidence? Is the outlook for the future that pessimistic? Where is there some reliable source of information?

The Bible has proven reliable throughout the centuries. Its prophecies have gradually unfolded down through the ages. Unlike the failed predications of the psychics, the prophecies of the Bible have been fulfilled with uncanny accuracy for the last 3,500 years.

One of the clearest evidences of the Bible's inspiration is the ability to foretell future events. Fulfilled Bible prophecy verifies the truthfulness of God's word. God does not guess. He knows!

The prophet Isaiah put it this way:

"Remember the former things of old, for I am God, and there is no other. I am God and there is none like me, declaring the end from the beginning and from ancient times things that are not yet done" (Isaiah 46:9,10).

The prophet Amos adds these incredible words:

"Surely the Lord God will do nothing, unless

He reveals His secret to His servants the prophets" (Amos 3:7).

The word "surely" means certainly, definitely, without a doubt. Here is something we can rely upon. When we look into the future we are not staring in the dark.

The apostle Peter echoes His assurance in these words:

"We also have the prophetic word made more sure which you would do well to heed as a light that shines in a dark place, until the day-dawns and the morning star arises in your hearts" (2 Peter 1:19).

Of all the books of the Bible which shed light on the last days, the Bible's last book, Revelation, is the most complete. In Revelation, God unfolds amazing last-day events which will dramatically affect you and me. Revelation's incredible predications guide us through the maze of false prophecies so common in our world.

The Revelation unfolds the plans of God and unmasks the plans of Satan. Of all the books of the Bible none has stimulated more discussion and fired the imagination more than Revelation. Even some biblical scholars are mystified in trying to unravel the meaning of:

◆ The four horsemen of the apocalypse.
◆ The heavenly book with seven mysterious seals.
◆ The harlot woman riding on a scarlet-colored beast.
◆ The magnificently beautiful woman in white standing on the moon with a crown of 12 stars on her head.
◆ The deceitful Antichrist, the mark of the beast and the mysterious number 666.
◆ The seven last plagues and the Battle of Armageddon.

The Bible deciphers the prophetic code. You can be prepared for the future as never before. As we open the book of Revelation together, a new confidence and certainty will be yours. Revelation's mysteries will be solved. The pieces will fit together like a puzzle and you will see yourself in the picture of a glorious tomorrow.

A SOURCE OF RELIABLE INFORMATION

Let's begin with the first verse of Revelation:

> "The revelation of Jesus Christ—which God gave to Him to show His servants—things which must shortly take place. And he sent and signified it by His angel to His servant John" (Revelation 1:1).

The title of the book means "a revealing," or "unfolding." Some people believe the book of Revelation is closed. Others believe it is too complicated to understand. The very title of the book indicates something is about to be revealed, not something to be kept hidden.

In the last chapter of this last book of the Bible, the angel tells the author of the book, John the apostle:

> "Do not seal the words of the prophecy of this book, for the time is at hand" (Revelation 22:10).

Revelation's prophecies are not sealed. They are not closed. The angel expressly said, "Do not seal the words of the prophecy of this book."

His revelation comes with the signature of God's approval: it is the revelation of Jesus Christ. Let's go back to our first verse again:

> "The Revelation of Jesus Christ, which God gave Him to show His servants-things which must shortly take place. And He sent and sig-

nified it by His angel to His servant John"
(Revelation 1:1).

Where did Jesus get it? From God!

Who did Jesus give it to? His angel.

What did the angel do with it? Brought it to John.

John wrote it in His book called Revelation "to show
His servants [God's people] things which must shortly take
place" (Revelation 1:1, 2).

The book of Revelation is not some personal opinion
or some psychic's view of the future. Its prophecies come
directly from God. It has the signature of heaven. God himself offers a triple blessing for those who study His book:

> "Blessed is he who *reads* and those who *hear* the
> words of this Prophecy, and *keep* those things
> which are written in it" (Revelation 1:3, italics
> supplied).

The prophecies of Revelation are life-changing. Your
life will be changed for the good forever as you study
Revelation. That's God promise.

Every book has a central theme. Here is Revelation's
key theme:

> "Grace to you and peace from Him who is and
> who was and who is to come." Revelation 1:4

Jesus "was"—

> He existed with the Father from eternity. He is
> the eternal Christ. Jesus was – He came to
> earth as our Redeemer, our Savior, our Lord.

Jesus "is" —

> He is alive, resurrected from the dead. He is
> our friend. He understands. He cares. Jesus is.

Jesus is "to come" —

> He is coming to take us home. All of creation is standing on tiptoe awaiting the coming of the King. That's the theme of the book of Revelation.

John adds:

> "Behold, He is coming with clouds, and every eye will see Him" (Revelation 1:7).

Russel Baker, a popular newspaper columnist, failed to grasp this end-time hope. His view of the future was foggy. Without Revelation's hope of this Jesus who is to come, Baker wrote these words:

> "I am sitting 93 million miles from the sun on a rounded rock which is spinning at the rate of a thousand miles an hour, roaring through space to no one knows where, to keep a rendezvous with nobody knows what, for nobody knows why.

> "And all around me whole continents are drifting aimlessly over the planet. I am sitting here on this spinning, speeding rock surrounded by four billion people, eight planets, one awesome lot of galaxies, nuclear bombs enough to kill me 30 times over, and mountains of handguns and frozen food, and I am being swept along in the whole galaxy's insane dash toward the far wall of the universe.

> "And as I sit here, 93 million miles from the sun (alone), I am feeling absolutely miserable."

The book of Revelation climaxes with the greatest

event in the history of the ages—the coming of Jesus.

- ◆ We are not cosmic orphans.
- ◆ Our planet is not destined for self-destruction.
- ◆ We will not be reduced to some spinning globe of nuclear-holocaust, ash.
- ◆ Famine and pestilence will not have the final word on a planet struggling for survival.
- ◆ Earthquakes, tornadoes, fires and floods will not dash our hopes and destroy our joy of an eternal tomorrow.
- ◆ Heart disease and cancer will no longer claim their victims.
- ◆ Tears, disappointments and heartache will come to an end.

In chapter 5, John describes a mysterious scroll and an awesome judgment scene, but the prophecy ends with all of the redeemed praising God, singing:

> "Blessing and honor and glory and power be to him who sits on the throne, and to the Lamb, forever and ever" (Revelation 5:13)!

Beyond all of earth's end-time heartaches, the saved are singing songs of deliverance. They have been redeemed!

In Revelation, chapters 6 and 7, seven cryptic seals are opened one after another. A time of great tribulation bursts upon the world, but look how the scene ends:

> "These are the ones who come out of the great tribulation. . . .Therefore they are before the throne of God, and serve Him day and night in His temple" (Revelation 7:14, 15).

The tribulation does not destroy them. They come

through unscathed with their faith stronger, praising God.

In Revelation 8 and 9, seven trumpets of tragedy blow. One disaster follows another in rapid succession throughout history. The judgments of God fall upon the earth. Disaster follows disaster. But the seventh angel sounds:

> "The kingdoms of this world have become the kingdoms of our Lord and His Christ, and He shall reign forever and ever" (Revelation 11:15)!

Every one of Revelation's prophecies ends in the same place—a place called eternal hope and joy. The book of Revelation is a Revelation of Hope.

Beyond the natural disasters, beyond conflict between nations, beyond famines, beyond ethnic conflicts and escalating worldwide political tension, beyond an uncertain economy, there is hope.

> Hope in a new society.
> Hope in a new leader.
> Hope in the coming of the Lord.

The 13th chapter of Revelation foretells the rise of the powerful Antichrist power. It unfolds a time when no man can buy or sell. It discusses the mark of the beast and the mysterious number 666. But in Revelation 14, at the end of this sequence, the apostle shouts with joy:

> "And I looked, and behold, a white cloud, and on the cloud sat One like the Son of Man, having on His head a golden crown, and in His hand a sharp sickle" (Revelation 14:14).

John looks away from the beast. He does not focus his attention on an economic boycott when no man can buy or sell. He is not seized with terror as the result of an international death decree. He looks and sees Jesus returning in glory. The aged apostle is secure in the blessed hope.

The book of Revelation ends with the coming of our Lord! In Revelation 19, "He is the King of Kings and Lord of Lords." Revelation's ending is dramatic, awesome, and glorious:

> "And God shall wipe away every tear from their eyes; there shall be no more death, nor sorrow, nor crying; and there shall be no more pain, for the former things have passed away" (Revelation 21:4, 5).

The Almighty God triumphantly proclaims throughout the whole universe:

> "Behold, I make all things new" (Revelation 21:5).

God will create a new world, and He can "make all things new in your life." This powerful, almighty God, who gives us hope as we face the future, longs to fill our heart with hope. He longs to make all things new in your life. He can place within your heart—

◆ a new sense of joy.
◆ a new sense of purpose.
◆ a new sense of spiritual power.
◆ a new sense of forgiveness and mercy.
◆ a new sense of happiness.

Would you like to say with me:

> "Oh, God—the God who will create a new heaven and earth—make my heart new also!" ❏

2
Revelation's Greatest End-Time Signs

On September 8, 1985, 16-year-old Sean Sellers and a companion entered the Circle K convenience store in Oklahoma City and opened fire on Robert Bowers, the 35-year-old clerk minding the store.

Sean described the murder to Jerry Johnston, a Christian author, in these words: "I squeezed the trigger and heard him scream. I hit him. He was still living, he got back up and my friend cut him off. I guess he got confused, because he ran almost right into me. He almost knocked me down. And when he was just about two feet from me, I squeezed the trigger again and the bullet entered through his heart and through his lungs. Blood was completely splattered on the opposite wall and he hit the ground. Then we walked out. We didn't take any money. We didn't take any merchandise. We just took the life of an innocent man for Satan."

Sellers states that he laughed after shooting Bowers. Giggling, he said, "Like it was a fantastic prank since he'd had no clue what we'd come there for." A friend said Sellers admitted he wanted "to see what it felt like" to kill somebody.

The 16-year-old killer wasn't even a suspect in the case until six months later when he killed his parents. He was angry at his mother because of her interference in his relationship with his girlfriend, a high school dropout. He said he had performed an occult ritual beforehand and, "There was nothing but cold hatred in me."

On the evening of March 5, 1986, Sean entered the bedroom of his parents and shot his father in the head while he slept. Next, he pointed the gun at his mother's head and squeezed the trigger. Her head raised up, he shot her a second time, and he walked out. Sean took a shower, got dressed, and went to a friend's house for some sleep.

For years, Sean Sellers was the youngest man on death row in the state of Oklahoma. Then, on February 4, 1999, just a little over a year ago, Sean Sellers, was executed by lethal injection, the first US murderer put to death in 40 years for crimes committed at age 16.

Did that story shock you? Did it surprise you? Probably not. Because if you've been reading your own daily newspaper, you're probably beyond being shocked at what evil hearts of men and women are capable of doing.

When did it come to this? When did our society quit enjoying the "Leave It To Beaver" show and become transformed into a lawless world that knew no bounds?

Long ago, Jesus sat on a hillside with His disciples and predicted such a time as this. In Matthew 24 the disciples came to Jesus privately. They asked Him, "What will be the sign of Your coming, and of the end of the age" (24:3)?

Here, Jesus outlined the signs which would precede His Second Coming. In addition, these signs in miniature would precede the destruction of Jerusalem in the first century. In 70 AD, Titus, the Roman general, attacked, overthrew, and totally devastated the city of Jerusalem.

Jesus used the Roman destruction of Jerusalem by fire as a symbol of the final destruction of the world by fire. The events which led up to the destruction of Jerusalem would be present at the end-time on a much larger, grander, more magnificent scale before Jesus' return in the end-time.

Here is something amazing. When we compare Jesus' prediction in Matthew 24 with the predictions in the book of Revelation, they provide an incredibly accurate picture of our day.

He was speaking about events of our time.

Signs in the world of religion.

Signs in the world of politics.

Signs in the world of nature.

Signs in the world of social life.

And today, these signs are being played out in the headlines splashed across our daily newspapers. Let's examine each of these signs individually.

SIGNS IN THE WORLD OF RELIGION

Jesus said:

> "For *many* will come in My name, saying, 'I am the christ,' and will deceive many" (Matthew 24:5 emphasis supplied).

Many will come saying they are Christ and will deceive many. He said that in the end-time's trauma and uncertainty—thousands in their search for meaning would turn to *cults*. They would turn to false christs and false prophets. Claiming to be prophets, these false christs would deliver messages they said were from above and recruit many to follow them. Jesus continued:

> "For false christs and false prophets will arise and show great signs and wonders" (Revelation 21:4, 5).

Read how the Book of Revelation confirms this prediction: "He performs great signs, so that he even makes fire come down from heaven on earth in the sight of men. And he deceives those who dwell on the earth by those signs which he was granted to do in the sight of the beast" (Revelation 13:13, 14).

Deception is part of Satan's plan:

> "For they are the spirits of demons performing signs, which go out to the kings of the earth and of the whole world to gather them to the battle of that great day of God Almighty" (Revelation 16:14).

One thing is for certain—these false christs will not come with a sign around their necks saying, "We are false christs and false prophets." They will simply lead, and those who are looking for a leader will follow.

False religions have increased phenomenally in our generation. Books on the occult and astrology are selling in the multimillions throughout America. Universities offer students classes in ESP, psychic phenomena, and the occult. Many young people who were raised in Christianity have cast aside the truths of their youth and are being drawn to spiritualism and the occult. Cults are recruiting those who are searching.

In March, 1997, 39 members of the Heaven's Gate cult produced a farewell video and then took their own lives. They believed that trailing the Hale-Bopp comet was a spacecraft coming to take them to the next level. The victims were found with purple cloths over their heads and shoulders.

In trying to identify the 39 bodies, police set up a toll-free number for relatives to call. In 24 hours, they fielded calls from over 1500 anguished relatives who had been out of contact with their loved ones for months or even years and suspected they might be part of the cult.

Jim Jones of the People's Temple who led nearly

1000 to their death in the jungles of Guyana as they drank cyanide laced Kool-Aid.

David Koresh led his followers to a fiery death in Waco, Texas.

Or think of those Swiss cults whose members burned themselves to death or a Japanese cult's planning nerve-gas attacks on Japanese subways.

Cults are everywhere, proclaiming they have messages from God, seeking to control the mind, deceiving those who would believe. There are Bible-based cults, UFO cults, Satanist cults, New Age cults, Eastern cults.

When Sean Sellers killed the convenience store clerk and six months later, his parents, he had been participating in rituals invoking demons to enter his body. He would speak to the demons and say, "My body is a sanctuary for you, please come in." Is it any wonder he did what he did?

Fortunately, he became a Christian and began a religious ministry from prison. "All I want to be is a Christian, Christlike," he wrote in his Internet journal. "I dream of heaven." But his stay of execution was denied, and 29-year-old Sean Sellers died for Satanic acts committed when he was a mere boy.

The Bible predicts a mighty false revival just before the coming of Jesus. There will be increased interest in astrology and communication with the dead. Over two thousand newspapers in the United States now carry astrology columns. Psychics are commonplace in storefronts— guiding participants through channeling, ESP, auras, crystal balls and palm reading.

Or over the phone—you can call 1-900 numbers and psychics will tell your future—for a fee. You can click on Internet sites and be guided through numerology, tarot cards and dream interpretations.

In these last days, it is important to know the Bible truth—because if you don't stand for something, you'll fall for something.

SIGNS IN THE WORLD OF POLITICS

Jesus continued:

> "And you will hear of wars and rumors of wars. . . . For nation will rise against nation, and kingdom against kingdom" (Matthew 24:6, 7).

How many wars can you remember? World War I, World War II, the Korean War, the Vietnam War, the Arab-Israeli Wars, the war in Bosnia, the Gulf War, Kosovo, southern and northern Ireland, all over Africa from Rwanda and Somalia to the Sudan, the Congo. The list goes on and on. I found one source that estimates 180 million people have been killed in the 20th century—a far greater total than for any other century in human history.

Indeed, Jesus was right when He said there would be wars and rumors of wars, nation would rise against nation, kingdom against kingdom.

Speaking of our time, the Apostle Paul declared:

> "For when they will say, 'Peace and safety!' then sudden destruction comes upon them. . . . And they shall not escape" (1 Thessalonians 5:3).

Have you noticed how fragile peace treaties are these days? Peace treaties fail because they are based on frail human promises. When Jesus, the Prince of Peace, fills the heart with His peace, it makes a dramatic difference.

And do you think there is greater stability in the world since the demise of the Soviet Union? Actually, there is less. In August of 1999, 60 Minutes II aired a program about Russia's Secret Cities, revealing that between 1940 and 1960, Russia recruited thousands of people from all over the Soviet Union to live in 10 "secret cities." These cities have been closed off from the rest of the world—no one has been allowed in and the residents have not been allowed out. For years, the residents were given the best food, the best clothes, the best housing. While conditions throughout the Soviet Union were grim, the residents of the secret cities lived like kings.

What these people have been doing inside these secret cities has been called "The biggest threat to our national security today." Even as the US has downsized our nuclear weapons, these secret cities have continued to produce plutonium, the key ingredient in most nuclear weapons. Over the past 40 years, the factories in one city alone produced 40 tons of plutonium, enough for over 10,000 nuclear bombs.

Today, a secret Siberian city generates enough plutonium to make a nuclear bomb every three days. And this city, we are told, is built inside a mountain so that if everything else were destroyed by a nuclear bomb, the city would still be intact to make more nuclear bombs.

But that's not the scary part. It has been more than eight years since the Soviet Union collapsed, and during those eight years the economic conditions have been incredibly shaky. As a result, workers in these secret cities are not being paid on a regular basis. Some have not been paid for three, four, five months. These people are angry and feel betrayed. Most of all, these people are hungry.

According to US Energy Secretary, Bill Richardson, we know that terrorists and rogue governments have come to Russia seeking to buy plutonium to make nuclear bombs.

In September of 1998, six nuclear scientists published

an article in *The Bulletin of theAtomic Scientist* about the threat these nuclear cities pose. They said:

> "Nothing the United States does to build improved security systems is likely to be enough if the guards continue to go unpaid and the economies of these nuclear cities continue to collapse around them."

If we did not have the hope of the Bible, the hope that Jesus would come again soon, these would be scary times.

Notice how Revelation puts it:

> "The nations were angry and Your wrath has come, and the time of the dead, that they should be judged. And that You should reward Your servants the prophets and the saints. And those who fear Your name, small and great. And should destroy those who destroy the earth" (Revelation 11:18).

Jesus will come at a time when the human race has the capacity to destroy itself. With unchecked nuclear weapons, we now have the capacity for self-destruction. This is certainly one of the greatest signs of the coming of Jesus.

Broadcasting from Hiroshima in 1945 after the atomic bomb was dropped, William Ripley stated, "I am standing on the place where the end of the world began." What would Ripley say today—at a time of unprecedented nuclear power?

Jesus pointed forward to our day when He emphatically declared:

> "Men's hearts failing them from fear and the expectation of those things which are coming on the earth, for the powers of heaven will be shaken" (Luke 21:26).

But we do not have to be afraid. We will not be destroyed in a nuclear holocaust. These are signs that Jesus is coming. We can look beyond what's going on around us to what's going on above us.

SIGNS IN THE WORLD OF NATURE

Jesus turns His attention to the natural world: "There will be famines, pestilence, and earthquakes in various places" (Matthew 24:7).

Do we see famines today? Look to North Korea. In the last four years, North Korea has experienced the worst rainfall in the past century. As a result of massive flooding and landslides, North Korea is experiencing a famine of extraordinary proportions. Millions are facing starvation. The North Korean government estimates 55,000 people have died from the famine in the last three years. Non-governmental agencies place the toll as high as three million.

Look to Sub-Saharan Africa. The UN Food and Agriculture Organization reports nearly 10 million people are in need of emergency food. In Somalia alone, one million people are facing serious food shortages, with over 400,000 at risk of starvation.

Look to Afghanistan. More than one million people need food assistance in Afghanistan because of a sharp reduction in cereal production due to a shortage of irrigation water. The country relies on snow for irrigation and they had the mildest winter in 40 years.

Look to Jordan. They have been hit by the worst drought in decades, affecting hundreds of thousands of people. Food security for about one-quarter of the country's population of 4.75 million is now threatened.

The UN reported last fall that 15 countries were facing unfavorable prospects for their current crops, while a total of 38 countries faced shortfalls in food supplies that would require emergency food assistance.

Experts estimate that for more than a billion people in the world today, about a sixth of the world's population, chronic hunger is an ever-present part of daily life. Ten thousand people a day, or more than 3.5 million people per year, die of starvation.

"There will be famines and pestilences" Jesus said in Matthew 24:7. What are pestilences? They are strange diseases on crops or strange diseases that run rampant among human beings. Pestilences can be caused by nature or pestilences can be caused by the carelessness of human beings.

The Centers for Disease Control and Prevention cites that American industry emits more than 2.4 billion pounds of toxic pollutants into the atmosphere each year and that an estimated 50,000 to 120,000 premature deaths are associated with exposure to air pollutants. The air we breathe is filled with pestilences. Strains of diseases are developing a resistance to known antibiotics and new diseases for which science has not found a cure.

Jesus said there would be earthquakes in the last days. Today we have 4,000 seismograph stations in the world that record 12,000 to 14,000 earthquakes per year—that's approximately 35 earthquakes per day.

> Some earthquakes that caused significant loss of life are listed here by their location, date, magnitude and approximate number killed:

> Tangshan, China; July 28, 1976; 7.8 to 8.2; 240,000
> Yokohama, Japan; September 1, 1923; 8.3; 200,000
> Gansu, China; December 16, 1920; 8.6; 100,000

Northern Peru; May 31, 1970; 7.7; 70,000
Northwest Iran; June 21, 1990; 7.3 to 7.7; 50,000
Chillan, Chile; January 24, 1939; 8.3; 28,000
Northeast Iran; September 16, 1978; 7.7; 25,000
Northwest Armenia; December 7, 1988; 6.9;
    25,000
Guatemala; February 4, 1976; 7.5; 22,778
Valparaiso Chile; August 16, 1906; 8.6; 20,000
Central Mexico; September 19, 1985; 8.1; more
    than 9,500
Northeast Afghanistan; February 4, 1998; 6.1,
    5,000
Northern Iran; May 10, 1997; 7.1; 1,500

The "big one" is on its way scientists tell us. All of this is preliminary to the dramatic earth shaking events at the coming of our Lord.

All of nature seems to be out of control. Nature's storms and the unusual weather patterns shout at us that something out of the ordinary is going on.

The list of natural disasters goes on and on reminding us of Jesus' words: "Men's hearts failing them from fear and the expectation of those things which are coming on the earth" (Luke 21:26).

SIGNS IN THE WORLD OF SOCIAL LIFE

We've looked at signs in almost every area of life, signs abundantly fulfilled. But no signs are more obvious or inescapable than those in the social world.

Jesus plainly predicted: "But as the days of Noah were, so also will the coming of the Son of Man be. For as in the days before the flood, they were eating and drinking, marrying and giving in marriage, until the day that Noah entered the ark" (Matthew 24:7).

And what was life like in Noah's day? Moral values fell through the basement, marriage vows were broken, divorce was common, the social and moral fabric of society in Noah's day disintegrated. Standards that were once the norm, God's standards, were no longer accepted.

What about today? How is the moral fabric of society in the 21st century? I don't have to tell you—you know. Living together outside of marriage is commonplace. There isn't even a stigma attached to it in most social circles. It's almost expected.

The National Centers for Health Statistics reports that in 1940, 89,500 babies were born to unmarried women, or less than four percent of all births. The number more than doubled by 1955, then doubled again by 1970, and has tripled since then. Now 30.1% of all births in America are to unmarried women.

What about divorce rates? Between 1970 and 1996, the divorce rate quadrupled, from 4.3 million in 1970 to 18.3 million in 1996. The marriage rate has fallen nearly 30% since 1970 and the divorce rate has increased about 40%.

Today's culture says truth is a matter of taste, and morality is an individual preference. Society has lost its belief in objective right and wrong.

Like Noah's time, we live in a nation of violence. Recently *USA TODAY* conducted a survey: "What do you think is the best way to combat the wave of violence sweeping the nation?"

Violence is sweeping our nation. In April of 1999, two students wearing black trench coats, massacred 23 teachers and students at Columbine High School in Littleton, Colorado. All over the country there were copycat attempts.

And it's no wonder. Children watch an average of three hours of television per day and by the time they're

12, they've witnessed 1,400 murders on the tube. Between November 1996 to November 1998, the Parents Television Council says violence on prime time TV increased another five percent; foul language increased 30%; and sexual content increased 42%. No wonder our moral values are decaying! Children mimic what they see—and so do adults, for that matter!

Jesus must come soon or we will destroy our planet through pollution, we will destroy our society through nuclear bombs, we will destroy our culture through immorality and violence.

SIGNS IN THE WORLD OF KNOWLEDGE

In 1,500 places, the Bible predicts the time of the end and the Second Coming of Jesus. Tturn to the book of Daniel just for a moment. Daniel in the Old Testament and Revelation in the New are the great prophetic books of the Bible.

Every time you boot up your computer I want you to think of a prophecy in Daniel: "But you, Daniel, shut up the words, and seal the book until the time of the end; many shall run to and fro, and knowledge shall increase" (Daniel 12:4).

Knowledge about the prophecies of Daniel would be increased. Knowledge in general would increase.

Knowledge has never increased as fast as it does today.

In the medical world, delicate surgeries are per-formed today that weren't even dreamed of a decade ago. Astronomers know more about what's above us, geologists know more about what's beneath us, biolo-gists know more about what's within us. It is estimated that 80 percent of all the scientists who have ever lived are alive today. The scientific material they produce every 24 hours would take one person a lifetime to read.

Think of transportation. I know people who are reading this page may even remember traveling by horse and buggy. In your lifetime, you have seen the advent of the Model T and the first airplane. And you have seen the first man walk on the moon and all kinds of space shuttles catapulted into space. You've gone from fountain pens to E-mail. You've gone from party-line telephones to cell phones the size of your palm.

Not to mention the world of computers. Technology is growing so rapidly in that area that by the time the common person, like me, figures out how to use the computer he has, the technology is obsolete and the computer is outdated.

And not only is knowledge increasing exponentially, the accessibility of that knowledge is phenomenal. If you wanted to know something years ago, you had to go to a public library and spend hours of research, or go to a special medical library or law library.

Today, knowledge is accessible at the click of a button—a mouse button. Anything you want to know? Boot up your computer, log onto the Internet, and it's there.

In 1988, there were approximately 33,000 Internet host sites. Ten years later, by 1998, there were 36.5 million—a thousand percent increase in websites in 10 years. In a four-year time period from December 1994 to December 1998, America Online subscribers increased from 1.5 million to 15 million.

So tomorrow morning, when you log onto your computer, remember—that mouse button points to the hope we have in Jesus' soon return.

Daniel's prophecy—"and knowledge will increase"—is speaking especially of the knowledge of God's words, the truth about Jesus and His soon return.

The Bible predicts a powerful worldwide spiritual revival before the coming of Jesus:

> "And this gospel of the kingdom will be preached in all the world as a witness to all nations, and then the end will come" (Matthew 24:14).

The aged John, writing from a barren, rocky island in the Aegean Sea adds:

> "Then I saw another angel flying in the midst of heaven, having the everlasting gospel to preach to those who dwell on the earth—to every nation, tribe, tongue and people" (Revelation 14:6).

This is a remarkable prediction. Before the coming of Jesus, unprecedented doors of opportunity for the proclamation of the gospel will open around the world. Totalitarian regimes crumble; oppressive governments collapse; unusual doors to preach the gospel open. Miraculously, tens of thousands hear God's Word. I have seen these prophecies fulfilled before my eyes.

Imagine Russian Army trucks delivering 20,000 Bibles to the Kremlin Palace Congress Hall—The Palace of Atheism—for thousands to study God's Word.

Imagine thousands gathering in Moscow's Olympic Stadium to eagerly listen to the gospel.

Imagine preaching throughout the former Communist countries of Poland, Hungary, Yugoslavia and Romania to tens of thousands. These prophecies are being fulfilled in our day.

Recently, I conducted a series of gospel meetings in Bucharest, Romania in the former Congress Hall of Communism. These meetings were sent by satellite to over 200,000 people.

A spiritual revival has broken out in Africa. Millions of Africans are coming to Jesus. I personally witnessed thousands sitting in torrential downpours eagerly absorbing God's Word.

It's happening throughout South and Central America. Crowds are pouring into auditoriums and soccer stadiums to hear God's Word.

In Santiago, Chile, our meetings were held in the National Ministry of Defense building in the nation's capitol. So many people came the last night that the authorities locked the doors because the auditorium was so packed.

In India, scores of former Hindus are turning to God's Word. I watched as over 1,000 were baptized in Madras, India, recently.

God is doing something special in China. In spite of fierce persecution, the church continues to grow. God is on the move.

From the islands of the sea to the massive metropolitan cities, God is on the move. From poverty-stricken hovels to multi-million dollar mansions, God is on the move. Prophecy is being fulfilled. The prophetic signs of Jesus' soon return are being fulfilled all around us.

Is there anything in your life which would keep you from being ready for His soon return. Jesus longs to save you. He longs to have you live together with Him forever.

This is no ordinary time. God's final call is going out all over this planet. Millions around the world are responding. This is a day of opportunity. This is the time to prepare for His soon return. Why not fully commit your life to Him, right now? ❏

3
REVELATION'S BIGGEST SURPRISE

Have you heard of the competition going on right now for the X-Prize? At least fourteen individuals or companies have thrown their hats into the ring for the $10 million dollar prize. In case you're interested in joining them, here are the rules:

- ◆ Be the first group to launch three civilian passengers 62 miles into space.
- ◆ Return them safely and in good health as reasonably defined and judged by the X-Prize Review Board.
- ◆ Re-launch them fourteen days later using the same vehicle.
- ◆ You cannot use a government grant to build your space vehicle, and any goods or services you use must be available to other entrants on similar terms.
- ◆ You must notify the X-Prize Rules Committee of the take-off and landing location along with the date of the launch at least 30 days in advance, and you must carry on board an X-Prize-provided flight recorder to monitor the flight profile and altitude achieved.
- ◆ No need to worry if you are not an American, the competition is international in nature and open to all qualifying entrants who agree to abide by the rules.

Are you ready to enter the competition? While some of us might laugh and think this is straight out of a Jetson's cartoon or the latest Star Wars movie, more than a dozen space visionaries are spending a substantial amount of time and money developing a strategy to win the $10 million dollar prize.

This contest is all part of the development of Space Tourism, a budding industry that expects to book us on space vacations within the next 10-20 years. One travel agent has already taken about 100 reservations, including a few customers who have put down $600,000 deposits in anticipation that space tourism will soon become a reality.

In 1999, half a dozen conferences were held around the world where space tourism was seriously discussed—in Japan, Germany, London, Amsterdam, Washington, D.C., and aboard the Queen Mary in California. They held seminars on dealing with pollution in space, developing global laws in space, real-estate claims in space, obligations of coming to the rescue of a vehicle in distress in space and studying physical and emotional reactions to being in space. There's a lot of nitty-gritty to be hammered out before space travel is possible!

If all of this intrigues you, you might want to begin saving now, because the estimated cost of the first of these vacations is $50,000.

If you are interested in space travel, and you don't have the $50,000 to invest in a week-long vacation, how about an eternity-long vacation that is being offered to you for free? God's ultimate reward for the redeemed is far more exciting than any journey on some multi-million dollar space shuttle.

John heard Jesus say:

> "And behold, I am coming quickly, and My reward is with Me, to give every one according to his work" (Revelation 22:12).

Christ offers us the ultimate space journey.

One of those chapters in the Bible that tells us when we should expect to take this journey is Daniel 2.

Speaking of Daniel's predictions, Jesus declared: "Whoever reads, let him understand" (Matthew 24:15).

If you want to understand the end-times, you must understand Daniel's prophecies. If you want to understand the book of Revelation, you must first understand Daniel's prophecies.

In Daniel 2 is an ancient prophecy that predicted who would rule the world, how each ruler would rise and fall, and how our world would eventually end. It began when Daniel was alive on earth—when a king dreamed of world events that spanned 2,500 years. Those events have come to pass with such precision that only the hand of God could have been involved. It is a prophecy that proves beyond a shadow of a doubt that God is in control of history. It is a prophecy that has been almost totally fulfilled—almost, but not quite. And when you look back over more than 2,000 years of prophecy that have been fulfilled, you can look ahead with assurance at the last little bit that remains to be fulfilled.

Let's listen to Daniel tell his story:

> "Now in the second year of Nebuchadnezzar's reign, Nebuchadnezzar had dreams; and his spirit was so troubled that his sleep left him" (Daniel 2:1).

Who was this Nebuchadnezzar who had dreams he couldn't remember? He was the king who ruled the great Babylonian Empire from the massive walled city of Babylon, more than 600 years before Christ. The city covered 500 acres on both sides of the Euphrates River.

This river flowed under the walls and through the city. Babylon was located in the area of the world known as the Fertile Crescent, which had an intricate system of canals that irrigated lush crop lands. Nebuchadnezzar is the king who built the luxurious Hanging Gardens—one of the Seven Wonders of the Word—for his wife who had been brought up in the mountains and now missed her homeland. In these terraced gardens, fragrant flowers and fruit trees blossomed and water cascaded through an extremely advanced system of drainage.

At the center of great Babylon, Nebuchadnezzar built a 300-foot shrine to the pagan god Marduk. He plated the walls and roof of the building with gold. The altar was solid gold. The throne and footstool were solid gold. Archaeologists estimate Nebuchadnezzar used eight and a half tons of gold in his shrine to Marduk.

Amid all of this opulence, success and power, Nebuchadnezzar had a dream he could not remember. I'm sure you can relate to Nebuchadnezzar's experience—waking up in the morning, knowing that you had a dream and trying in vain to remember it. But I doubt if you ever took it to the extreme that Nebuchadnezzar did. The Bible tells us that he called together his magicians, astrologers, sorcerers and Chaldeans and asked *them* to tell *him* what he had dreamt.

The Chaldeans replied:

> "O king, live forever! Tell your servants the dream, and we will give you the interpretation" (Daniel 2:4).

They figured they could analyze the dream and make up some sort of interpretation once they knew what the dream was. But interpretation wasn't yet the problem—remembering it was the first step!

King Nebuchadnezzar was upset. He saw through what they were trying to do. He demanded:

> "Tell me the dream, and I shall know that you
> can give me its interpretation" (Daniel 2:9).

If you can't tell me the dream, the King is saying, how am I supposed to trust you to give me its meaning! You're supposed to be able see into the future! Prove it to me now! Tell me what I dreamed.

The Chaldeans protested: "There is no man on earth who can do what you ask" The situation began to heat up, but Nebuchadnezzar would not back off. He knew his dream was important, and he wanted to know what it meant. He became so angry that he decreed that if the wise men could not tell him his dream and its interpretation, then all wise men in Babylon should be destroyed!

One of the men, Arioch the king's captain, was sent to kill Daniel. (Earlier, Daniel had been taken into captivity when Babylon attacked Jerusalem. Because he had been identified with other Hebrew young men as gifted in wisdom. He had been trained as a servant for the king and was recognized as a "wise man.") Now, when Daniel asked why he was to be killed, Arioch told him the story of the dream. The Bible says that Daniel went in to see the king and asked for time that he could pray to the God of heaven who reveals all secrets. He had utmost confidence that God would solve the problem —not confidence in himself that he could figure it out, but confidence in God to reveal it.

In a night vision, God *did* reveal the dream and its interpretation to his servant Daniel. Daniel prayed a wonderful prayer of thanks to God:

> "I thank You and praise You," he said. "You have

given me wisdom and might" (Daniel 2:20-23).

Daniel did not claim any of the glory for himself. He knew where his wisdom came from, and he was quick to give thanks to the God of heaven.

And then Daniel went in to see the king and he told him that no wise man, no astrologer, no magician, no soothsayer could reveal the dream. "But there is a God in heaven who reveals secrets," Daniel told the king, "and He has revealed to King Nebuchadnezzar what will be in the latter days." God was very clear with Daniel that the dream the king had dreamed actually revealed events that would occur in the last days of earth's history. It foretold events that would occur at the *close* of earth's history. The dream starts back in the days of Nebuchadnezzar, and it goes forth generation after generation after generation to the last days of earth's history.

Daniel went on to tell the king what he had dreamed:

> "You, O king, were watching; and behold, a great image! This great image, whose splendor was excellent, stood before you; and its form was awesome. This image's head was of fine gold, its chest and arms of silver, its belly and thighs of bronze, its legs of iron, its feet partly of iron and partly of clay. You watched while a stone was cut out without hands, which struck the image on its feet of iron and clay, and broke them in pieces. Then the iron, the clay, the bronze, the silver, and the gold were crushed together, and became like chaff from the summer threshing floors; the wind carried them away so that no trace of them was found. And the stone that struck the image became a

great mountain and filled the whole earth"
(Daniel 2:31-35).

The King was excited! "Yes, that's it! That's it!" he
cried. "That's *exactly* what I saw! But Daniel, what does it
mean?"

Does Daniel begin to stutter and say, "Well, I know
what you dreamed, but I don't know what it means"? Did
God bring him only halfway and leave him there? Of course
not! God told Daniel the dream and He told him the interpretation! This is a dream not only for Nebuchadnezzar, but
a vision for us as well, and God has made it simple for us
to understand. There is no guesswork. It is all spelled out
clearly. Note how Daniel began the interpretation:

> "You, O King, are a king of kings
> . . . . you are this head of gold" (Daniel 2:37,38).

History books tell us that the Babylonian Empire
was the dominant world power from 605 BC to 539 BC.
History books tell us that King Nebuchadnezzar's
kingdom was splashed with gold. Remember how lav-
ishly gold was used in Bel-Marduk's temple? In that one
temple alone, Nebuchadnezzar used 18 tons of gold.
There is no better way for God to describe the
Babylonian Empire than by using the symbolism of gold.

Nebuchadnezzar was happy with this interpretation.
He liked being the head of gold. He wanted the head of
gold to last forever, but that was not to be, for Daniel went
on. "After you shall arise another kingdom" (Verse 39).

At the time Nebuchadnezzar had this dream, he was
secure as the world leader, no reason to suspect that it
would not always be so. But he was to be overthrown by
a kingdom represented in Daniel 2:32 as "the chest and
arms of silver." Just a few pages ahead in your Bible,

Daniel 5:28, the next world-ruling power is referred to as the Medes and the Persians. Again, a fitting symbol: the two arms joined at the chest to show two kingdoms—Medes and Persians. The Medes and Persians ruled the world from 538 BC to 331 BC.

The story of how the Babylonians were overthrown is told in Daniel 5. King Belshazzar, grandson of King Nebuchadnezzar, hosted a feast for a thousand of his lords. He called for the gold and silver vessels captured from the temple in Jerusalem to be brought to him. From these holy vessels that had been used in temple services to worship the God of heaven, he drank wine. In the midst of this drunken party, a mysterious, bloodless hand appeared and wrote words on the wall: MENE, MENE, TEKEL, UPHARSIN.

The interpretation of these words, spelled doom for the mighty Babylonian Empire:

> "MENE: God has numbered your kingdom, and finished it; TEKEL: You have been weighed in the balances, and found wanting; PERES: Your kingdom has been divided, and given to the Medes and Persians" (Daniel 5:26-28).

That very night, the Medes and Persians diverted the Euphrates River that ran under the massive walls of Babylon. They marched their armies straight down the dry riverbed and came up inside the city. One hundred and fifty years in advance, Isaiah not only foretold, in chapters 44 and 45, exactly how Babylon would be overthrown, he named the leader of the army who would do it—Cyrus. They were overtaken in one night by the Medo-Persian army, led by Cyrus, just as the Bible predicted, just as Nebuchadnezzar saw in his dream.

The Medes and Persians ruled the world for nearly two centuries. But Nebuchadnezzar's dream doesn't end there, and neither does history. Time marches on, one kingdom replacing another kingdom, just as God foretold in the dream of Nebuchadnezzar.

The next kingdom is described in Daniel 2:32 as the belly and thighs of bronze. More than two hundred years in advance, Daniel actually names Greece as this third kingdom which overthrew the Medes and the Persians (Daniel 8:21). Once again, an appropriate representation. The Greek army was led by Alexander the Great, a young man who marched his men 11,000 miles, conquering almost all of the then-known world before he died of malaria at the age of 33. What did Alexander's men wear into battle? Bronze breastplates, bronze helmets, bronze shields, bronze swords. Once again, God chose a fitting metaphor to describe the kingdom that would rule the world from 331 BC to 169 BC.

But history doesn't end with this third kingdom. Greece did not rule the world forever, for there was a fourth metal after the gold of Babylon, the silver of the Medes and Persians, the bronze of Greece. The next kingdom is represented by iron:

> "And the fourth kingdom shall be as strong as iron" (Daniel 2:40).

The last kingdom to rule the entire known world is described as iron. In 168 BC the iron monarchy of Rome overthrew the Greeks.

So inescapably did the prophetic portrayal correspond to its historical fulfillment that the great English historian Edward Gibbon, though not a Christian or Bible-believer himself, wittingly or unwittingly used scriptural language in his monumental *History of the Decline and Fall of the Roman Empire* when he wrote:

> "The images of gold, or silver, or brass, that might serve to represent the nations and their kings, were successively broken by the iron monarchy of Rome."

Just as legs form the longest part of the body, Rome had the longest reign of any other of the world powers. Little by little, Rome rose to power, fighting many wars and enslaving many people. By the time Jesus was born, most of the then-known world was under Roman rule. You will remember that Joseph and Mary were on their way to pay taxes to the Roman ruler, Caesar Augustus, when Jesus was born.

For more than 500 years, Rome appeared to be invincible—her flag waving from the British Isles to the Arabian Gulf, from the North Sea to the Sahara Desert, from the Atlantic to the Euphrates and beyond.

But were the Romans the last ruling empire of the world? What did the Bible predict?

Daniel wrote:

> "Whereas you saw the feet and toes, partly of potter's clay and partly of iron, the kingdom shall be *divided*" (Daniel 2:41 emphasis supplied).

How did the Roman Empire break up? Was it overcome by another world power as had happened in the preceding thousand years? If this prophecy is to be right, it must predict what actually happened in history—that the legs of iron would *not* be succeeded by a fifth world-ruling power.

History confirms that this seemingly unconquerable Roman Empire crumbled for two reasons—from within and from without. From within—wealth poured into

Rome through taxes collected from all over the world. The simple Roman life was replaced with luxury and pomp. The political world brewed with corruption, crime infiltrated the streets, the work ethic was lost, sexual immorality was rampant. And as the mighty Roman Empire weakened from within, Rome was attacked from without and divided into ten major tribes.

Ten is not a coincidence. The God of the Bible looked down through the ages of history and foresaw this division of ten. Therefore, this time period of history is symbolized by the ten toes of Nebuchadnezzar's image. These ten tribes were the Alamanni who settled in what has become Germany, the Franks who settled in France, the Anglo-Saxons in England, the Visigoths in Spain, the Suevi in Portugal, the Lombards in Italy, and the Burgundians in Switzerland. Originally the Vandals, Ostrogoths, and Heruli took over parts of the Roman Empire, but they were eventually destroyed.

Daniel 2:42,43 predicted history from the time of the downfall of the Roman Empire to the end of time. No matter how many battles are fought around the world, no matter how many Hitlers try to conquer the world, no matter how many Napoleons, no matter how many Charlemagnes, no matter how many times men try to unite the world as one kingdom, they will not succeed. In vain world leaders seek to conquer the world. The Bible says that just as iron and clay will not mix together, so the world will not be united under one ruler again.

Why is it important that you know about the dream of an ancient king? Simply this—the image in Nebuchadnezzar's dream portrayed the time line of history down to our day. Once you realize that the Bible can be trusted with the past, you will know without a doubt that the Bible can be trusted with things still to come.

Where are we living today? In the toenails of history! Every part of this prophecy has come to pass except for one.

> "You watched while a stone was cut out without hands, which struck the image on its feet of iron and clay, and broke them in pieces. . . .The God of heaven will set up a kingdom which shall never be destroyed. . . . It shall break in pieces and consume all these kingdoms, and it shall stand forever" (Daniel 2:34,44).

History has followed this prophecy like a blueprint and will continue to do so. The political workings of this planet are not random. God has been guiding and controlling it all along, and only one kingdom remains to rule the world—God's kingdom. That rock, cut out without hands, is the one kingdom which will rule forever..

John, in Revelation speaks about this coming kingdom:

> "And there were loud voices in heaven, saying, 'The kingdoms of this world have become the kingdoms of our Lord and of His Christ, and He shall reign forever and ever" (Revelation 11:15)!

Today we can have hope, because tomorrow is in the hands of the same God who has been guiding history from one end of the time line to the other.

Do you want to some day explore space, but not as a tourist who has to return to earth? Do you want to see what's out there, but not with the hefty price tag of space tourism?

History has played itself out. There is only one

kingdom left to be established. Soon Jesus Christ, the Messiah, the one who paid such a remarkable visit to this planet 2000 years ago, is going to pay us another visit. And He is going to make a grand entrance the second time. The heavens will rumble with a great shout as trumpets blast and angels sing. Christ and the heavenly hosts will swoop down in a cloud of glory to gather together those who have been faithful. First the dead will rise up, and then the living, to be forever with the Lord.

It's coming! I plan to take this journey with Jesus.

It's coming! Commit to Jesus that you will be part of it.

It's coming! So be ready.

It's coming! So look up. ❏

4
REVELATION'S STAR WARS
THE BATTLE BEHIND THE THRONE

An interesting phenomena has been sweeping through this country during the last few years. It's especially apparent in Los Angeles, the entertainment capital of the world. This city is full of people dreaming of making it big, finding their starring role. But very different types of characters have been getting the spotlight lately. Who? Angels.

Angels have definitely made it to prime time. They star in a hit CBS series called "Touched By An Angel." They make appearances in feature films. They are the subject of several best-selling books.

Angels are one of the dominant themes of the book of Revelation. The book opens with Jesus sending His angel to John to reveal to him the truths of Revelation.

Angels reveal God's message in each age of human history to God's church in Revelation 2 and 3.

Four angels standing on the four corners of the earth hold back the final winds of destruction from totally devastating the earth before the coming of Jesus (Revelation 7).

Angels blow the trumpets of destruction in Revelation 8 and 9. A mighty angel comes down from heaven to encourage God's people and loudly proclaim God's last message for the world in Revelation 10.

Three angels are pictured swiftly carrying God's urgent, end-time message to "every nation, tribe, tongue, and people" (Revelation 14:6) to prepare them for the coming of Jesus.

Angels are major characters in the book of Revelation. They are heavenly beings commissioned by God, invisible to human eyes, but nonetheless real.

Revelation reveals a titanic struggle between good and evil, between Christ and Satan. Good angels exist, but so do evil angels.

Frank Peretti wrote a novel about angels that caused a sensation in Christian circles. The book, *This Present Darkness*, painted a graphic picture of the struggle between good and evil angels. The plot revolved around various characters in a small town and the moral choices they had to make. But the real action took place in the supernatural realm where the forces of good and evil battled.

Peretti did his best to imagine what that other, supernatural world might be like. I want to tell you about an angelic conflict outlined in Revelation that overshadows anything we human beings can imagine.

This battle is supremely important because it's really a battle about who God is. It's a battle about human destiny. And we're all involved, whether we realize it or not.

The book of Revelation tells us that a war broke out in heaven. Combat erupted in paradise. Angel armies lined up for a dramatic showdown.

Now, how can you have war in heaven? That seems impossible. But it happened:

> "And war broke out in heaven: Michael and his angels fought against the dragon; and the dragon and his angels fought, but they did not prevail, nor was a place found for them in heaven any longer. So the great dragon was

cast out, that serpent of old, called the Devil
and Satan, who deceives the whole world; he
was cast to the earth, and his angels were cast
out with him" (Revelation 12:7-9).

A BATTLE FOR THE THRONE

War in heaven. Angels involved in combat. Christ and
Satan warring in heaven? Christ winning. Satan losing.
Satan and his angels thrown out of heaven.

This brings up other perplexing questions. Before we
ask, "Why was there war in heaven?" we might ask,
"What was the dragon doing in heaven in the first place?
What was Satan doing there? Where did he come from?"

Well, fortunately we can find some clues in the Bible.
In fact, we're able to piece together a kind of pre-history of
Satan.

We find the first clue in the book of Ezekiel. This
prophet once communicated a message from the Lord
about the king of Tyre. But in the prophecy we see that
God is also talking about someone else. The exalted king
represents an angelic creature:

> "Thus says the Lord God: You were the seal of
> perfection, Full of wisdom and perfect in
> beauty. . .You were the anointed cherub who
> covers; I established you; You were on the holy
> mountain of God; You walked back and forth
> in the midst of fiery stones; You were perfect
> in your ways from the day you were created;
> until iniquity was found in you" (Ezekiel
> 28:12-15).

Here we have a being described as "the anointed
cherub who covers." This was an angel, anointed for a

special task. In the Jewish temple, the covering cherubs stood over the mercy seat, the throne of God. This angel had a special place near the throne of God. He was the "seal of perfection, full of wisdom, perfect in beauty."

The picture of him walking back and forth in the midst of fiery stones, suggests someone who existed near the glory of God, near the brilliance of the Holy One. But something happened to this wonderful angel: "Iniquity was found" in him. He allowed sin to enter his life. How? What kind of sin? What kind of sin could enter paradise? Ezekiel wrote:

> "Your heart was lifted up because of your beauty; You corrupted your wisdom for the sake of your splendor." (Ezekiel 28:17).

This angel became wrapped up in his own splendor, mesmerized by his own beauty. Now let's think about this for a minute. There's nothing wrong with appreciating your own talents and abilities. There's nothing wrong with feeling good about yourself. So how did this angel cross the line? How did he cross the line from a sence of self-worth to "iniquity?" How was his wisdom corrupted?

We get our second big clue in Isaiah. And here this angel had a name:

> "How you are fallen from heaven, 0 Lucifer, son of the morning! . . . For you have said in your heart; 'I will ascend into heaven, I will exalt my throne above the stars of God; I will sit on the mount of the congregation, on the farthest sides of the north; I will ascend above the heights of the clouds; I will be like the Most High'" (Isaiah 14:12-14).

Lucifer, wise, splendid Lucifer, son of the morning. This angel developed an attitude. He wanted a higher position. Being near God's throne wasn't enough. He wanted a throne "above the stars of God." Inhabiting God's glory wasn't enough. He wanted to "ascend above the heights of the clouds."

In his perfection Lucifer already was "like the Most High." But now he wanted *to be like the Most High in another sense.* He wanted to be as powerful as the Most High. He wanted to have the authority of the Most High. He wanted to be as exalted as the Most High.

LOVE IS THE ANSWER

That's what started it all. That's how this angel began his tragic fall, a fall that would pull a lot of other angels down with him. The apostle John, the same John that wrote this book of Revelation, emphasizes something often in his letters. We have three of these letters in the New Testament. This is what John wrote:

> "Love is of God; and everyone who loves is born of God" (1 John 4:7).

> "This is love, not that we loved God, but that He loved us" (1 John 4:10).

> "God is love" (1 John 4:8).

John tells us that God is love. That's the foundation of His government. Love was all around Lucifer. But Lucifer turned away from love. He got so wrapped up in his own glory that he took in less and less of the love of God. And that started a vicious cycle. The less love Lucifer experienced, the more he needed to exalt himself, and the more he exalted himself, the less love he felt.

Finally, Lucifer began to see God as a rival! His

twisted mind began to picture God as the enemy. The prophet Ezekiel tells us that this rebellious angel thought he was as wise as a God (Ezekiel 28:6). Why should God have all the power and authority? Lucifer began to think he could do just as good a job at running things.

Try to imagine what kind of disturbance this caused in heaven. Imagine a place where jealousy and slander and malice don't exist—had never existed! It has never occurred to anyone to question the wisdom and love of God. And suddenly, this brilliant Lucifer, this cherub so near the throne of God, starts making remarks. He wonders why God has to have all the glory. He wonders why every created being has to obey God. Maybe there's an alternative. Maybe there's a better way to run the universe.

Lucifer questioned God's fairness, appearing so reasonable, so wise. On the inside, pride and greed had taken over. He'd cut himself off from love. But on the outside he remained a brilliant angel of light. And evidently Lucifer persuaded many other angels to join his rebellion. One-third of the angels joined him over who had the right to run the universe. A great battle developed around the throne of God

Now we come to God's response. What should He do with Lucifer? What should He do with this challenge? Many may wish that God had simply destroyed Lucifer. Why? Because if this was the origin of evil, if Lucifer was the first to cut himself off from God's love, then why not nip it in the bud? Why not destroy evil before it had a chance to spread? Why not eliminate evil before it spread to other worlds?

Good question. Why didn't God just execute Lucifer? Think for a moment. Think about what that would have said to all the watching angels.

Suppose that the mayor of Los Angeles, sitting in his office in City Hall, has come under attack by a city councilman. The councilman accuses him of being unfair, arbitrary and dictatorial. He claims the mayor does not really have the citizens' interests in mind at all but is using his office to further his own selfish purposes.

Now how should that mayor respond if the charges were false? What if he called on a SWAT team from LAPD to track down the councilman? Would that clear his name? What if he ordered National Guard units to surround the man at his home? Would that solve the problem?

You see the point, of course. God's reputation and credibility were at stake when Satan delivered his haughty challenge. The question raised was: "Is God really just? Is His way really best?" Eradicating the opposition wouldn't have answered that challenge.

Instead, God chose a wiser course. He would allow sin to exist in the universe for a period of time. When it had been fully demonstrated that rebellion against God does not bring happiness, but rather sickness and disaster; when the whole universe could see that God's way brings joy and Lucifer's way death, then and only then would God destroy all evil.

The answer is that God is love! And love takes the long view. God draws us to Himself with cords of kindness. Love does not coerce. Remember, Lucifer was the first to challenge God's fairness. He claimed there was an alternative, a better way. He claimed that God's power was arbitrary. If God had killed him, would that have settled the question?

Love does something different. Love doesn't force. Love lets people see for themselves, decide for themselves.

God wants us to love Him for who He is. And that can only happen if we really do have free choice. But God had to set limits. He had to set limits on what Satan could do.

John wrote:

> "So the great dragon was cast out, that serpent of old, called the Devil and Satan, who deceives the whole world; he was cast to the earth, and his angels were cast out with him" (Revelation 12:9).

Lucifer—who turned into Satan—was cast out of heaven to earth. And here on earth is where he began to tempt human beings into following him. When Lucifer challenged God, God told him, in effect, "Okay, set up your alternative system. Let the whole universe see what happens. Let all created beings see what happens in a world cut off from love."

No one back then, except God, knew what a disaster Lucifer's alternative would be. No one knew how much suffering and misery it would create. The universe, including us, had to see that for ourselves. We had to know that God's way is best—beyond the shadow of a doubt—because that's the only way God could solve the problem of evil once and for all. That's the only way He could ensure that evil would never plague the universe again. He wants every question to be answered, every doubt settled. That's the fact that lies behind the great conflict between good and evil all around us.

Why did God's angels have to battle Satan's angels? Because God set boundaries around Satan. God allowed Satan to attempt his alternative system, but He didn't permit him to wreak havoc through the whole universe. Satan was excluded from heaven. And that's part of love too. Love doesn't coerce or manipulate, but love does confront when necessary. Love sets boundaries. Love doesn't lay down in the face of evil.

Satan was banished from God's throne, from God's glory. But he didn't leave heaven willingly. He tried to defy God's boundaries. That's why there was war in heaven.

That's the sad story of Lucifer. That's what happened when pride and greed took root inside the best and the brightest creature in heaven.

PLANET EARTH JOINS THE CONFLICT

This brings up yet another question. How did this particular planet, planet Earth, get involved? Was it created simply as a dumping ground for Satan? Were human beings doomed to suffer under his dominion?

The book of Genesis tells us that everything was "good" when God created this world, and that included the first human beings. Everything was perfect in Eden. But God made human beings free, moral beings, just as He'd given the angels free choice. They could choose to listen to God or choose to wander away from Him.

When Eve wandered over to the forbidden Tree of the Knowledge of Good and Evil, Satan, disguised as a serpent, had the opportunity to spread His lies. Eve told him that God had said she would die if she ate of this tree. But Satan replied:

> "You will not surely die. . . For God knows that in the day you eat of it your eyes will be opened, and you will be like God, knowing good and evil" (Genesis 3:4, 5).

Satan was essentially saying, "You will have greater

happiness if you follow me. God is restricting your freedom." Tragically, Eve and her husband Adam accepted that lie. Today we can see the results of that lie all around us. Satan's alternative is not anything like what that serpent in Eden advertised. We live on a planet in rebellion, a planet full of decay and death.

After Adam and Eve ate of the forbidden tree, they were filled with guilt and anxiety. When God came looking for them in the garden, they hid from His face. And we've been running and hiding ever since. Sin produces alienation between us and God, alienation between people. The seeds of the first war were planted in the hearts of the parents of the human race when they sinned. The reason there is abuse in the home; the reason there is so much animosity in this world is that sin has infected the human heart. When man is alienated from God, he becomes alienated from his fellow humans as well. That's the answer to the fundamental question we have in a world of suffering and tragedy. It's the answer to why.

THE ORIGIN OF SUFFERING

Jesus emphasized that answer in one of His parables. In Matthew 13, verse 24, Jesus talked about a field that was perfectly tilled and prepared for seed. And He pictured a good man who planted the seed in the field and was looking forward to an abundant harvest. But some time later, a servant discovered that weeds had popped up everywhere in the wheat field, and he raised a question:

> "Sir, did you not sow good seed in your field?
> How then does it have tares" (Matthew 13:27)?

That's the question every person faces at some time in his or her life. If God is good, if He made this world to blossom for His children, why do we see so many tragic weeds? In Jesus' parable the master answered that question very simply. He said, "An enemy did this."

Where does suffering come from? Where do sickness, heartache and anxiety come from? Jesus' answer is: They didn't happen because the master of the field was irresponsible. He planted good seed. He didn't sow sickness and suffering and death. An enemy of God and man came in the night and sowed seeds of destruction.

The Bible consistently identifies this enemy as Satan. He is the one who rebelled against God and unleashed the whole sin problem. In Scripture, the devil isn't some fairy- tale figure who flits around with a pitchfork. He is a very real being who causes very real tragedies.

And do you know something? The devil is going to have a very real ending—a permanent ending. We can be assured that his long war against God will fail in the end.

Revelation reveals the beginning of this war, and it reveals its ending:

> "And the devil, who deceived them, was cast into the lake of fire and brimstone" (Revelation 20:10).

Ezekiel the prophet adds:

> "Therefore I brought fire from your midst; it devoured you, and I turned you to ashes upon the earth. . . . You have become a horror and shall be no more forever" (Ezekiel 28:18, 19).

That's the fate that awaits the villain of the book of Revelation. He will be finally, completely, and totally destroyed.

God gives us great assurances about how things will

turn out, but He also gives us great assurances about how we can live right now; how we can live successfully, even in a world scarred by the work of Satan.

God Had a Plan

God didn't abandon us to our fate because the human race rebelled against Him. From the very beginning when sin first entered our world, He had a plan. He showed us a way out. Look back at Genesis where God gave a message of warning to the serpent who seduced Adam and Eve.

> "And I will put enmity between you and the woman, and between your seed and her Seed; He shall bruise your head and you shall bruise His heel" (Genesis 3:15).

God's promise is that we don't have to continue to be victimized by the serpent, by Satan. He will put enmity between us and the evil one. We can get out from under his control. How would this happen? It would happen through the offspring of the woman, the promised one. He would destroy the oppressive power of Satan.

Revelation, chapter 12, echoes the same great assurance. That's the chapter which pictures that great war in heaven. And it shows us Satan as a great dragon who tries to deceive and persecute God's people. But look how Christians can confront Satan:

> "And they overcame him by the blood of the Lamb and by the word of their testimony" (Revelation 12:11).

The blood of the Lamb is the weapon that overcomes Satan—every time. We will discuss this more in our next chapter.

If you've every wondered, "Why doesn't God do something about the sickness and sin and heartache in our world?"—the answer is: He has done something—in the gift of His Son. Jesus can give us the ability to live triumphantly, even in a world dominated by sin.

Let me give you one wonderful example of how that happens. Let me tell you about the triumph of John McCain and other POWs. He spent five and a half years as a prisoner of war in Hanoi during the Vietnam War where he and many other pilots endured terrible suffering. But there came a day, McCain remembers clearly, when they were able to rise above the abuse and isolation.

It was Christmas Eve, 1971. A few days earlier McCain had been given a Bible for just a few moments. He furiously copied down as many verses of the Christmas story as he could before a guard approached and took the book away.

On this special night the prisoners had decided to have their own Christmas service. They began with the Lord's Prayer and then sang Christmas carols. McCain read a portion of Luke's gospel in between each hymn.

The men were nervous and stilted at first. They remembered the time about a year earlier when the guards had burst in on their secret church service and began beating the three men who were leading out in prayers. They were dragged away to solitary confinement. The rest of them were shut up in 3x5 foot cells for 11 months.

But still the prisoners wanted to sing on this night. And so they began: "O, come all ye faithful; joyful and triumphant." They sang barely above a whisper, their eyes glancing anxiously at the barred windows.

Huddled below a naked light bulb, they appeared to

be a rather sorry congregation. These men who had once been superbly fit officers now looked gaunt and broken. They shivered in the damp night air. Several shook from fevers. Some were permanently stooped as a result of torture. Others leaned on makeshift crutches. But they kept singing, "O come ye, o come ye to Bethlehem. Come and behold Him, born the king of angels . . . "

And as the service progressed, the prisoners grew bolder. Their voices lifted a little higher until they filled the cell with "Hark, the herald angels sing" and "It came upon a midnight clear."

Some of the men were too sick to stand. But others propped them up on a platform and placed blankets around their trembling shoulders. All wanted to join in the songs that now seemed to make them indeed joyful and triumphant.

When they came to "Silent Night," tears rolled down their unshaven faces. John McCain wrote:

> "Suddenly we were 2000 years and half a world away in a village called Bethlehem. And neither war, nor torture, nor imprisonment . . . had dimmed the hope born on that silent night so long before."

As the prisoners in that North Vietnamese cell sang with feeling the final refrain, "Sleep in heavenly peace, sleep in heavenly peace, " they realized that a transformation had taken place. John McCain expressed it this way:

> "We had forgotten our wounds, our hunger, our pain. We raised prayers of thanks for the Christ child, for our families and homes . . . . There was an absolutely exquisite feeling that our burdens had been lifted. In a place designed to

turn men into vicious animals, we clung to one
another, sharing what comfort we had."

Friends, all of us, at some point, have to make the big
choice. We have to choose between two forces in this
world. One force will try to turn us into vicious animals.
Another force will work to ennoble our hearts.

We have to choose between pride and love, between
self-centeredness and serving God. We have to choose
between opening our hearts and closing our hearts. We
have to choose whose side we are really on. In every
heart there is a throne. In every heart there is a battle for
supremacy. In every heart there is a struggle for control.

That war that began in heaven still goes on. It's a
conflict that reaches into our hearts. The battle lines don't
always stand out clearly, but they are battle lines. Two
forces are clashing. They lead in opposite directions. And
we do make important choices—all important choices on
who will be supreme in our lives.

We all can lift up a song of triumph, a song of defiance against the enemy "who has done this."

Yes, joyful and triumphant, even in the midst of sor-
rows and cares. That's our privilege. Such a life becomes
our privilege as we place our faith in the One born King
of Kings on that silent night in the little town of
Bethlehem.❏

5
REVELATION'S PEACE MAKER

The researchers at a prestigious university on the east coast of the United States were studying the central nervous system. As part of their experiments, they were attempting to discover how much stress an individual was capable of handling. What is the ultimate threshold of stress tolerance? How much pressure can we handle without breaking?

The researchers selected lambs to use in their experiment. They believed they could draw parallels between human beings and lambs. They placed a lamb in a feeding pen with twelve feeding stations. The researchers hooked up an electrical stimulus to each feeding station. The researchers were able to observe the lamb, but the lamb was not able to see the researchers.

As the lamb munched on hay at the first feeding station, the researchers shocked the lamb. The poor lamb flinched, twitched and ran. The researcher observed something significant. The lamb would never return to the feeding station where it had been shocked. The researchers continued the experiment. Soon they shocked the lamb at every possible feeding station. The lamb staggered to the center of the pen—quivering, shaking, trembling and fell over dead with a nervous breakdown. The load of anxiety was too much. The stress levels were too high. The burden too great.

The researchers then took this lamb's twin and put it in the same pen. But there was one difference. They put the lamb's mother in the pen with him. As this second lamb calmly munched on its lunch of hay at one of the feeding stations, the researchers shocked him. Immediately the lamb ran. Do you have any idea where this lamb ran? To mother, of course. He snuggled up close to mother. To the researchers' absolute amazement, after a few minutes in the security of mother, the little lamb returned to the feeding station it had been shocked at. The researchers shocked it again. This time the lamb simply looked at mother and kept right on eating.

At times when our burdens are the greatest, when guilt is eating away our joy, when sin's condemnation is robbing us of our peace, when we are loaded down with a sense of frustrating failure, we also have a place of refuge.

Jesus, the Center of Revelation

The very first words of Revelaton are "The revelation of Jesus Christ" (Revelation 1:1). That's how John's prophecy got its name. It is a revelation from Jesus and about Jesus. A few verses later, lest there be any doubt about who is at the center of this book, John presents Jesus Christ as:

> "The faithful witness, the firstborn from the dead, and the ruler over the kings of the earth. To Him who loved us and washed us from our sins in His own blood . . . be glory and dominion forever and ever" (Revelation 1:5, 6).

John focuses on Jesus as the "Alpha and the Omega, the Beginning and the End" (Revelation 1:8). He is always present. He is there when we need Him most.

Where is Jesus pictured? In the midst of the lampstands. What are these lampstands? According to Revelation 1:20, "The seven lampstands. . . are the seven churches."

Jesus is pictured walking among His people. He knows our burdens. He understands our trials. He is there when the shocks of life strike. He understands. He can lift the burden. He can remove the difficulty. He can take away the guilt.

Later in Revelation, chapter 5, Jesus makes His appearance as the only one in heaven and earth who can open the scrolls of judgment and redeem us.

Jesus is the male child born of a virgin to challenge Satan head-on. He is our mighty Savior (Revelation 2:5)!

In chapter 14, Jesus is not pictured as a babe in Bethlehem but as "the Son of Man" with a sickle in His hand to reap earth's final harvest:

> "And I looked, and behold a white cloud, and on the cloud sat One like the Son of Man, having on His head a golden crown, and in His hand a sharp sickle" (Revelation 14:14).

Here is the Christ who wants to deliver His people from a doomed planet.

Later, Jesus, the triumphant hero, receives great praise, along with God the Father, on a sea of glass (Revelation 15:3,4).

In Revelation, chapter 19, Christ makes a different appearance—as a bridegroom! He is preparing for a great marriage supper with His people.

Then a few verses later, He comes riding out of the sky on a white horse, the Faithful and True, the Word of God. Again he's the great deliverer coming to our rescue (Revelation 19:11).

In Revelation, chapter 21, we find that Christ is the one who makes all things new. He creates a new heaven and a new earth.

In Revelation, chapter 22, Christ is enthroned in the New Jerusalem and he repeats a wonderful assurance to us; "I am coming quickly" (verses 12, 20).

Jesus Christ is the hero of the book of Revelation. He makes dramatic appearances. He is our Creator, our Redeemer, our Lord, our Intercessor and our coming King. He prevails in every conflict.

But one symbol dominates in the book of Revelation. One picture of Jesus keeps flashing out at us through all His other roles. And it's this one: Jesus is the Lamb of God. Jesus is described as the Lamb 27 times in Revelation.

This is how John saw Him:

> "And I looked and behold, in the midst of the throne . . . stood a Lamb as though it had been slain, having seven horns and seven eyes, which are the seven Spirits of God sent out into all the earth" (Revelation 5:6).

This Lamb is declared to be worthy to open that sealed scroll. Revelation 13:8 tells us this Lamb is the one slain from the foundation of the world. And we keep seeing this figure.

In chapter 14, the Lamb reappears. The redeemed surround His eternal throne and praise Him forever.

In the next chapter, faithful believers are standing on what looks like a sea of glass, and they sing the song of the Lamb, crying out:

> "Great and marvelous are Your works . . . Just and true are Your ways, O King of the saints" (Revelation 15:3)!

Another scene of end-time visions rushes by and Jesus appears again, riding out of the sky on a white horse, leading the armies of heaven. Revelation ends with a picture of heaven and the New Jerusalem and the Lamb at its center.

Jesus Christ, the Lamb of God, stands at the center of the book of Revelation. And what's remarkable is this— the Lamb is up against all kinds of evil, vicious forces. They are represented by a seven-headed beast, a fiery red dragon, a seductive harlot, a corrupt empire called Babylon, and a scary assortment of disasters.

The Lamb is put into the thick of all this conflict. You wouldn't think He'd have much of a chance against all those fearsome characters. But this is the bottom line.

> "These will make war with the Lamb, and the Lamb will overcome them, for He is Lord of lords and King of kings; and those who are with Him are called, chosen and faithful" (Revelation 17:14).

Friends, Revelation has a wonderful message for us. It's a simple, profound message. The Lamb will win. He's going to prevail over everything that can be thrown against Him. And we can win with Him!

Let's look at why this Lamb prevails over all opposition.

THE SANCTUARY LAMB SLAIN

The slain lamb is a symbol of Christ, an innocent, righteous Christ, crucified on the cross. Although His sacrifice was symbolized in the Old Testament by various ceremonies, it was symbolized most powerfully by the slaying of a lamb.

Imagine with me what the ceremony would have

meant to one individual struggling with a burden of guilt.

In the early morning light, a man named Eliud walks through the encampment of Israel. Passing tent after tent of his own tribe, he knows that friends, relatives and strangers follow his steps. They know where he is going. Eliud is leading a small lamb. Perhaps he has to pick it up and carry it in his arms. It's pure white, spotless. His children have played with it since its birth.

But Eliud is going to the tabernacle to slit this animal's throat. An ache in his memory drives him there; a sin that's been gnawing at his bones. He has to make it right. So he keeps walking, eyes straight ahead.

At the entrance to the outer court of the tabernacle, Eliud waits with others who have brought their sin offerings. He watches as the priests perform their ancient ritual. And then it's his turn.

Eliud kneels beside the lamb and places one hand around its neck. A priest approaches. Eliud places his other hand on the lamb's head and confesses his sin. He tries not to look in the animal's trusting eyes. Quickly its head is lifted. There's a swift flash of the knife. Dark blood spurts out on the ground. The lamb kicks once and then falls limp.

Priestly assistants then take the carcass toward the large altar. They drain the blood into a trench at its base. Then they place the slain animal on the grating and flames begin to consume it.

As Eliud watches the black smoke curl up toward a perfect blue sky he feels for a moment that his own life has been whisked from the plunging blade. He's been rescued. This spotless sacrifice points to a divine forgiveness. And that grace is as real to Eliud as the blood that still stains his hands.

That is what happened at the Hebrew tabernacle, at the altar of burnt offering. What did it all mean?

1. People were accepting responsibility for their wrong doing. They were facing up to it squarely, confessing it. No denials, no excuses. That's why people brought their lambs to the temple. They were accepting their guilt.

2. But they were also acknowledging something else—the fact that they couldn't atone for their sin. They couldn't really make up for it. Certainly they could provide restitution where that was possible. They could never do enough to change the past.

That spotless lamb slain, was an act of faith—faith in the fact that another would take their guilt. Another would make atonement.

That lamb pointed forward to a holy event. When Jesus came to the Jordan River, John confidently proclaimed: "Behold! The Lamb of God who takes away the sin of the world" (John 1:29)!

The lamb, without spot or blemish represented Jesus, God's lamb. The Bible states it clearly, "The wages of sin is death" (Romans 6:23). Without Jesus, the guilt of sin crushes out our lives. Sin's ultimate wage is death.

In the Old Testament, when the guilty sinner confessed his sin, the guilt was symbolically transferred to the innocent lamb. The lamb bore the sinner's guilt. The death penalty now hung over the head of the lamb. The sinner now was free. The lamb bore the guilt. The sinner could live. The lamb must die.

The blood of lambs could not save us from sin. It pointed forward to One who would save. The writer of Hebrews describes these prophetic animal sacrifices and what they accomplished:

"How much more shall the blood of Christ, who through the eternal Spirit offered Himself without spot to God, purge your conscience from dead works to serve the living God" (Hebrews 9:14)?

Christ offered Himself on the cross as a sacrifice for sin. And only that sacrifice can cleanse guilty hearts. That's the real secret behind the power of the Lamb of God. That's why he will ultimately prevail. He doesn't just win a victory over the forces of evil. He wins a decisive victory over sin itself—at the cross. He wins a victory over human guilt and misery—at the cross. The Lamb brings us peace not just by overcoming foes, but by creating forgiveness.

Friends, people need forgiveness today. We need it desperately. Because guilt does terrible things to us, guilt can rob us of peace and destroy our lives. Because we've been struggling with the internal consequences of our wrong-doing since history began, we have developed all kinds of ways of dealing with guilt. All kinds of do-it-yourself strategies.

DENYING WRONG DOING

Sometimes we try simple denial. We try to pretend that the wrong isn't there, that it never happened.

Once a company found itself in the middle of tense negotiations with union leaders. Company officials insisted that workers were abusing sick-leave privileges. The union denied it.

One morning at the bargaining table, the company's negotiator held up the sports page of the local newspaper. He pointed to a picture showing an employee winning a golf tournament in town. "This man," the negotiator declared, "called in sick yesterday." But there he was in the paper beside a caption describing his excellent golf score.

After a moment of silence, a union man spoke up. "Wow," he said. "Think of what kind of score he could have had if he HADN'T been sick!"

Nice try. We can deny. We can try to cover our deceptions or our misbehavior. But it usually doesn't take us very far. Our sins have a way of finding us out. So when denial fails, people often fall back on excuses. We try to explain away irresponsibility.

At one university, two psychologists tried a simple test. They gathered a group of students in a room, and in the adjacent room they staged what sounded like an accident. A woman fell down and screamed, "Oh, my foot. I can't move it. Oh, my ankle. I can't get this thing off me!" The woman's voice could be clearly heard by all the students. But almost no one offered to help.

What really surprised the psychologists, however, was the explanation these people gave afterwards. Most said, "I didn't really know what happened." Others claimed that "it wasn't serious."

Excuses keep guilt at bay—for a while at least. Sometimes our excuses reaches monstrous proportion. John Gacy was convicted of murdering scores of children in his home near Chicago. Twenty-seven bodies were found in the crawl space under his home. How did he respond as he faced death by lethal injection? Gacy said, "In my heart, as God is my witness, I haven't killed anyone."

"It wasn't really me." "I couldn't help myself." Those are excuses that have become all too common recently. But justifying wrong breaks down just as our denial does. Eventually the weight of guilt becomes too great for these flimsy excuses.

Still, there's one final strategy left us in our do-it-yourself attempts to deal with guilt. And that is—making up for it, atoning for what we've done. Now this may sound rather noble at first, but it leads people down a self-destructive path.

Mr. Konrad grew up in a very religious home. Through most of his childhood he tried very hard to please God. But he always felt guilty about falling short. And his harsh, rigid parents didn't offer much help.

Mr. Konrad became a rather successful businessman, and he gave generously to charities. In fact, he gave to the point of sacrifice. At one point he got it into his head that some local church leaders were destroying true religion. He spent thousands of dollars in a campaign to denounce them.

Mr. Konrad kept trying to do the right thing. But he could never do enough. He could never give enough. He could never sacrifice himself enough. Those terrible guilty feelings persisted. And finally they overwhelmed him. Mr. Konrad had to be admitted to a mental institution.

While there, he deliberately burned his hands and feet on a radiator and even gouged holes in his feet and the palms of his hands. He was imitating the crucifixion. He just couldn't stop his tortured efforts to atone for wrong by *doing* something.

Unresolved guilt can drive us to such extremes. It can destroy our emotional health. We've been looking for answers in all the wrong places.

Ultimately forgiveness can only come from one source—it has to be God who forgives. When we fail morally, the pardon has to come from the Lawgiver. In our innermost hearts we know that forgiveness has to come from a higher source. Our friends can comfort, but they can't really solve our guilt problem. Psychology can help us adjust and cope, but it can't really deal with our guilt.

It took the cross to create pardon and grace. Christ was pouring out His life on the cross, the spotless Lamb of God. He was taking on our guilt and giving us His righteousness, His right standing with the Father. That's why the sacrifice of the Lamb is so powerful. That's why it can become the source of great peace.

Paul makes this plain:

> "For He made Him who knew no sin to be sin for us, that we might become the righteousness of God in Him" (2 Corinthians 5:21).

Christ never sinned. He lived a spotless, perfect life. But He became sin. He assumed the guilt of sin for us.

We find peace at the foot of the cross. We find it as weak, undeserving human beings who look up at a crucified Christ. We find it by reaching out in faith toward this Savior, just as Eliud placed his hand on the lamb's head. We find it when we look down and see that our hands, too, are stained with blood. We're involved. We're participants. It's our sin that required this great sacrifice. And it's our lives that Jesus wants to rescue.

The book of Revelation emphasizes this truth over and over again. John pictures the redeemed standing at the throne of God with songs of praise singing:

> "For You were slain, and have redeemed us to God by Your blood out of every tribe and tongue and people and nation" (Revelation 5:9).

Remember who is going to win in the end—the Lamb

of God. He will prevail over every other force in the world. And we can win with him! We can win by accepting his incredible sacrifice for us. How do we do that? Let me tell you how you can experience forgiveness and divine acceptance and the right to eternal life even while you are reading this page.

Forgiveness is a gift. The whole New Testament is electrified by this theme. You can almost hear the apostle Peter joining in the chorus:

> "You were not redeemed with corruptible things, like silver or gold . . . but with the precious blood of Christ, as a lamb without blemish and without spot" (1 Peter 1:18, 19).

All the silver and gold in the world, all the good deeds in the world, won't bring you an inch closer to forgiveness. It's only the precious blood of Christ that counts—His sacrifice. Redemption is a gift. And it's a gift, only in Jesus Christ.

A lot of us have a hard time grasping this—not because it's a complicated concept, not because it's hard to understand—but because of the shape of our hearts. Our hearts just don't naturally fit around this idea of grace. So many of us have been shaped by dysfunctional, broken families. So many of us have tried so hard to earn a parent's affection or approval. So many of us get stuck trying to control others or manipulate others in order to get the love we need. That's what has shaped our hearts.

And this grace business just doesn't fit. We know the right words. We may even nod our heads in agreement— yes, forgiveness is a gift in Jesus Christ. But the reality goes right by us. We can hear about God's love a thousand times and still figure out a thousand ways to try to earn it. The people who need grace the most are the ones who react against it the most.

Friend, if we don't grasp grace in our hearts, then we haven't grasped anything. If this fundamental fact doesn't become real for us, then all our talk about God or faith or religion means very little.

Here are five simple steps you can take to receive this gift of eternal life:

1. Accept the fact that God loves you and wants to save you (Jeremiah 31:3).
2. Recognize that you cannot save yourself (Romans 3:23, 24).
3. Believe that Jesus can and will save you. (John 3:16).
4. Confess your sins to Jesus and believe you are forgiven (1 John 1:9).
5. Claim His gift of eternal life and decide to serve Him forever (1 John 5:11, 12).

In 1992 I was invited to conduct a series of prophecy lectures inside the Kremlin Palace just off Moscow's Red Square. The palace auditorium seats 6,500 people. The auditorium was jammed for two sessions each evening. The doors of freedom were open. These former Communists were now eager to hear God's word. Tens of thousands opened their hearts to Jesus.

In one meeting I spoke on Revelation's Lamb—how to find freedom from guilt, peace of mind and eternal life in Jesus. I described Jesus dying on the cross with blood spurting from His hands and feet. I described the crown of thorns jammed into his head with blood running down His face. I described the wrenching agony Jesus experienced when darkness engulfed the cross and all Jesus could experience was separation from the Father.

I made a strong appeal for the audience to accept this Jesus and receive eternal life. Between sessions I was resting in a small office, and the door swung open. A large Russian man burst into the room. I estimate he was in his late 20's. His hair was long. He was unshaven. He had a scar about five inches long on his left cheek. He was yelling in Russian. I thought I was being attacked. My translator stepped in-between us. This young man was a criminal. He had been arrested more than 20 times. Now with tears in his eyes he longed for forgiveness. This Russian criminal wanted to find Jesus.

We talked, we shared. I opened my Bible and read him John 3:16:

> "For God so love the world that He gave His only begotten Son, that whoever believes in Him should not perish but have everlasting life."

Tears filled his eyes and ran down his cheeks. He opened his heart to accept Christ. A new peace radiated from his countenance. Joy flooded his entire being. His eyes sparkled with a sense of forgiveness. He was now a child of God.

Friends, the good news is what it has always been. Forgiveness is a gift. Eternal life is a gift. And if we don't get it as a gift, we just don't get it. It's available to you at anytime.

That's the great anthem of the New Testament. It's there from those early chapters when a baby was laid in a manger—God Almighty placed into our hands. And it's there in the very last chapter of the Bible where the apostle John urges us to take the free gift of the water of life:

> "And the Spirit and the bride say, 'Come!' And

let him who hears say, 'Come!' And let him who thirsts come. And whoever desires, let him take the water of life freely" (Revelation 22:17).

This is the most wonderful piece of news that has ever been announced on this planet. Forgiveness is a gift. And that gift is in Jesus Christ. Please let this gift begin reshaping your life.

Have you come to the foot of the cross where the guilt problem is solved once and for all? Why not come there just now? Come to the hero of the book of Revelation. And call Him your Lord. ❏

6
REVELATION'S POWER LINE

A new revolution in psychoactive drugs is happening today. Scientists are linking more and more mental states to specific genes in our heads. It seems that we're approaching a day when there will be a pill for every problem. A pill for turning depression into joy. A pill for turning anxiety into peace. A pill for turning anger into kindness.

Are we going to find all our answers in pharmaceuticals? Or will the new wave of biological psychiatry smash us into a brick wall?

Scientists have been using brain imaging—MRI, CT and PET scans—to peer into the structure and activity of the brain. They've found that heroin addicts are more likely to have an abnormally long version of a gene on chromosome 11. The same type of gene is also common among impulsive thrill-seekers.

Researchers identified a shortened gene on chromosome 17 that results in a build-up of serotonin in the brain. And this abnormal gene seems to make people more neurotic, more anxious or depressed.

Other scientists linked obsessive-compulsive disorder to a gene on chromosome 22. People with this gene suffer from a build-up of brain chemicals that keep delivering the same message over and over.

But that's not all. Most recently scientists have been discovering links between abnormal genes in our heads and personality traits or behaviors that are just a little bit odd. There's a hitch in the brain related to worrying too much. Another one connected to the blues. Another one identified with being overly concerned with a tidy desk or neat house.

A little hitch somewhere in the brain produces a personality quirk. A larger abnormality in the same place in the brain produces a corresponding mental illness. So a person who's overly suspicious probably has one or two abnormal genes in a certain chromosome. A person who's schizophrenic has all nine or ten abnormal genes.

Finding a biological basis for the way we act has had a huge effect on the way we deal with life's problems. It's had a huge impact on the counseling profession. If we're worried or depressed or angry because the chemicals in our brains are out of whack, then why not just straighten out the chemicals?

That's what therapists have been trying to do with the new wave of psychoactive drugs. These drugs are being prescribed for all kinds of symptoms these days.

A teenage girl who's unhappy with the way she looks will get regular doses of an anti-depressant. A mother who's insecure and over-protective will get a prescription for a drug that calms anxiety.

As we enter the 21st century, it does seem like there's going to be a pill for everything—a pill for every problem. Psychoactive drugs are on a roll. One big reason is the Prozac phenomenon. After this anti-depressant went on the market, people began telling remarkable stories of how their lives had changed dramatically.

This drug seemed to be transforming human beings. And that made a lot of people wonder—if a pill can do all this, do we still need God? Are psychoactive drugs going to make God obsolete in the 21st century?

What are we to make of this? Do pills do what God cannot? Is divine power going to become obsolete in the 21st century?

Well, let's take a closer look at exactly what God does in an individual's life. Let's look at how His Spirit, the Holy Spirit, works in our minds. And we'll compare that with what psychoactive drugs do. I think you'll be amazed. There is a divine power which provides radical, life-transforming changes. Let's turn to the book of Revelation.

Did you know that there is one dominant image of believers in the book of Revelation. They are characterized in one certain way—more than any other. They are called "overcomers". Revelation pictures hard times and cataclysms in the end-time. It pictures evil powers like the dragon and beast warring against believers.

♦ But believers overcome.
♦ Believers are delivered.
♦ Believers win.

It starts in the beginning of Revelation.

♦ Revelation 2:7 — "To him who overcomes, I will give to eat from the tree of life."
♦ Revelation 2:11 — "He who overcomes will not be hurt by the second death."
♦ Revelation 2:17 — "To him who overcomes, I will give some of the hidden manna."
♦ Revelation 2:26 — "He who overcomes . . . to him I will give power over the nations."
♦ Revelation 3:12 — "He who overcomes, I will make him a pillar in the temple of My God."
♦ Revelation 3:21 — "To him who overcomes, I will grant to sit with Me on My throne."

The book of Revelation pictures believers as overcomers. They overcome adversity. They overcome evil.

We see the same theme later in the book. Speaking of Satan, the accuser, the enemy, John says:

> "They overcame him by the blood of the Lamb and by the word of their testimony" (Revelation 12:11).

And at the end of the book, this same picture of believers emerges:

> "I will give of the fountain of the water of life freely to him who thirsts. He who overcomes shall inherit all things, and I will be his God and he shall by My son" (Revelation 21:6,7).

Believers overcome in the worst of times, under the most trying conditions. That is part of the message of the book of Revelation, friends. It's telling us that we weak, sinful human beings can be overcomers. We don't have to live defeated lives. We don't have to be intimidated by the forces of evil in this world.

I have seen God radically transform people around the world. Their lives have been changed forever.

◆ Drunkards made sober.
◆ Thieves become honest.
◆ Money-grabbing businessmen transformed into unselfish, compassionate husbands and fathers.
◆ Angry, bitter people renewed in spirit.
◆ Prostitutes and lust-filled men transformed.
◆ Hearts filled with hatred—now filled with love.
◆ It's a miracle—a miracle of God's grace!

What God does in human hearts is remarkable. The apostle Paul shouts it in these words:

"If anyone is in Christ, he is a new creation: old things have passed away; behold, all things have become new" (2 Corinthians 5:17).

How does it happen? The Bible calls this experience "the new birth" or being "born again." To be born again means to be radically transformed from deep within by the power of the Holy Spirit. It means to have:

◆ a new way of looking at things
◆ a new power operating in your life
◆ new desires
◆ new impulses
◆ new joy and peace in your life.

Discussing this radical change with Nicodemus, Jesus commented:

"That which is born of the flesh is flesh and that which is born of the Spirit is spirit. Do not marvel that I said to you, 'You must be born again.' The wind blows where it wishes, and you hear the sound of it, but cannot tell where it comes from and where it goes. So is everyone who is born of the Spirit" (John 3:6-8).

The human mind cannot understand it. We become overcomers through the Spirit. We are born again. We are powerfully changed by God's Spirit working within our brain cells. A new power operates in our lives. The Spirit helps us to uproot anger, bitterness, lust, and addictions and replaces them with love, joy, peace and long-suffering.

The Holy Spirit's power liberates us from the bondage of habits which destroy our souls. The apostle Paul states it this way:

> "And where the Spirit of the Lord is, there is
> liberty" (2 Corinthians 3:17).

The Spirit's power frees us from the chains of sin which bind us.

Drug medication deals only with symptoms. They deal with bad feelings or impulses. If a person is depressed, then certain pills can sometimes ease that depression. Other pills may, in certain circumstances, ease anger or anxiety. But no psychoactive drug can show you *why* you're depressed. Or what lies behind your anger or your anxiety.

Pills just treat symptoms. And many times those symptoms are telling us we need to deal with a deeper problem. But we want to deal with the symptoms. Many in the counseling community are concerned about that. They're very concerned about our rush to just medicate the mind.

Pills don't give us wisdom. They don't give us the insight we need to deal with our problems and grow through them. But the Holy Spirit works in us to do precisely that. He is the Spirit of Revelation, and His revelations can produce dramatic results. Paul said:

> "Now we have received, not the spirit of the
> world but the Spirit who is from God, that we
> might know the things that have been freely
> given to us by God" (1 Corinthians 2:12).

Let me give you a dramatic example. A young woman named Eileen was admitted to the hospital, convinced that she had multiple sclerosis. She showed many of the symptoms. But neurological tests revealed no traces of the disease. When psychiatrist William Wilson told her about this, she became angry. Eileen still continued to insist that she did have multiple sclerosis.

During later visits, Dr. Wilson discovered that this young woman was really suffering from a long bout with depression. She had a lot of anxiety and stress in her life. But for Eileen, having a physical problem seemed a whole lot better than having a mental problem.

Dr. Wilson had come to believe that a relationship with God can help in a person's healing. Eileen seemed quite interested in this idea. She wanted to know how she could have a Christ-centered life.

So the psychiatrist talked about learning to trust Christ as Savior and surrendering one's will to Christ as Lord.

Here is Revelation's key to receiving the liberating power of the Spirit in your own life and what Eileen needed:

> "And let him who thirsts come. And whoever desires, let him take the water of life freely" (Revelation 22:17).

Dr. Wilson explained to Eileen that as she made a conscious act of her will to surrender her life to the lordship of Jesus Christ, a wonderful change would take place in her whole life.

About a week later, Eileen asked Jesus to enter her life. And she prayed to be filled with the Holy Spirit. After that, Dr. Wilson encouraged Eileen to ask God for wisdom to understand her illness—whatever it was.

Eileen prayed and her depression suddenly intensified. But in this pain, the lights came on. She finally realized that her real problem was depression, not the multiple sclerosis she was so sure she had.

Dr. Wilson continued counseling with Eileen and

praying with her. Her symptoms began to go away. And soon she was ready to go home.

But back at the house, surrounded by her old environment, that horrible feeling of depression began to overwhelm her again. She felt nauseated. She could hardly focus. This went on for two hours until finally she collapsed to the floor. Eileen struggled, but she couldn't move. It seemed that all her old symptoms were back.

But at that moment something struck her—a revelation. She realized that deep inside, she was really still struggling against God. She had been so stubborn. She hadn't fully surrendered her will to Him.

So Eileen cried out "I give up." She asked God to forgive her pride and to enable her to serve Him. Eileen soon began to face each day with anticipation and joy.

Friends, pills can relieve symptoms. But only the Holy Spirit can enlighten. Only the Holy Spirit can help us grow.

Sometimes drugs are required to lift certain kinds of depression. We can be thankful for those drugs just as we're thankful for insulin or penicillin.

But we need more than just being rid of some bad feelings. We need to understand. We need to grow. We'll always need to do that. And that's why the Holy Spirit will always be there for us.

Now let's look at something more that God's Spirit does inside human beings. The Spirit fills up our lives with good things, with good qualities. Paul wrote:

> "But the fruit of the Spirit is love, joy, peace, longsuffering, kindness, goodness, faithfulness, gentleness, self control" (Galatians 5:22, 23).

Love, joy and peace—those are qualities the Holy

Spirit reproduces inside us. In Ephesians Paul says that the fruit of the Spirit is in all goodness, righteousness and truth (Ephesians 5:9).

In writing to Timothy, Paul says:

> "For God has not given us a spirit of fear, but of power and of love and of a sound mind" (2 Timothy 1:7).

The Holy Spirit fills us with good things. That's how we keep growing. To the Galatians Paul said:

> "He who sows to the Spirit, will of the Spirit reap everlasting life" (Galatians 6:8).

The Spirit moves us down a path that leads to abundant life—everlasting life.

In Ephesians, Paul talks about the Spirit strengthening us in our inner being so that we can grasp the height and length and breadth of God's love:

> "That He would grant you, according to the riches of His glory, to be strengthened with might through His Spirit in the inner man" (Ephesians 3:16).

Please give your attention to this! You can be strengthened with the mighty power of God inside of you!

You can be different than you are now! You don't have to be what you are!

A miracle of God's grace can take place in your life. You do not need to struggle with the same habits over and over again. When life presses you down, when you struggle with impulses which seem uncontrollable, when you feel too weak to try—remember the apostle Paul's words:

> "Yet in all these things we are more than con-

querors through Him who loved us" (Romans 8:37).

God has called you to be a winner, not a loser.

I can think of no better example than the experience of my own father, James Finley. He was just another New York City slum kid, like thousands of others growing up in what was called "Hell's Kitchen." No home life to speak of, no money, no future. Dad had to learn about life on the streets. And for a long time, it seemed, he absorbed all the wrong lessons.

His mother was unstable. His step-father had a very small income as a part-time tugboat captain. The family was constantly having to move, constantly scrounging for life's necessities. As a boy, Dad had to get used to standing in line for free cans of beans and stew and wearing the khaki pants that announced to the world he was on home relief.

He attended 15 different schools in 11 years. It was almost impossible to keep up.

One Friday night, Dad went home and found that the doorknob on the front door wouldn't move. Then he noticed the white piece of paper taped there with a message: "We moved. New address: 110th Street, Harlem."

The pattern had started all over again. Only here, there weren't just fights, there were gang wars. There wasn't just poverty, there was desolation.

Dad picked up more and more signs around the house that he wasn't really wanted. So at the age of 17 he decided to take off on his own. At first, he hid out in the house of a friend named Skip. Skip let him stay in the attic and sneaked up his meals.

Later he went to live with a stepbrother in Jersey City. He did manage to find odd jobs here and there. But he'd gotten into a habit of petty theft. He told himself that he only took things he really needed.

Finally, my father tried what seemed to be the ultimate escape—the Navy. He joined up at the age of 17. He did find a measure of stability in the military discipline. But as a sailor, he was mainly interested in freedom—staying out late, going from bar to bar, no badgering parents around. He even became involved in car theft.

There was a point in my father's life when the battle became just too strong. He sensed an emptiness within. He realized the need for divine power to transform his life. He opened his heart to the power of the living Christ. He surrendered to the claims of the Spirit. He opened His heart to God's life-transforming power.

Dad didn't just get out of Hell's Kitchen. Hell's Kitchen got out of him. He did make the ultimate escape. The bar-hopping sailor who kept "borrowing" cars became a beloved and respected father and community leader.

The important question, of course, is—*how* did it happen? How did such a change come about?

Dad dropped to his knees and repeated the words of that hymn to God: "And though all men should forsake Thee, by Thy grace I'll follow Thee." My father truly escaped from Hell's Kitchen because he truly made a commitment. He stopped saying that he'd like to find out if this religion bit was real—someday. He stopped giving it occasional glances from the distance.

Jim Finley made a commitment, heart and soul. "And though all men should forsake Thee, by Thy grace I'll follow Thee."

The God of Scripture *is* a God of great transformations. He *can* help people escape the worst circumstances, the narrowest lives. But what makes the difference between just getting out of Hell's Kitchen and Hell's Kitchen getting out of us is the commitment we make. That's how we become overcomers.

Friends, the Holy Spirit is with us for the long haul. He's there for us. The big question is, are you there for Him? Are you allowing God's Spirit into your life? Maybe you're still resisting on some level, like Eileen did for so long. Maybe you just want to get rid of the symptoms. Maybe you're running away from a deeper problem God wants you to deal with.

Isn't it time to surrender to the Lord who can help you understand and grow? Isn't it time to give your will into the hands of the One who can fill you with good things? ❏

7

REVELATION'S MOST AMAZING PROPHECY

Twelve thousand feet above Phoenix, Arizona, Debbie Williams and a half-dozen friends poised briefly in the open door of an airplane. Then they dove out into the clear blue skies. These experienced sky divers planned to link into a mid-air formation. A few seconds into her free-fall, Debbie went into a corkscrew, a fast dive to catch up with four others below her.

But she miscalculated her descent and slammed into another diver. The 50-mile-per-hour impact knocked her unconscious. She bounced away, limp as a rag doll.

Debbie was plummeting toward earth, with her parachute unopened, and no way to open it. She flew past instructor and jump-master Gregory Robertson. He noticed the blood covering her face.

Immediately, Gregory forced his body into a "no-lift" dive: head tucked into his chest, toes pointed, and arms flat at his sides. Now he was diving at 180 miles per hour. When he looked up to check, Debbie still seemed to be falling away from him.

But Gregory kept going, as the horizon came up to meet him, trying to dive faster, and faster. He maneuvered his shoulders ever-so slightly to guide his descent toward the unconscious young woman.

And then, he was there beside her, looking for all the world like superman without a cape. Gregory reached out and grabbed Debbie's reserve cord. Yanking it hard, he quickly moved away. Her chute opened and she began drifting slowly toward the ground. At 2000 feet, only 12 seconds from impact, Gregory opened his own chute.

Debbie and superman both survived. Debbie would recover fully from her injuries and remain always grateful to the one who'd miraculously snatched her from a fatal impact.

We are rushing headlong toward an impact with the end-time; we're speeding toward a collision with the final events of earth's history. Wars and rumors of wars keep rushing at us. Devastating earthquakes have dramatically increased. The social fabric is falling apart. Violent crime is on the rise. Immorality is commonplace. And the gospel is going to all the world, sweeping through whole empires where it once was shut out. All these things are rushing at us. They are signs that history is coming to a climax.

We're plummeting toward ground zero. And a lot of people don't have a parachute. Even more are simply unconscious; they don't realize that the horizon is rushing up to meet them. They grow limp in the face of climactic, end-time events.

But even at this late hour, God has planned a mid-air rescue. That's right. He knows the human race is spinning rapidly toward its date with eternity. He knows the destiny of millions will soon be decided forever. And so, even as we fall headlong, seconds from impact, He's devised a way to help us pull our rip cord.

God's mid-air rescue is described in Revelation, the last book of the Bible. This preview can lift us up with great hope in these last days. This is what the Apostle John saw happening near the close of time:

"Then I saw another angel flying in midair, and

he had the eternal gospel to proclaim to those
who live on the earth—to every nation, tribe,
language and people" (Revelation 14:6, NIV).

What a dramatic picture! God attempting to rescue
every person on planet Earth! Here is a heavenly messenger flying in midair, coming to our rescue.
Throughout Revelation, angels are pictured bearing messages from heaven to earth. This book of Revelation is
full of symbols. The fact that angels bear this message
highlights its urgency. Here is an urgent, end-time message directly from God.

This angel is the first of three angels who are proclaiming God's three last messages. They are the words
He shouts at us, seconds from impact.

God has always sent messages to warn his people of
sweeping events that would affect millions. What happened before the Flood? Did the heavens just pour down
rain without warning? No, Noah, in fact, preached for 120
years. He warned that a flood was coming that would
destroy life on the earth. He pleaded with people to take
refuge in his ark.

What happened before the great Egyptian famine?
God sent a messenger to prepare those people. Joseph
saw what was coming in a dream. He had the Egyptians
stockpile supplies to meet the famine.

God doesn't play games. He's not out to catch us off
guard. He wants us to be prepared for what is coming.
The prophet Amos put it this way:

> "Surely the Lord God does nothing, unless He
> reveals His secret to His servants the
> prophets" (Amos 3:7).

In Revelation, God is sending a message through his

angels that something of cataclysmic proportions is just over the horizon: "Something big is coming. Open up your eyes. But you don't have to be afraid. I will be with you. I will provide you with a way of escape. I will show you a safe place. Keep your eyes on me and I will tell you what to do."

So, what is this big event God wants us to focus on? If you look at this chapter carefully, you will see something very important in verse 14. What is it? You see the Son of Man with a golden crown on His head and a sharp sickle in His hand. "The harvest of the earth is ripe," an angel says. This is the Second Coming. This is the final judgment, when history climaxes and all human destinies are sealed.

So obviously the messages that come right before this are vitally important. They are God's last warning, God's final appeal, God's last altar call! He's telling us exactly how to open our parachutes as the end of time rushes up to meet us.

Let's take a closer look at the message of the first angel:

> "Then I saw another angel flying in midair, and
> he had the eternal gospel to proclaim to those
> who live on the earth—to every nation, tribe,
> language and people" (Revelation 14:6, NIV).

Whom is this message for? Does it say it's aimed at Canadians or only those who speak Spanish? Is it targeted only at those who live in big cities? No it's to go to every nation, to every tribe, to every language, to every people. This message is to leap across geographical boundaries and ethnic barriers. It is God's universal message for the whole world.

The message begins with an angel having "the everlasting gospel" to preach. The gospel doesn't change. The good news that saved Paul is the same good news that will save the last person on earth. There's only one parachute ever made that can rescue sinful human beings—Jesus' love, Jesus' salvation. There is an old gospel hymn that says, "Jesus saves, Jesus saves." And He does, friends.

So all that these three angels say must be understood in the context of the gospel. Forces are unleashed at the end of time that try to distort and compromise the gospel. That's what these warnings are about.

Both panic and lethargy are real dangers as we approach the end. Either can prevent us from grasping the gospel, from pulling the rip cord. So let's try to identify this "everlasting gospel" as clearly as we can from the words of Scripture.

When the Apostle Paul wanted to define "the gospel which I preached to you," he summed it up this way:

> "For I delivered to you first of all that which I also received: that Christ died for our sins according to the Scriptures, and that He was buried, and that He rose again the third day according to the Scriptures" (1 Corinthians 15:3, 4).

The everlasting gospel, as outlined in these verses, contains four key elements.

First, Jesus Christ died for our sins. He, our Creator, a sinless being, voluntarily marched down that bloody road to Golgotha. He placed his wrists on the cross. He allowed soldiers to pound spikes into his limbs. He did this on our behalf. Christ voluntarily took the penalty of sin so we wouldn't have to. In the most well-known verse in the Bible, Jesus put it beautifully when He said,

"For God so loved the world that He gave His
only begotten Son that whoever believes in Him
should not perish but have everlasting life"
(John 3:16).

This is the essence of the gospel. Christ died for our
sins. His death was for us.

Second, at the cross, Christ also laid down his perfect life as a substitute for our sinful life. His righteousness is credited to us. We are forgiven and accepted in
Jesus Christ. We can enter heaven because of the welcome He receives.

Third, Christ rose from the dead. He came through
the ordeal of the cross victorious. He triumphed over the
forces of evil. Three days after his broken body was taken
down from the cross, He arose. An angel rolled the stone
away from his tomb and he walked out.

Fourth, Christ ascended to the Father in heaven. He
comes before God to present his sacrifice on our behalf.
He wins for us pardon and acceptance.

The most important question you will ever face in
your life is this one—What must I do to be saved? It is
the most important question at this very moment in your
life; it is the most important question when you take your
last breath.

Friends, the cross gives us a clear answer to that question. It's the solution. It restores our broken relationship
with God.

Jesus didn't die on the cross simply to help us feel
better. He sacrificed himself because we are doomed; we
are in deep trouble; our sins separate us from the life-
giving God. We have a big moral problem.

Christ gave himself up on the cross in order to rescue
us from eternal death. That's the inevitable result of sin.

We are sinners, and we are responsible before God for what we do and what we become. We are accountable before Him. Our moral failures carry consequences.

That's our basic problem. We can't see the problem if we just keep saying, "I'm OK, everything's fine. I'm not any worse than most other people." If we don't understand our sinfulness, our self-centeredness, we won't understand our urgent need for a solution, for rescue. We won't see the day of final judgment rushing up to meet us. If we won't pull the ripcord, the everlasting gospel can't save us. So God flies down through the heavens, in the person of these three angels, and shouts final instructions in our ears. "Please listen," He says, "listen to what I am telling you. Let's pull the rip-cord together!"

That's the backdrop for this message of the first angel in Revelation 14. He proclaims in a loud voice,

> "Fear God and give glory to Him, for the hour of His judgment has come; and worship Him who made heaven and earth, the sea and springs of water" (Revelation 14:7).

The message has three parts.

- ◆ First, it tells us what we're supposed to be doing.
- ◆ Second, it tells us why we are supposed to do it.
- ◆ Third, it tells us what has happened that makes this command so critically important.

First, let's look at what we're supposed to be doing. The message tells us to fear God and give glory to Him. What does it mean to fear God? We'd better know if a messenger from heaven is telling us we're supposed to be doing it.

To fear God means to stand in awe of Him. To stand in awe means to deeply admire, revere and respect. If we respect someone, we long to please or obey them. Throughout the Bible, fearing God or respecting God and obeying God are linked together.

Soloman says:

> "Let us hear the conclusion of the whole matter. Fear God and keep His commandments, for this is the whole duty of man" (Ecclesiastes 12:13).

> "My son, do not forget my law, but let your heart keep my commands. . . . Fear the Lord and depart from evil" (Proverbs 3:1,7).

God's last-day message is an urgent call to obey God at a time in earth's history when millions have the idea that they are responsible only to their own "inner sense" of right. Today, the common belief is—"I can do whatever I choose; I am only accountable to myself; no standard or right or wrong exists outside of my own mind."

The book of Revelation gives us an urgent call—"Fear God"—obey God. There is a standard outside of your mind.

John put this into sharp focus:

> "Here is the patience [endurance] of the saints; here are those who keep the commandments of God and the faith of Jesus" (Revelation 14:12).

In the last days of earth's history, God has sent an urgent, loving, truth-filled message calling us back to obedience to Him. Throughout history, God has had a people who have been faithfully obedient to Him.

John says there is more: "Fear God and give him glory" (Revelation 14:7). What does that mean?

Giving God glory means honoring God in everything we do. Glory is a word reserved for the highest form of adoration. To give God glory means that our entire lifestyle is surrendered to reflecting His will for us.

Paul clarifies what it means to glorify God with these words:

> "For you were bought with a price; therefore glorify God in your body and in your spirit, which are God's."

> "Therefore, whether you eat or drink, or whatever you do, do all to the glory of God" (1 Corinthians 6:20; 10:31).

Here is a powerful concept: glorify God in all of your actions. You do not give God glory by placing abusive substances in the body which destroy. You do not glorify God by polluting your mind with this world's filth. You glorify God by saying, "Lord, my body is yours. My mind is yours. My spirit is yours."

Now to the second part of this message. The angel tells us *why* we are supposed to do this; *why* we should fear and glorify God.

The Bible tells us repeatedly to worship God for one reason: quite simply, He's the Creator. What does the angel say here?

> "Worship Him who made heaven and earth, the sea and springs of water" (Revelation 14:7).

God created the mind-boggling, wonderful complexity of life on this planet. God created everything out there in the stars, everything you can see through the Hubble telescope—and more. God created everything you can see through the most powerful electron microscope. He spoke, and from nothingness, complex life-forms assembled.

The very reason we worship God is because He created us, John says:

> "You are worthy, O Lord, to receive glory and
> honor and power; for You created all things
> and by Your will they exist and were created"
> (Revelation 4:11).

In an age when the popular, so-called scientific view is that the human race evolved over millions of years from single-celled amoebas and simple life-forms to complex forms of life called human beings, God calls our society back to worship Him as the Creator.

Earth's final conflict, earth's last spiritual war, will be centered on this subject of worship. Revelation 14:7 calls us to worship the Creator. Revelation 14:9 calls us to avoid worshipping the beast.

These two worships—worshipping the creator and worshipping the beast – will form the heart of a titanic struggle between the forces of good and evil. The coming economic boycott, the enforcement of the Mark of the Beast, the mysterious #666 all have to do with this final battle over worship.

We will fully explain the significance of what it means to worship the Creator and how to avoid receiving the Mark of the Beast in future chapters.

But for now, let's move to the third part of this message. This tells us what has happened that makes our allegiance, our worship, so critical. The angel proclaims that the hour of God's judgment has come.

Now, many people shy away from the idea of a divine

judgment, believing it's pretty scary to stand before God to give account of what they have done. Some even believe it contradicts the idea of a loving, accepting God. He just forgives period, they say; He doesn't need to sort things out in a judgment.

Let's step back a moment and get a broader perspective on this subject. Let's start with the very first verse in the book of Revelation:

> "The Revelation of Jesus Christ, which God gave Him to show His servants things which must shortly take place" (Revelation 1:1).

So, who is this book of Revelation revealing? Jesus Christ. If you want to get to know Jesus, read the gospels, read about His life. But don't stop there if you want the whole picture. The book of Revelation is a revelation of Jesus too. It shows us Jesus in the end-times. And it shows Jesus involved in judgment. But here's the good news: the gospel of Jesus, the good news of His salvation, is also involved in the judgment. We need to understand that.

The truth of the gospel does not remove the truth of the judgment. No. The truth of the gospel is the answer to the truth of the judgment.

What is this judgment all about anyway? Remember that, at the beginning of time, a rebel angel challenged God's character. Lucifer claimed that God was unfair, unjust. He made this accusation before the whole universe.

Now, thousands of years have gone by. The watching universe has seen the results of Satan's way, Satan's work on this planet. They've seen the cruelty, the suffering, the abuse, the horrors of war. The universe has also seen all the things God has done to warn people about the results of sin, all the things He has done to save us.

But there are still questions, big questions. Has God been fair in his dealings with every individual? Has everyone truly had a chance to make a decision about eternity?

The judgment answers those questions. In the judgment, as cases are reviewed, everyone gets a chance to see that God has been fair and just. Everyone can see that anyone who is lost is lost because of his own choices. God has done everything He can to save them.

At the end of time, the whole universe will joyfully proclaim in one chorus of praise:

> "True and righteous are His judgments" (Revelation 19:2).

The judgment is also about dealing with sin once and for all. God has to draw a line at some point and say, "Enough!" He doesn't want sin and suffering to go on forever. He won't let destructive behavior go on forever unchecked. And so He has appointed a time when the door is closed on wickedness, a time when sin ends.

But He will do this openly and fairly. He will allow everyone to see exactly how He's reached His decisions.

Here is something incredible. Revelation 14:7 says,

> "The hour of His [God's] judgment has come."

The coming of Jesus is later pictured in Revelation 14:14 when the Son of Man comes in the clouds. God's judgment hour precedes the coming of Jesus. According to Jesus:

> "Give everyone according to his work" (Revelation 22:12).

If Jesus is coming to give out His reward, a judgment must precede His coming to determine who will receive a fair reward. The decisions we make today are settling our eternal destiny. The choices we make today determine where we will spend eternity.

A day will soon come when our characters are settled due to the choices we have made. John describes it this way:

> "He who is unjust, let him be unjust still; he who is filthy, let him be filthy still; he who is righteous, let him be righteous still; he who is holy, let him be holy still" (Revelation 22:11).

Sin is a deadly disease, let loose on this planet. God is going to eradicate it. But he will do that only at the point when every person has made a choice, when people have chosen between allegiance to Satan or allegiance to God. A time is coming when those choices will seal destinies forever.

Jesus is coming back, not to destroy sinners, but to destroy sin. That's why he has given us this urgent message about his judgment, about worship and allegiance. We are rushing headlong toward an impact with the end of time. We are speeding toward a collision with the final events of earth's history. The judgment is upon us. And too many have been lulled into a false sense that everything is business as usual, that just drifting along is good enough.

This planet is going down just as surely as the Titanic sunk to the bottom of the Atlantic. We have to get into a lifeboat. We have to find a safe place. God has sent up the flares. He's prepared plenty of lifeboats. But we have to get in. And sometimes we have to let go of things in order to get in. Titanic passengers couldn't take their foot lockers with them. They had to leave things behind.

Sin will not be in heaven. And if we just refuse to let go of something self-destructive, if we're more interested in hanging on to that, then what can God do?

We need to let go of the things that hold us back and grab firmly God's hand. We can trust Him to get us into the lifeboat. He's provided a wonderful rescue in Jesus Christ.

Do grab hold of that hand, extended all the way down to you. There will be great rejoicing in heaven that you accepted His rescue plan. ❑

8
REVELATION REVEALS HOW JESUS WILL COME

There's something wonderfully hopeful about watching astronauts in their space shuttle—human beings tinkering in the vastness of space as if it were their garage or back yard.

Recently we all watched in amazement as the space-shuttle crew managed to rescue a damaged satellite—retrieving it from the vastness of space, locking it into place in the shuttle cargo bay, and repairing the complex instrument before sending it on its way again. Seeing those astronauts drifting in slow motion, their white space suits gleaming against the enormous blackness of space—gave us pause for reflection. It was an inspiring achievement.

For those of us watching here on earth, space-shuttle flights have served, more than anything else, as a window to a breathtaking glimpse of our universe.

Everything is on a grand scale out there. Eternity seems so much closer when you escape the gravity of Earth.

The space shuttle helps us think seriously about our basis for hope as human beings. What's our place in the universe? When, if ever, will eternity touch this planet?

I see a sharp contrast between the kind of hope inspired by the space shuttle and the kind of hope inspired by popular religion today. The achievements of the space program are inspiring because they're tangible and specific; all the complex details—the flow of rocket fuel, the humming of computers, the astronaut check list—it all fits together like clockwork.

Religious hope today, however, tends to be vague and shapeless. People have *hunches* about life after death; people *imagine* something about what heaven might be like. We don't have much that's specific or tangible. Some hope for a light at the end of the tunnel. Some believe that mankind will somehow stumble into love and peace.

This kind of vague hope maybe OK on a greeting card. But what about when you come face to face with death? What about when some malignant tumor or serious heart condition brings it all home, and suddenly you feel lost, weightless, severed from your life line?

Vague hope doesn't do much for us then. We need something tangible and specific to cling to.

Now you may be thinking that religious hope is always going to be a shot in the dark. After all, it's not scientific. We can't really *know* what lies beyond the grave, some say.

Let me ask you: Do you think our Creator is scientific? Would He make a good scientist? Maybe you've never thought of God in that way. But if He's the Creator of all living things, doesn't that make Him wiser than all our scientists combined? Certainly He's capable of being precise and specific if He so chooses. Certainly He can carry out His end-time plan like clockwork; He can make it fit together as smoothly as a space-shuttle flight.

My point is this: God *has* laid out His end-time plan for our world in the Scriptures. He's specific. He's eager to tell us what's coming in the future, what we can hope for.

So our typically vague religious hopes and God the Creator just don't mix. He's communicated clearly; why should we rely on hunches? He's painted for us a bright, focused picture of hope; why should we try to imagine a light at the end of the tunnel?

Much of God's wonderful picture is in the book of Revelation. Revelation gives us a look at the event that will bring human history to a climax. And it pictures that event in various ways.

Here's one of those pictures:

> "And I looked, and behold, a white cloud, and on the cloud sat One like the Son of Man, having on His head a golden crown and in His hand a sharp sickle" (Revelation 14:14).

Here Jesus Christ is coming in glory, coming to a world that is ripe for the harvest. Christ is coming to take his followers home to heaven.

Here's another picture:

> "Then I saw heaven opened, and behold, a white horse. And He who sat on him was called Faithful and True. . . And the armies in heaven clothed in fine linen, white and clean, followed Him on white horses" (Revelation 19:11, 14).

Jesus Christ comes down as a triumphant general leading the hosts of heaven to rescue his people from a doomed planet.

The Kingdom of God will have finally burst upon this planet:

> "The kingdoms of this world have become the kingdoms of our Lord and of His Christ, and He shall reign forever and ever" (Revelation 11:15).

Christ is coming to take us home! Christ is coming to reign forever and ever! That's the central event in the book of Revelation, blessed hope of the New Testament.

Let's look at exactly *how* this event will happen. What exactly is involved in this Second Coming of Jesus Christ? What will happen to us as a result? Fortunately the Bible gives us clear answers.

Paul helps us:

> "Behold, I tell you a mystery: We shall not all sleep, but we will all be changed—in a flash, in the twinkling of an eye, at the last trumpet. For the trumpet will sound, the dead will be raised imperishable, and we will be changed. For the perishable must clothe itself with the imperishable, and the mortal with immortality" (1 Corinthians 15:51-53, NIV).

Please remember: this is the God of the universe talking through His messanger; this is not some mystic speculating about the future. Mortal human beings will be changed; we'll be clothed with immortality in the twinkling of an eye. God will re-create us as imperishable beings.

When? At the last trumpet. In his first letter to the Thessalonians Paul writes that Jesus Christ will descend from the heavens with the trumpet call of God, and the dead will rise from their graves.

Human beings will meet eternity at the Second Coming of Jesus Christ. Those who've placed their faith in Him as Lord and Savior will face a wonderful new age of discovery.

New Testament hope is specific first of all because it centers on a specific person. The Second Coming is not about some UFO that's going to invade history. He's very much identified: Jesus Christ, Lord and Savior, coming in glory.

Scripture also tells us about an enemy who will try to

sabotage that plan. Speaking about the appearance of false christs, Jesus warned His disciples:

> "Men will tell you, 'There he is!' or 'Here he is!' Do not go running off after them. For the Son of Man in his day will be like the lightning, which flashes and lights up the sky from one end to the other" (Luke 17:23, 24, NIV).

Charismatic figures will arise in the last days, claiming to be Christ. Their miracle-working powers will seduce many people. They'll gain large followings. People will come to you excitedly, with a glow on their faces, saying: "We've seen Christ face-to-face! Come and see him."

What are we told to do? "Don't go running off after them." Christ won't suddenly appear on a talk-show in New York or as a miracle-worker on the streets of Paris. He won't rise up from somewhere down here; He'll be coming down from up there!

A family in Toronto woke up one morning to discover that their barbecue grill was missing from the patio. It was nowhere to be found; someone must have stolen it. But the next morning the barbecue was back in place, along with a note which read: "We just borrowed it; sorry for the inconvenience." Attached to the note were two tickets to a very popular play.

The delighted family went to the theater and had a wonderful evening out. But on their return they discovered that the barbecue bandits had cleaned out the whole house!

At some point the enemy is going to hand us tickets to the theater; we'll have a chance to see a charismatic, miracle-worker, someone who claims to be Christ. Don't go. The Antichrist wants to clean out your spiritual home.

How do we distinguish the real Christ from the false

christs in the end-time? Very simple. When Jesus Christ ascended into the sky following His resurrection, an angel told His watching disciples the following:

> "This same Jesus, who has been taken from you into heaven, will come back in the same way you have seen him go into heaven" (Acts 1:11, NIV).

Jesus is going to descend from the skies; it's going to be a visible event, as His ascension was; tangible and specific. The book of Revelation says, "Behold, He comes with clouds and every eye will see Him" (Revelation 1:7). Peter tells us the heavens will disappear with a roar and the earth will be burned up (2 Peter 3:10-12). Paul tells us the Lord Jesus will be revealed from heaven in blazing fire with his powerful angels (2 Thessalonians 1:7-10).

Jesus Himself describes the event:

> "For as lightning that comes from the east is visible even in the west, so will be the coming of the Son of Man . . . the Son of Man will appear in the sky, and all the nations of the earth will mourn. They will see the Son of Man coming on the clouds of the sky, with power and great glory" (Matthew 24:27, 30, NIV).

People can fake miracles; people can claim to be Christ. But no one can counterfeit the Second Coming. It will be unmistakably real. When the heavens above us explode, and ten thousand angels lift their voices, and the glory of God Almighty breaks through the clouds, no one will wonder who has come calling.

God has given us a very clear picture of His end-time plan. It is definitely not a picture of some secret, mystical event. It's not something that happens in our hearts, invisible to others.

Some people have misinterpreted a few Scripture texts and built up the picture of a Secret Rapture, where individuals are whisked away to heaven in a flash while others go about their business. Let's notice how Jesus' described His return:

> "But of that day and hour no one knows, no, not even the angels of heaven, but My Father only" (Matthew 24:36).

> "But know this, that if the master of the house had known what hour the thief would come, he would have watched and not allowed his house to be broken into. Therefore you also must be ready, for the Son of Man is coming at an hour when you do not expect Him" (Matthew 24:43, 44).

All the images in the Bible which discuss Jesus' coming as a thief do not emphasize a secret coming but an *unexpected* coming. Jesus is not coming secretly to a chosen few. He is coming suddenly when millions do not expect Him.

The Secret Rapture theory relies primarily on texts that speak of the Lord coming like a thief in the night. We are told to watch and be ready for the unexpected event. On the surface this seems to imply a secret, perhaps invisible event.

The problem for that theory is that texts about Jesus coming like a thief stand side by side with texts about Jesus coming in a blaze of glory. Peter mentions the two in the same breath:

> "But the day of the Lord will come like a thief. The heavens will disappear with a roar; the elements will be destroyed by fire" (2 Peter 3:10, NIV).

Obviously the Lord comes like a thief in the sense that the Second Advent will be a great surprise to those who aren't ready. It catches them off guard. But it is *not* a mystical or invisible event. There's nothing quiet or intangible about the heavens disappearing with a roar.

The launch of a space shuttle gives just a little taste of what that great event will be like. The long countdown . . . the final tense seconds . . . the blast of those enormous engines . . . the explosion of smoke . . . the rocket balanced and motionless for an instant . . . and then the steady rise into the heavens.

Every eye is fixed on that craft as it begins its journey into space. The dreams and hopes of countless Americans rise with the shuttle into the clouds.

Our Creator God has planned an event no less dramatic, no less eye-riveting. It will capture the attention of every living being on this planet. It may come as an incredible surprise to some. But it won't be quiet; it won't be secret; it won't be something vague and mystical.

The Second Coming is the definite, irreversible period that God places on history. It's the end of one kind of age and the beginning of an entirely new one where Christ's followers are clothed with immortality. It's the time when death, the final enemy is vanquished.

But we won't be able to make up for lost time when Christ bursts through the clouds. No second chances! Not a subjective event that we can put off until the "right time."

It happens at the same time for everyone. When Christ descends from the sky, our destinies will be sealed, our eternal future determined.

So it's vitally important that each of us should be in sync with God's plan. We can't just follow our hunches or our imaginations. We have to look carefully at what God is going to do.

In history books we learn that World War II officially began on September 1, 1939. But the first shots were actually fired six days earlier.

Hitler originally had planned to launch an attack on Poland on August 26. The evening before, several combat units were poised to strike. But last-minute political developments forced Hitler to postpone the invasion. Each of the combat units had to be contacted by radio and called home. But one unit could not be reached.

So at 12:01 a.m. on the appointed day, August 26, a unit led by Lieutenant Herzner moved out and captured a railway station at the town of Mosty. He also took a few Polish prisoners. When Herzner telephoned in his report he was told that he'd jumped the gun. On orders, he released his prisoners and returned to Germany.

Now this snafu should have made Hitler's intentions plain. But incredibly enough, the Polish government missed the sign; they let the incident pass without notice. And when the Nazis swept into the country on September 1, the Poles were taken by surprise.

We don't want to miss the signs of God's final invasion of human history. We don't want to be surprised by Christ's Second Coming as by a thief in the night. These are the specific events we can look forward to at Christ's Second Coming—in close sequence:

1. Seismic upheavals. Revelation 6:14; 16:18-20

> First there will be stupendous seismic upheavals; mountains and islands will be moved; and a great earthquake will shake the planet.

2. Righteous dead raised. 1 Thessalonians 4:16; John 5:28, 29

Paul tells us in Thessalonians, "The dead in Christ shall rise first." All who sleep in their graves will hear Christ's trumpet-like voice and rise up to eternal life.

3. Righteous living translated. 1 Thessalonians 4:17

The righteous who are alive will be caught up together with the resurrected and ascend toward Christ, who is flashing across the heavens in glory.

4. Immortality bestowed. 1 Corinthians 15:53

Both the righteous resurrected dead and the translated living will receive the gift of immortality.

5. The wicked are destroyed. Revelation 19:11-21

Those who have deliberately and persistently rejected God's call of mercy will be destroyed. The glory of Christ which is a thrilling sight for His friends, seems like consuming fire to His enemies.

6. The righteous welcome the returning Christ. Isaiah 25:9

As Christ's followers ascend toward their Lord their boundless happiness echoes the words of the prophet: "This is our God; we have waited for Him, and He will save us . . . we will be glad and rejoice in his salvation."

7. The righteous journey to heaven. John 14:2, 3

Finally, the righteous begin a wonderful

journey with Christ toward their heavenly home. They remember His words of promise: . . ."I go to prepare a place for you. . . . I will come again and receive you to Myself, that where I am, there you may be also."

This is the hope each one of us can cling to if our faith in Christ is secure. It's not something vague or speculative. It's specific; it's clear; it's a plan as comprehensive as the plan to put man in space. God has told us exactly how He will return; and exactly what will happen at His return.

You can imagine what it will be like—

Somewhere, in a small family cemetery on the wind-swept prairie, the earth breaks open. The flowers that a grieving mother has placed by the tombstone are laid aside. A tiny coffin opens up and a baby's voice begins to cry out. Instantly an angel darts from the sky and gathers the infant in his arms. In another instant he's beside the mother, who's been gazing in stunned silence at the heavens.

She stares at her son for a second. The last time she looked at his precious face it was pale and full of pain. His breath had come in little gasps as he fought a losing battle against a deadly disease. His flesh is now warm and pink; his eyes bright as it looks in the mother's face.

And trembling, this woman takes her baby and hugs him close, too happy for words. When she turns to thank the angel--he's already off on another mission.

Somewhere, in a city cemetery, a young couple find themselves standing beside their own open graves. At first, they're completely disoriented in the bright light around them. They have no idea how they got there. The last thing they remember is a big truck heading straight at them. They were on their way to their honeymoon. Did they somehow survive the accident? No, those are their names on the tombstones.

Then they look up and catch their breath. The man and woman reach for each other as they stare at the heavens. This is it! This is Jesus Christ appearing. This is the One they dedicated themselves to in their wedding ceremony. And now the whole planet is lit up with His presence. Now they know that they will never, ever be parted again. They will have an eternity to grow in their love.

In the last few minutes of Earth's history, this planet will be shaken with countless resurrections. And everywhere you'll hear the cries of recognition with loved-ones torn apart by tragedy, falling into each other's arms.

Now, it really does seem, to believers, that their joy knows no bounds. They can't possibly contain it all. They're clutching loved-ones who were once torn from their side by death. But something else happens, the most wonderful event of all.

Believers begin to notice that their feet are no longer on the ground. They feel weightless. They are rising to meet this spectacle in the heavens. Many of the joyful reunions, in fact, happen in mid-air—families embracing on their way to meet Jesus.

And now the face of the Savior is really close. The joyful voices of believers rise up to meet the trumpet sound and the call of angels echoing from the cloud.

Rising up to meet the Lord of Lords, the Prince of Peace, the Wonderful Counselor, the Good Shepherd! Rising up to meet the Creator of all life! Rising up to meet an eternal destiny with Jesus! What inexpressible joy!

These are the last moments, the last seconds of human history. Where will you be during the last minutes of Earth's history? What will you be experiencing?

Will it be unimaginable terror? Or inexpressible joy? You may feel rather indifferent about God right now. You may not think faith is so important. But one day soon it will make all the difference in the world. One day soon it will divide humanity eternally, into two groups. Revelation, the Bible's last book, describes two classes at our Lord's return.

One group will experience the Second Coming of Christ as a horrifying surprise. They will be praying for the rocks to fall on them:

> "And the kings of the earth, the great men, the rich men, the commanders, the mighty men, every slave and every free man, hid themselves in the caves and in the rocks of the mountains, and said to the mountains and rocks, 'Fall on us and hide us from the face of Him who sits on the throne and from the wrath of the Lamb! For the great day of His wrath has come, and who is able to stand'" (Revelation 6:15-17)?

The second group will experience it as a wonderful deliverance, as a fulfillment of all they've lived for. They will be singing ecstatically:

> "This is our God, we have waited for Him and He will save us" (Isaiah 25:9).

> "Great and marvelous are Your works, Lord God Almighty! Just and true are Your ways, O King of the saints" (Revelation 15:3).

Please don't put off an encounter with Jesus Christ until it's too late. Make your commitment now. This is your invitation.

Think of what it will be like to look up and see the

first sign of Christ's return: that unusual cloud in the distance that keeps getting brighter, and, yes, closer. It will be as tangible as the gleaming space shuttle floating into our atmosphere for a landing. Every eye fixed on it. Everyone waiting breathlessly as it comes closer and closer to you and me.

Yes, God our Creator will someday soon descend from outer space and make a spectacular appearance. That's the great hope, shining through the New Testament. That's the hope that can lift us above our dreary days and out of our darkest night.

In the prophecies of the Bible we are given a remarkable space window. We do get a glimpse of eternity coming closer; we can find our place in the universe. And we will understand clearly how God will overcome His and our final enemy—death.

Perhaps you're in desperate need of hope right now. Maybe you've lost a family member in a car accident. Perhaps you've had to say a painful good-by at the bedside of a beloved Mother or Father. Or you've had to walk down a cold, impersonal hospital corridor, knowing that your child has very little chance of pulling through.

Whatever your dark shadow is, please remember that God's hope is brighter. Jesus is coming soon to put an end to all of our dark shadows.

Don't you want to be a part of that great victory? Don't you want to be one of those who rise to meet the Lord in the air, united with departed loved ones?

Choose today to make Jesus, the coming Lord your personal Savior. ❏

9
REVELATION PREDICTS THE
TIME OF THE END

For decades, America has represented the last hope for desperate causes, the final stand of individuals threatened by a hostile majority. The United States Supreme Court is a majestic symbol of law and justice. It suggests to millions the ideal that, in the end, right will prevail.

The Supreme Court's rulings have sometimes been very controversial; some believe it has blundered badly in recent times. But the principle this court stands for remains: Individuals have an opportunity to appeal their case all the way to the top, all the way to the Supreme Court.

But what about the most important judgment of all. The final judgment. Could there possibly be a way for an individual to appeal God's verdict? Is there a Supreme Court behind the voice that thunders out, separating for all eternity, the sheep from the goats?

Think about some of the images in Scripture used to describe God's judgment. God Almighty seated at His Great White Throne, decreeing the destiny of humanity, sentencing some to hell, welcoming others into heaven. Mountains melt like wax when He comes to judge the peoples. The whole earth trembles before His majesty; a stream of fire flows as the verdict is about to be read.

On that day, some even among those who've given many Bible studies and seminars or cast out devils in the

Lord's name will be told, "Depart from me, you workers of iniquity."

The final judgment is obviously all in God's hands. He is the sovereign ruler over all. In the end we will all appear before Him, and Him alone, to give account for what we have done.

To many people, this is a terrifying prospect. Our eternal destiny decided, as it were, in the wink of an eye; with the flick of His wrist, God assigns us either with the sheep or with the goats. No other decision could ever be as important, and yet no other decision seems so completely out of our hands.

Some may have even wondered: Can there be any appeal to this final verdict? Can we get a word in perhaps, before the final, divine gavel falls? Perhaps explain something about why we were so mean to our parents, or why we stopped going to that church?

Is God really acting alone in the final judgment or is there a Supreme Court to which we may make a final appeal?

Let's see what Scripture can tell us. The prophet Daniel gives us a very dramatic portrayal of a judgment scene in the seventh chapter of his book:

> "As I looked, thrones were set in place, and the Ancient of Days took his seat. . . Thousands upon thousands attended him; ten thousand times ten thousand stood before him. The court was seated, and the books were opened" (Daniel 7:9, 10, NIV).

Isn't it interesting that it says, "thrones were set in place." Thrones—in the plural. Evidently the Ancient of Days, God Himself, permits other heavenly beings to preside with him in the judgment. That idea is further supported by the phrase, "The court was seated."

Daniel's vision almost suggests robed Supreme Court justices filing in to their stately chairs behind the high bench to hear oral arguments. Evidently God's final decision regarding individual human destinies isn't just a matter of divine decree. He is willing to carry this out in a courtroom setting, accompanied by others on their thrones, and in front of thousands upon thousands of witnesses.

In other words, God's final judgment is an open affair, not a private decision. When that supreme court in heaven is seated, Daniel tells us, the "books" are opened. Although God is omniscient and doesn't need to be reminded of the facts, He has chosen to make the final judgment a matter of public record; the evidence is down in black and white.

Read what John the Revelator saw in vision:

> "And I saw the dead, great and small, standing
> before the throne, and books were opened.
> Another book was opened, which is the book
> of life. The dead were judged according to
> what they had done as recorded in the books"
> (Revelation 20:12, NIV).

It's apparent that the Almighty doesn't merely want to satisfy Himself in the judgment; He also wants to satisfy all those who witness the proceedings. Evidence is presented for all to see.

That's one thing that is apparent in the rulings handed down from the U.S. Supreme Court. Those nine justices take great care in writing their decisions, because they know that the principles they express will become the basis for future law. Each Supreme Court justice has a staff of law clerks who conduct a great deal of research on the issues surrounding a particular case. They want as many facts on hand as possible before making their historic decisions.

I get the impression of a similar principle at work in the divine supreme court that presides in the end-time. A thorough work of investigation goes on when the court is seated and books are opened. Apparently, facts are made very clear in each case before a final verdict is rendered. That is, before God in His wisdom separates the sheep from the goats. Before the saved and the lost are sent off to their two destinies, He graciously chooses to go over the evidence in an open and thorough investigation.

Picture this final investigation as it is highlighted in the Bible's longest most amazing prophecy. We learn where this judgment takes place and when it began. We will understand why we are living in the end-time of God's judgment hour. And all this can give us a valuable perspective on how to live our lives, in preparation for that judgment hour.

Revelation contains vivid scenes of the hour of God's judgment. But it doesn't tell us much about its timing. To discover when the judgment begins we must turn to the prophetic book of Daniel. Daniel unlocks several mysteries in Revelation. God designed these two books to be studied together.

Let's look first at *where* the judgment takes place:

> "I watched till thrones were put in place, And the Ancient of Days was seated; His garment was white as snow, And the hair of His head was like pure wool. His throne was a fiery flame, Its wheels a burning fire . . . A thou-

sand thousands ministered to Him; Ten thousand times ten thousand stood before Him.
The court was seated, And the books were
opened" (Daniel 7:9, 10).

Daniel's attention was directed to heaven, to the
throne room of the universe—to a kind of supreme court
in heaven's sanctuary.

The books were opened. The final judicial investigation begins in heaven.

When did it begin? Let's try to answer that question.
You may recall that John tells us:

"Fear God and give glory to Him, for the hour
of His judgment has come" [Note that the text
doesn't say "will come" at some future time,
but "has come"] (Revelation 14:7).

Also, Revelation 14:6-12 clearly states that before
Christ returns, a message will go to all the world
announcing the judgment hour.

So, we need to look for a type of judgment that
occurs *before* the second coming of Christ. The prophet
Daniel gives us the time frame in the Bible's longest and
most amazing prophecy:

"For two thousand three hundred days; then
the sanctuary shall be cleansed" (Daniel 8:14).

Let's look at what this means, "the sanctuary shall be
cleansed."

We need to understand something about the ceremonial system in the Old Testament. Since the time of
Moses, the Jews followed a detailed worship program that
centered on their earthly sanctuary service, either in the
portable tabernacle or in the Hebrew temple. These sacri-

fices and offerings were modeled after a pattern God gave to Moses. The services of the earthly sanctuary were to serve as an illustration of the plan of salvation. God wanted certain truths to stand out clearly. The offering of a lamb without blemish, for example, pointed forward to the Lamb of God, Jesus Christ, who laid down his sinless life as a sacrifice on our behalf.

Two main services were connected with the sanctuary—the daily service and the yearly service. Here's what happened in a typical daily service. A person who had sinned brought a sacrifice to the temple. He confessed his sin over the animal and the animal was killed. A priest caught the blood in a basin, poured most of it out at the base of the altar of brass, then took the rest of it into the sanctuary. In this way, sin was symbolically transferred from the sinner to the substitute, to the sanctuary. Again, that innocent slain lamb pointed forward to Christ's ultimate sacrifice on our behalf.

Now, in a sense, this stream of sacrificial blood flowed all year, bringing sin into the sanctuary. And that's why the yearly service was required. On the tenth day of the seventh month of the religious year, the Hebrews participated in the Day of Atonement. *That's when the sanctuary was cleansed.*

> "In the seventh month, on the tenth day of the month, you shall afflict your souls, and do no work at all . . . For on that day the priest shall make atonement for you, to cleanse you, that you may be clean from all your sins before the Lord" (Leviticus 16:29, 30).

Actually, this soul-searching began ten days before the Day of Atonement. Ten days before, silver-trumpet blasts announced the coming of that solemn day. Those who deliberately ignored the warning were shut off from the camp.

This cleansing of the sanctuary in the Old Testament was an illustration of something that would happen before Christ's coming. Those daily sacrifices pointed forward to the sacrifice of Christ. The cleansing of the sanctuary pointed forward to something else. Daniel 8:14 says that after 2300 days, the sanctuary shall be cleansed, referring to a judgment that takes place before the end of Earth's history. The earthly ceremonies described in Leviticus 16 are shadows of God's judgment in the heavenly sanctuary which will take place just before Jesus comes again.

During the Old Testament's Day of Atonement, two goats were used—the "Lord's goat" and the scapegoat.

The Lord's goat was sacrificed. The high priest took its blood into the sanctuary, through the veil into the most holy place. He sprinkled the blood on the mercy seat that rested on a chest called the Ark of the Covenant. This chest contained the original, divinely etched Ten Commandments. It represented the throne of God in heaven where Jesus represents His people today.

The high priest before the mercy seat was standing in the very presence of God. He represented Jesus Christ, our heavenly high priest, who appears before God on our behalf.

After the Lord's goat was sacrificed in this way, the scapegoat was led into the wilderness to wander until it died. This represented the death of Satan, the originator of sin. Each year, the Hebrews were reminded of the sacrifice of the Savior and of the ultimate elimination of sin from the universe. Each year they participated in a service that prepared them for God's ultimate judgment.

So, this is what we can say: The cleansing of the sanctuary in Daniel 8:14 is about the Day of Atonement; it refers to a very specific process of judgment.

But when did this process begin? Let's look at the time frame of the prophecy. Daniel says, after 2300 days the sanctuary will be cleansed.

Daniel himself didn't really know what that meant. He was perplexed. But God, being who he is, sent an angel to explain things. God said:

> "'Gabriel, make this man to understand the vision.'. . .So he came near where I stood: and when he came, I was afraid, and fell upon my face: but he said to me, 'Understand, son of man, that the vision refers to the time of the end'" (Daniel 8:16, 17).

Notice three points these verses make. They shed light on the 2300-day prophecy.

First, the vision extends to the close of time, to "the time of the end."

Second, the 2300 days applies to God's heavenly sanctuary. Why? Because the earthly system of sacrifices, obsolete after the death of Christ, were all fulfilled.

Third, the 2300 days represents a time period couched in the symbolic language of apocalyptic prophecy.

First, let's remember that a day represents a year in Bible prophecy. Ezekiel 4:6 tells us: "I have laid on you a day for each year." So we can safely say, the 2300 days represents 2300 years.

The angel Gabriel explained more to Daniel about the 2300 days. That time period was broken into two segments. First, he says in Daniel 9:24:

> "Seventy weeks are determined for your
> people and for your holy city."

Seventy weeks relate to "your people," the Jews.
Seventy weeks equal 490 days, or, in prophecy, 490 years.
In this time period, the Jews had the opportunity to accomplish the work God gave them. This was their final chance.
God would have to use other means to accomplish His purposes if they failed.

Those seventy weeks, 490 years, are determined, cut
off from the 2300 days or years. That leaves us with 1810
years remaining. The remaining 1810 years would lead to
an event called the "cleansing of the sanctuary" or the
time of judgment.

Now let's look at the master key for unlocking this
entire time prophecy:

> "Know therefore and understand, That from
> the going forth of the command to restore and
> build Jerusalem until Messiah the Prince,
> there shall be seven weeks and sixty-two
> weeks . . . " (Daniel 9:25).

When Daniel received this prophecy, his people, the
Jews, were exiles, captives in Babylon. Jerusalem lay in
ruins. The angel told Daniel this time prophecy would
begin when the final, imperial decree was officially
given, allowing the Jews to return to their homeland and
rebuild Jerusalem.

We have a precise date for that event. Artaxerxes,
King of Persia, made that decree in the fall of 457 BC.

So now we have a starting date. The seven weeks, or
490 years, began in 457 BC. And the 2300 days or years
began in 457 BC.

Do you know what we discover if we follow this time

line? We find that Daniel foretells with remarkable precision the dates of the baptism and death of Jesus. It also foretells the time when the gospel would be rejected by the Jewish nation and proclaimed to the Gentile world.

Notice what the prophecy says: sixty-two weeks plus seven weeks from the decree to restore Jerusalem until the coming of the Messiah. That's a total of 69 prophetic weeks, or 483 literal years.

So with these momentous events in mind, let's go back to our starting point, 457 BC. That's the decree that starts everything. Now let's add 483 years to 457 BC. Remember in BC we're counting backwards. It takes us to 26 AD. But remember there was no zero year in history. Historians record time from 1 BC to 1 AD. So we must add a year, coming up with AD 27.

What happened in AD 27? That's exactly when the Messiah, Jesus Christ, the anointed one, began His public ministry following his baptism. It happened in the fall of AD 27, in the fifteenth year of the reign of Tiberius.

This remarkable prophecy gives special meaning to what Jesus often proclaimed in his preaching, "The time is fulfilled." The time had indeed been fulfilled, with incredible accuracy.

That 69-week prophecy, given approximately 500 years before the birth of Christ, pinpointed the exact date of Christ's baptism.

Now, the ministry of Christ lasted precisely three-and-a-half years. Guess what? This too was predicted by Daniel:

> "And after the sixty-two weeks, Messiah shall be cut off . . . Then he shall confirm a covenant with many for one week; But in the middle of the week He shall bring an end to sacrifice and offering." (Daniel 9:26, 27).

The Bible predicted that in the midst of this last week—the seventieth week allotted to the Jewish nation—sacrifices would stop, come to an end.

Remember the 69th week ended in AD 27. One last prophetic week remained. In other words, seven years remained. Note "in the middle of the week" there would be an end to sacrifice. What's the middle of the prophetic week? Three-and-a-half years. Add three-and-a-half years to 27 AD. That brings us to AD 31.

Amazingly, at this precise time, during the feast of Passover, in the spring of AD 31, Jesus was crucified. the Jewish sacrificial system no longer had any meaning. Christ, our Passover Lamb, had been sacrificed.

That's what happened "in the middle of the week," the last prophetic week of the period allotted to the Jews. What about the end of the week? Three-and-a-half more years, after AD 27? What happened in AD 34?

As it turns out, that's when the first Christian martyr, Stephen, was stoned to death by the Jews. Jewish leaders were sealing their rejection of the gospel. The gospel then went to the Gentiles. That's how the 70 weeks, or 490 years allowed to the nation of Israel were concluded.

Centuries in advance, the prophet Daniel had laid all this out. The exact time of Christ's baptism, the exact time of Christ's crucifixion, the exact time the gospel went to the Gentiles. The seventy weeks cut out of the 2300 day prophecy are clearly accounted for.

But what about the remaining time of that prophecy? After we advance 70 weeks, or 490 years from the starting point, 457 BC, we still have 1810 years left.

Now add 1810 years to AD 34—where we left off. We come to 1844. What did the Bible predict would happen then, at the end of the 2300 day/year prophecy?

The sanctuary would be cleansed; the judgment hour would begin in the heavenly sanctuary.

That's the message Daniel reveals. It is a solemn truth to consider. We are living in the judgment hour. God's final investigation began in 1844. God considers His judgment so important that He pictures an angel flying in the midst of heaven announcing with a loud voice:

> "Fear God and give glory to Him, for the hour
> of His judgment has come" (Revelation 14:7).

The Lord looks over the "books" recording the deeds of human beings throughout history. Names are reviewed and cases examined. Someday when this awesome task is completed, Christ will descend to earth to claim his own.

We are indeed living in the judgment hour, heading toward the climax of history. So let me ask you: Do you have confidence today about how your case will be decided in that final investigation in heaven? Or are you worried about being in the judgment hour?

Even if God does carefully weigh all the good and bad in that final investigation, most of us would probably still feel we're on very shaky ground. Only the most mis-guided egotist would claim that he has earned a spot in God's holy heaven—while staring up at those thrones of God's Supreme Court.

Friends, we need more than justice; we need more than fairness. We're all guilty when confronted with the standard of God's holy law. And that standard is not going to bend for any of us. Just as the Supreme Court justices of the United States are called to uphold the Constitution, and apply it consistently, so our Sovereign God will uphold His law.

So what hope is there? The answer is suggested by

one of the most celebrated cases to ever appear before America's highest court: Gideon vs. Wainwright.

Clarence Earl Gideon was arrested by police in a small Florida town for breaking and entering a poolroom. He was charged with a felony. Gideon, a homeless indigent, could not post bail and could not pay for a lawyer when his case came before the local court. He asked that the court appoint a counsel to serve in his defense.

The judge denied Gideon's request. He explained, "Under the laws of the state of Florida, the only time the Court can appoint Counsel . . . is when that person is charged with a capital offense."

So Gideon attempted to defend himself in the trial. He was convicted and sentenced to five years in prison. While incarcerated this man didn't just idle away his time, he began to study law; although he'd not had a great deal of formal education, he became quite an authority. Most importantly, Gideon ran across the Sixth Amendment to the Constitution, which states that an accused person shall have the right to counsel for his defense in all criminal prosecutions.

So he appealed his case to higher state courts, asking, in carefully written petitions, that they declare his conviction invalid because he'd been refused his constitutional right to counsel. No one chose to rule in his favor. But eventually Gideon's case reached the Supreme Court.

By that time, 22 other states had filed "friends of the court" briefs urging that the "right to counsel" be made a requirement throughout the United States. Justice Hugo Black was chosen to write the court's unanimous decision. He emphasized the fact that, in America, a fair trial means that "every defendant stands equal before the law." If only the rich could provide themselves with legal counsel, then others could not be guaranteed equal protection under the law. The Supreme Court ruled in Gideon's favor.

And so, because this one homeless man persevered in his petition, the Sixth Amendment guarantee of the right to counsel is made secure for every individual in America.

Now, what does this have to do with our predicament, as we face that divine Supreme Court at the end of time? See what the Apostle John tells us:

> "My dear children, I write this to you so that you will not sin. But if anybody does sin, we have one who speaks to the Father in our defense—Jesus Christ, the Righteous One" (1 John 2:1).

John tells us that we will have expert counsel on that day; Jesus Christ Himself will speak in our defense. Many translations say, "we have an advocate before the Father." That's the good news in the judgment. We won't stand alone before the holy tribunal; God Himself, in the person of our Advocate Jesus, will be standing right beside us.

What will this advocate do, exactly? How will He defend us? Will He, when our acts of insensitivity come to light, remind the judge of the times we were kind? Will He attempt to balance the picture by presenting our good side?

I do not believe that this is our Advocate's role. Let's read the very next verse:

> "He is the atoning sacrifice for our sins, and not only for ours but also for the sins of the whole world" (1 John 2:2, NIV)

His great speech on our behalf is the speech of Calvary, the evidence of the cross. I believe that on the day of judgment Christ will say, "Yes, this person is guilty of sin. He has fallen short of Your glory. But now he's been adopted as our son. He has accepted My sacrifice for sin on his behalf. He has chosen to ask our help in overcoming his sins. Therefore I ask that You accept Him into heaven on the basis of My perfect life, lived on earth."

That is what our Advocate can say on our behalf. He is going to win the case; He's going to win every time.

You see, God's Supreme Court is interested in justice, in upholding the law, but it's also focused on something more: the believer's Bill of Rights. All those who commit their lives to Christ as Lord and Savior are given incredible privileges, incredible rights. Our long record of good and bad deeds will no longer be used against us. We pass out of judgment and into life. We have the right to call on the righteousness of Christ.

Many years ago in Germany, a young musician named William Herschel played in the royal band of Hanover. His superior talent won him much admiration. But when war came and he had to huddle in trenches as the cannon roared all night, young William was overwhelmed with terror. One night he couldn't take it any more and fled the battlefield. Knowing that the penalty for desertion was death, he kept fleeing—all the way to England.

There, William started a new life for himself. He became a great organist and also began to study astronomy. The years passed; William was finally able to build his own telescope, and he spent night after night scanning the heavens. One evening he located a bright heavenly object that he couldn't identify. As it turned out, William had discovered a new planet. Soon the world was acclaiming his discovery, and the King of England sent for him.

As William approached Windsor Castle for his appointment, however, he was filled with a terrible dread, instead of joyous anticipation. For the King of England then was none other than George of Hanover, the man in whose army he'd served long before, the man who would recognize his name as that of the infamous deserter.

As he sat in a chamber, waiting for his audience with the king, a servant approached and presented him with an envelope. With trembling hands, William opened it. Would he finally look at his long awaited condemnation? Instead, William found a full and complete pardon for his act of desertion.

Overjoyed, William was ushered into the presence of the king. The monarch told him, "Now that you are pardoned we can talk freely, and you shall come and live at Windsor and become Sir William Herschel."

When your appointment with the King of the Universe comes, on that final day of reckoning, you need not tremble with fear. You don't have to worry about some past act of indiscretion, some terrible mistake coming up to condemn you. God has already written out a pardon full and free. All those who have looked up at the bright, morning star of Jesus Christ, all those who have seen him rise in their hearts as Savior and Lord, will find that the past is wiped away. Only Christ's grace will stand in that Supreme Court. Only His merits will count. But they are more than enough to win us a place in the King's Castle, an eternal home in heaven.

Your name can be written in the book of life right now. The Judge of the Universe can write out your pardon right now. Why not pass from judgment and into life. ❏

10
REVELATION'S ANSWER TO CRIME, LAWLESSNESS AND TERRORISM

Most people have tried to make their home a refuge from the stress of life. They've tried to make it a place of love and safety.

But futurists tell us that the home is headed for some dramatic changes. And families will have to adjust. It's more than a matter of Ozzie and Harriet simply getting laptops. The real question is: How will family values survive in the 21st century?

What will life be like in your home in the 21st century? How will things be different? What will remain the same? And how will this affect your ability to make the home a healthy, nurturing place for your family?

The first thing we hear from those who've been studying trends, sounds like good news. Most futurists agree that people will spend much more time at home in the 21st century.

In the closing decades of the twentieth century, the family home almost became a way-station to somewhere else. Mom and Dad often worked outside the home—single parents almost always had to. Parents and kids always seemed to be rushing through. They stopped for a quick bite to eat, or a change of clothes, and then hurried off to a soccer match or a late meeting at the office.

But in the future, many more people will be able to do their work at home, at their home computer. They'll be connected via the internet to a wide assortment of new businesses. More and more individuals will become free-lance workers and entrepreneurs.

In the next few decades, people will also do more of their shopping at home. They'll be able to surf the net for all kinds of goods and services—order catalogues, conduct transactions, make purchases—all at their keyboard. Television, telephone, computing, information—all these things will combine into one interlocking system—in your house.

So it looks like the home will be alive and well in the 21st century. That's the good news.

But there's also troubling news. And that relates to how easily unhealthy stuff can get *into* your home. There will be more and more avenues for incoming material that's dangerous or immoral. Recently we've seen examples of how quickly a virus or a hoax can spread to millions on the internet.

Even worse things can spread too.

Kids can access the most debasing kind of pornography on the internet.

Disturbed individuals can try to get a family member's name and address through e-mail.

Hate groups and bizarre cults are finding the internet a great way to spread their propaganda. Every wacko can now have a web site.

In the years ahead, popular culture will become a louder and louder voice in our homes—and make a bigger picture.

We'll soon be looking at high definition television screens that fill an entire living room wall. The images will look as sharp as photographs. Gorgeous images will dazzle us and seem to fill the whole room.

But what about the content? What about the messages that hit us so forcefully?

Read what one Gen-Xer named Greg thinks. As a nervous newly-wed he said this: "If you flip on the TV, you don't see families anymore. Family life is not part of the general TV menu. It takes a lot of faith to put a premium on marriage in your vision of life."

That's a cause for real concern in the 21st century.

Dr. Shervert Frazier served as Director of the National Institute of Mental Health. He expressed concerns in his book "Psychotrends." Dr. Frazier described what he called a "co-violent society." That's one which "celebrates mayhem while simultaneously condemning it." It ends up making violence seem amoral and inevitable.

In other words, the six o-clock news shows us a tragic picture of some kid sprawled on the street in a drive-by shooting. Nothing pretty about that at all. But then the eight o'clock movie shows us a hero mowing down or blowing up the bad guys in some new, spectacular, heart-stopping way. And that's entertainment. Soon it will splash all over your living room wall in living color.

We live in a world in which different values compete for our attention, and for our loyalty. It's pretty much an open marketplace. Your kids will see all kinds of beliefs and practices modeled in the programming that fills that high-definition TV screen. They'll be exposed to many different versions of right and wrong.

A major U.S. magazine recently described our nation as "America the Violent." Another article stated that 23,700 people were murdered in our country in one recent year. The average 18-year-old has witnessed 200,000 violent acts on television, including 40,000 murders.

We live in a dangerous world. One very important

part of protecting your family is helping them make good choices, helping them to be able to sort out values. They need to see for themselves the difference between the healthy and unhealthy, between the moral and immoral.

The question is, how do you make your values count—when so many others are bouncing off the wall? How do you do it in the 21st century?

Let's think about helping your family make wise choices. Start with a vitally important perspective that is highlighted in the book of Revelation. It provides a background for sorting out right from wrong. It's the proclamation of three angels that we've been keying-on in previous chapters. It's a vital one for our time:

> "Then I saw another angel flying in the midst of heaven, having the everlasting gospel to preach to those who dwell on the earth—to every nation, tribe, tongue, and people—saying with a loud voice, 'Fear God and give glory to Him, for the hour of his judgment has come; and worship Him who made heaven and earth, the sea and springs of water'" (Revelation 14:6,7).

This angel is introducing God's final message to a world hurtling toward a rendezvous with destiny, toward the end of time.

This angel has the "everlasting gospel" to preach to every person on earth. That's the good news of God's grace, of what Christ accomplished on the cross through his sacrificial death and what He wants to do in us through His Holy Spirit.

The angel who proclaims the gospel makes this specific call:

> "Fear God, give Him glory, because the hour
> of his judgment has come."

God is about to judge every individual on the planet. A day of reckoning is upon us. And God has a very clear standard on which He bases His judgments.

The apostle James, the brother of Jesus, puts it this way:

> "So speak and so do as those who will be
> judged by the law of liberty" (James 2:12).

The law of God is the standard of the judgment. It is a law of liberty by God's grace obeying that law frees us from sin's shackles, allowing God's grace to transform our hearts.

God's law, God's commandments are the unchanging standard of right and wrong. And that is what we need to acknowledge as our standard. We are accountable before God for our behavior, responsible for our choices.

Look at what John saw in heaven:

> "Then the temple of God was opened in
> heaven, and the ark of His covenant was seen
> in His temple" (Revelation 11:19).

When God commanded the Israelites in the Old Testament to build a sanctuary. He commanded them to make the ark of the covenant in which should go the tables of stone, or the Ten Commandments. John is showing us that the temple in heaven contains the real ark of the covenant, the real Ten Commandments. He is showing us that this moral law is the foundation of God's character.

Revelation's answer to moral chaos is found in heaven at God's throne, represented by the ark of His covenant that contains the Ten Commandments. The law of God is a transcript of God's character, a description of his will. It shows us clearly the difference between right and wrong. It shows us the basis on which God renders judgment.

But we've been losing that perspective, even among Christians in recent years. Believers don't want to talk about it too much. Many don't want to think about it at all.

And the truth is, part of the reason we are struggling to protect our families is that we've been running away from God's law of liberty for so long. Part of the reason we find it hard to help young people make wise, moral choices, is that we've been running away from God's law for so long.

We only want to "talk" about the gospel. We haven't realized how the judgment and the law are part of the gospel. The whole point of Christ dying on the cross was to put us in a right relationship with God's law. God's moral requirements loom large in the drama of salvation.

But we've largely lost sight of that. We've lost this sense of accountability before a holy God. We've lost the fact that there's a great standard for behavior. Read what John says about God's law:

> "Whoever commits sin also commits lawless-
> ness, and sin is lawlessness" (1 John 3:4).

Sin is not violation of my personal moral code of ethics. Sin is breaking God's moral code. Sin is violating heaven's code of conduct. I may not think it is sin. But that makes little difference. Sin is violating God's law.

We live in a time when most people are making up their own rules, looking for the truth only in their own hearts. And that comes across over and over in the programming that often fills our homes. It will only get worse in the 21st century.

So we need something big to counter that kind of thinking. We need something that will reinforce a different perspective. Think about it: the final judgment is big enough. That's an event big enough to fill the horizon. And it's an important event that tells us that our actions are measured against the absolute standard of God's law. It's an important event that helps us make wise, moral choices today.

Let's say your child has just watched a TV show in which the very cool main character uses a very clever deception to get what he wants. Maybe he pretends to be the star quarterback at school to get the pretty girl he's after. Maybe he sneaks off with his Dad's expensive sports car and passes it off as his own.

If your child watches enough of these episodes, he or she may begin to wonder: maybe I'd get farther ahead if I was a little more "creative" with the truth. Maybe honesty isn't all it's cooked-up to be.

If this youngster doesn't have a clear sense of accountability before God, it will be much easier to begin making up his own rules. If he doesn't understand that all we do is measured against the standard of God's law, it won't be hard to rationalize a few lies here and there to get ahead.

But that won't be easy if this young person knows that a holy God accepts and loves him—if he knows that this God wants the best for him—if he knows that this best is spelled out in God's commandments. Love always leads to obedience, never disobedience.

Jesus said, "If you love Me, keep My commandments" (John 14:15). Love does not lead me to do what I please, it leads me to do what He pleases.

John adds these powerful words:

"Now by this we know that we know Him, if we
keep His commandments. He who says, 'I know
Him,' and does not keep His commandments, is
a liar, and the truth is not in him" (1 John 2:3, 4).

When we are committed to Christ, when we gen-
uinely know Him, when our hearts are surrendered to
Him, the natural response is to obey Him.

Friends, here's the bottom line. The judgment makes
the thought of God's law bigger in our minds. You want
your family members to choose God's values when there
are many other values competing for attention. The judgment helps make God's values vivid. They're what Christ
fulfilled, at great cost. They're what God is calling us to
embrace as our own.

That's a perspective we badly need in the 21st century. We need this bigger picture; especially where moral
values shrink around us.

Let me share with you how God's law works on a
practical level. First of all, the law was intended to work
as a mirror, a very special kind of mirror. That law may
reflect specific problems in our lives, specific sins.

The Apostle Paul found that the law provides a
piercing diagnosis. In Romans 7:7, he wrote: "I would not
have known sin except through the law. For I would not
have known covetousness unless the law had said, "You
shall not covet." The apostle also adds, "By the law is the
knowledge of sin" Romans 3:20. God's law reveals what sin
is. It defines sin.

Of course, we are not saved by the law anymore than a
mirror can remove dirt. We are saved by grace: "For by
grace you have been saved, through faith, . . .not of works,
lest anyone should boast" (Ephesians 2:8, 9).

Salvation comes solely and only through grace. But grace does not lead us to disobedience, it leads us to obedience:

> "For sin shall not have dominion over you, for you are not under law but under grace" (Romans 6:14).

In this passage, Paul declares you will not be dominated by law-breaking because God's grace—His mercy to redeem you from your past guilt and His power working in your life—will enable you to obey God.

Grace and faith do not do away with God's law: "Do we then make void the law through faith? Certainly not! On the contrary, we establish the law" (Romans 3:31).

Grace never does away with God's commandments, it leads us to keep them. The apostle James tells us that we need the law as we do mirrors:

> "For if anyone is a hearer of the word and not a doer, he is like a man observing his natural face in a mirror; for he observes himself, goes away, and immediately forgets what kind of man he was" (James 1:23, 24).

Our psychological landscape today is littered with broken mirrors. We don't want to look at who we are; we'd rather have excuses.

But we desperately need to take that long look; we need to accept what the law tells us about ourselves. That's what God's absolute standard gives us. The truth, no distortions.

A mirror, however, can't make anyone more lovely. And the law, by itself, can't turn us into righteous people. Remember, it's the diagnosis only.

But what the law *can* do, is drive us into the arms of

the Great Physician. We see our weakness, we see our sin, and we cry out, "Help!" That's how, as Paul said, the law leads us to Christ. The psalmist says:

> "The law of the Lord is perfect converting the soul" (Psalm 19:7).

How does God's law convert us? It reveals our sin. It shows us our weakness. It leads us to Jesus. It makes us ready for the cure, ready for the forgiveness and grace that only Jesus Christ can bestow.

But for many people the law no longer does that. The law has lost its power. Even some churches have been teaching that God has no absolute standard or that His law is no longer relevant to contemporary needs. Some maintain that God's law has been done away with in order to make way for the Kingdom of Grace.

But society is learning the hard way that you don't really produce freedom by just throwing out the rules. Once you remove the standard of right and wrong, chaos follows.

Permissiveness hasn't worked. We all know that now. There is a great cry in the United States for a return to "traditional values." Political leaders constantly talk about their devotion to "family values."

But the next question is: whose family values? There were families out here on the streets during the L.A. riots—mothers and fathers carrying stolen liquor and appliances, their children trailing behind them. Different families obviously have different values. And even stable families can be pushed over the edge and into lawlessness during times of crisis.

We need something stronger than just "what I think is right," or "what you think is right." We need basic values that speak to us with authority. We need something that will stand as powerfully for lawfulness, as looters in riots stood for lawlessness.

That's why we need that formula God gave us centuries ago; it's a formula for a crime-free society. If this formula had been followed, the morning news and the evening paper would be filled with uplifting human-interest stories; you'd see no headlines of shocking tragedies.

That formula came at a particular time, in a particular place. The children of Israel had just been delivered form slavery in Egypt. They were camped near a mountain called Sinai. And God said this: Exodus 20:2, "I am the Lord your God, who brought you out of the land of Egypt, out of the house of bondage."

God began His vitally important communication, by first establishing His relationship with His people. He identified Himself as their deliverer, the One who opened up the Red Sea, the One who fed them with manna from heaven. Here was the Great Protector saying, "I care for you; you can trust me."

With this trust established, God wrote out His divine law. Through that law, God provided humanity with an *objective* standard of right and wrong, a standard that would ensure our peace and safety.

Thundering down from the summit of Sinai, He delivered these injunctions:

Thou shalt have no other gods before Me.
Thou shalt not make unto thee any graven image . . .
Thou shalt not take the name of the Lord thy God in
vain . . .
Remember the Sabbath day to keep it holy. Six days
shalt thou labor, and do all thy work: But the seventh day is the Sabbath of the Lord thy God . . .

Honor thy father and thy mother . . .
Thou shalt not kill.
Thou shalt not commit adultery.
Thou shalt not steal.
Thou shalt not bear false witness against thy
neighbor.
Thou shalt not covet.
(Exodus 20:3-17, KJV).

Here God summed up His primary principles. It's been estimated that more than 35 million laws have been drafted by human beings in an effort to control behavior. But in just ten brief precepts, the Almighty formalized a code that covers all human conduct.

And this code, Scripture states, was carved by the finger of God on tablets of stone. It was meant to last; it was meant to last forever.

God's law is the eternal standard of right for the universe. It gives us an *objective* standard on which to base our values. Individuals need that; families need that; societies need that.

If we're just making up the rules ourselves, then it's very easy to modify them as we go along. It's very easy to put them aside when the fires heat up. It's very easy to forget them when everyone else is looting.

Let me give you a practical example of how one simple principle from the Word of God can make a big difference. This principle relates to how values are shaped, and it's never been more relevant:

> "But we all, with unveiled face, beholding as in a mirror the glory of the Lord, are being transformed into the same image" (2 Corinthians 3:18).

We are transformed by beholding, by constant looking. We become what we look at. What our mind habitually focuses on, will begin to mold us. It will mold us for good—or for bad.

Think of that terrible tragedy in Littleton, Colorado. Two teenagers walked into their high school, loaded with bombs and weapons, and proceeded to shoot down their classmates—as many as they possibly could.

In the shock that followed, we all wondered: how could these youngsters engage in such cold-blooded, merciless killing? How could they laugh as the bodies sprawled around them? How could two teenagers have become so de-sensitized, so untouched by the suffering of others?

Do you know what these boys were doing in the weeks and months before the tragedy? They were playing a violent video game called "Doom" every afternoon. They'd become obsessed with it. The object of the game is to see who can rack up the most "kills."

The two boys also watched a movie called "Natural Born Killers" over and over. It's a depiction, in graphic detail, of a couple engaging in random murders.

Now, everyone who plays violent video games doesn't go out and mow down their classmates. Everyone who watches "Natural Born Killers" doesn't go on a killing spree. But it is also true that these games and films have serious consequences. One of God's commandments says, "Thou shalt not kill" (Exodus 20:13, KJV). If you fill your mind with scenes of violence, you likely will become violent.

Another one of God's commandments says, "You shall not commit adultery" (Exodus 20:14). If you fill your mind with sexually immoral, pornographic scenes, you are likely to be driven by lust. One of God's commandments says, "You shall not bear false witness" (Exodus 20:16). If you fill your mind with deceit, you are likely to become deceitful. The commandments are safeguards. They are God's value system.

The value system we choose dramatically affects how we live. To disregard God's value system—the Ten Commandments—is to destroy the very foundation of morality in our society. Take Littleton for an example.

The only solution to the problem of moral decay in our society lies deep within our own minds. Are we willing to allow God to place within our hearts and minds a love for His law? Are we willing to fully trust Him? When our impulses and desires pull in one direction, are we willing to surrender to the loving claims of His law, knowing His way is best?

Do you remember the film "Mutiny On The Bounty"? The "Bounty," a sailing ship, piloted by Captain Bligh was carrying precious cargo in the South Pacific when the crew mutinied. They set the ship on fire and headed for a small island called Pitcairn in their lifeboats. Although they hoped to establish their own Utopia, things went terribly wrong. Drunkenness, robbery, murder and rape governed the island. Warring factions developed between the men. Violent fights broke out.

After a few years only a few men, along with the women and children, survived. They were desperate. They needed some standard by which to govern the island. They needed some moral values with which to nurture their children. The needed some code of conduct to live by. Rummaging through their meager belongings someone found Captain Bligh's weathered, battered sea trunk. As they examined the contents, they discovered Captain Bligh's Bible. Fletcher Christian, the group leader, determined that they needed a dramatic change if they were going to survive.

Each morning and evening he read passages from Scripture to the entire group. The moral values of the Bible began to shape that little island. They accepted the Ten Commandments as Heaven's code of conduct. They asked God for a moral revolution within their own hearts to live in harmony with God's commands.

Slowly but surely that island began to change. Miraculously, lives were transformed. Robbery, rape and murder became only a memory. Pitcairn became a model community. The little island became a paradise of love. For years on Pitcairn there have been no jails, no crime, no police, no courts, no judges, no fighting, no murder, no divorce. The two hundred plus inhabitants have lived in harmony on that little speck in the South Pacific.

Why? They had been transformed by God's grace— so transformed that they lovingly obey His law. It had reshaped their values.

Would you like to open your heart to the Lord of the Ten Commandments? Would you like to say, "Jesus, in a world of lawlessness, I long to keep Your law." Would you like to ask Jesus to change you from within?

Why not do it now? ❏

11
Revelation's Eternal Sign

I n early 1991, the Cosmic Background Explorer (COBE) satellite sent back information to Earth that caused a sensation in scientific circles. This satellite had been hurled into space to peer into the depths of the universe.

But what it eventually produced was far more than pictures and measurements of distant stars. In effect, it sent us snapshots from the distant past, from what appeared to be the origin of the universe. And there we could make out the telltale sign of the Creator's fingerprints. Someone was there. Someone was there when it all began.

Astronomers, astrophysicists, cosmologists. These are not the sort of people you see jumping up and down with excitement too often. They usually spend their time in research centers going over bits of data that seem unintelligible to the rest of us. But something made them jump in April, 1992. Something really got their attention.

Stephen Hawking called it, "The discovery of the century."

Another scientist exclaimed, "It's the most exciting thing that's happened in my life as a cosmologist."

Another said, "They have found the Holy Grail of cosmology."

What was all the fuss about? Information coming back from the COBE satellite provided a final, critical piece in the puzzle of the origin of the universe. What the COBE satellite really did was to prove that the universe did indeed have a beginning. It came as close to proving this as is humanly possible.

Now, let me explain why this is important, and why this shook the scientific community. Let's say that your picture of the universe leaves no room for God. Let's say that, for whatever reasons, you simply can't believe that there is a personal Creator behind it all.

But what's the starting point? There has been only one answer to that question. It may not really be an answer, but it's the best people can do when they take God out of the picture. What they say is simply that the universe has always been there. It's eternal. Matter has always been there. That's the usual starting point.

When you get down to the basic question of origins, there aren't that many alternatives. You either start with God or you start with matter. You start with a God who is eternal, outside of time, who can create the complexity around us. Or you start with matter always being there, and slowly evolving into more and more complex things.

But, if the universe *hasn't* always been there, it had to have a beginning. Well, that pretty much narrows down the alternatives to one.

How did the COBE satellite fill in the picture of how it all began? How did it produce the final piece of the puzzle?

First, it measured temperatures in different parts of the universe. This provided a picture of how the universe is radiating or dissipating energy in the form of heat. It's known as the "microwave background radiation temperature." COBE indicated it to be very low and smooth—no big irregularities in temperature. This confirms the model of the universe beginning at one specific moment in time and radiating smoothly thereafter.

COBE also took measurements related to something called "exotic matter." It provided information about the proportion of exotic matter to ordinary matter in the universe.

According to Dr. Hugh Ross, author of *The Creator and the Cosmos,* the measured proportion exactly fit the proportion you would expect—if the universe had a beginning. That's what the COBE satellite told us. The Hubble Space Telescope also helped fill in the picture. It made measurements that confirmed this proportion of ordinary matter and exotic matter.

That's what caused the big stir. As one Berkeley astronomer put it: "What we have found is evidence of the birth of the universe . . . It's like looking at God."

Recent scientific data points in the direction of a Creator God. In the Bible's last book, Revelation, God is on center stage as Creator of the universe. Come with me to an amazing scene in the throne room of the universe.

For John a door suddenly stood open in heaven! A voice called; ringing out like a trumpet. The man heard the words, "Come up here," and he was invited into a very special place.

He walked through that door and found himself standing in front of a glorious throne. It rested on what appeared to be a sea of glass. Then he noticed a Being seated on that throne. He was so dazzling it seemed like a whole rainbow of colors spilled out from Him. It seemed like brilliant jasper and sardius and emeralds flashed in the light. Twenty-four officials in white robes were seated around that throne, each with a gold crown on his head. Four other living creatures declared ceaselessly, " Holy, holy, holy, Lord God Almighty, who was and is to come" (Revelation 4:8)!

This was a scene of joyful worship—a picture of heavenly beings lost in worship. Immediately after those living creatures gave glory and honor to God, the twenty-four elders fell down before Him, tossed their crowns at the foot of the throne, and declared:

> "You are worthy, O Lord, to receive glory and honor and power; for You created all things, and by Your will they exist and were created" (Revelation 4:11).

What I've just described was an unforgettable scene which the apostle John actually saw in vision. John, the author of the book of Revelation, walked through that open door and into God's throne room. He described this scene early in the book of Revelation because he wanted us to know that God is at the center of this book. And He is indeed an awesome God, a glorious God and worthy of praise. Why? Because He created all things. All things exist by His will.

This Creator makes another dramatic entrance a few chapters later in chapter 7. That's where John sees a great multitude standing before the throne of God, waving palm branches and crying out, "Salvation belongs to our God who sits on the throne." And those elders are still worshipping. They fall on their faces and declare:

> "Thanksgiving and honor and power and might, be to our God forever and ever. Amen" (Revelation 7:12).

God is the mighty God—the all-powerful God—the Creator. In chapter ten we find an angel making a solemn declaration to John:

> [He swears by] "Him who lives forever and ever, who created heaven and the things that

are in it, the earth and the things that are in it,
and the sea and the things that are in it"
(Revelation 10:6).

Revelation 14 gives us God's last warning message
to earth. Three angels fly down to earth to share the everlasting gospel in a special, urgent way. And this is what
the first one declares:

"Fear God and give glory to Him, for the hour
of His judgment has come; and worship Him
who made heaven and earth, the sea and
springs of water" (Revelation 14:7).

Scene after scene in the book of Revelation, picture
after picture, shows God as the all-powerful Creator. God is
not some vague shadowy essence on a distant galaxy. He is
not some abstract symbol. The book of Revelation provides
an incredible picture of God, the one who made heaven,
earth, sea and sky, plant and flowers. He is the Father of all
humanity. We are more than a biological accident. We are
His creation!

But you know what? Most people have lost sight of
that today. People on this planet have been cut-off from
this Creator God. He has shrunk in size, shrunk in power.
He is no longer worthy of our heart-felt praise and worship. He's only worthy of a quick nod heavenward.

Let me tell you about one of the main reasons that
has happened.

In 1831 a British ship called The Beagle sailed down
the western coast of South America. Its mission—to map
this part of the world more accurately. When the ship
docked at the Galapagos Islands, the naturalist on board
took a keen interest in the animals unique to the islands.
He gathered information on a variety of bird species,

their different beak shapes, coloring, etc. And his interpretation of that data would change the way most people look at the world.

The naturalist was, of course, Charles Darwin. And his theory—the origin of life by natural selection. His theory shocked Victorian England. A few observations on variation in species had apparently eliminated the need for a Creator. Now we had evolution. Soon God seemed no longer necessary.

But God has an answer to the problem of evolution. It is part of His final message for all people. Revelation calls us to "worship Him who made heaven and earth, sea and the springs of water" (Revelation 14:7).

How do we worship the Creator of heaven and earth? How does He remind us of His creative power?

All of the books of the Bible meet and end in Revelation. We will only understand the significance of the monumental issues in today's world if we understand the events at creation.

Revelation's final call for the entire human race to worship the Creator has its origin in Genesis—the book of beginnings. This theme of true worship—remembering the Creator—is a common thread throughout the Bible. It is one of the most important themes of Scripture. The heart of Revelation's final crisis is over true and false worship. Worshipping the Creator is at the center of it all.

Let's return to our origin so we can understand our destiny. Let's return to the book of beginnings, Genesis, so we can understand the book of endings, Revelation.

The amazingly intricate world as we know it today was created in six literal days. Starting with a dark shapeless mass, God dazzled it with light, enveloped it with atmosphere, salted it with seas, brightened it with plants, enlivened it with wild things—day by day looking upon his handiwork and saying, "It's good!"

And then came the crowning act of creation. Turning to the Father, the Creator said:

> "Let Us make man in Our image . . . in the image of God He created him; male and female He created them" (Genesis 1:26, 27).

Man could receive no greater honor! God could have shown no greater love! The human race is God's master-piece of creation—the object of His supreme love! And this love was meant to be shared, for God said:

> "Be fruitful and multiply; fill the earth and subdue it; have dominion over . . . every living thing that moves on the earth" (Genesis 1:28).

After the creation of Adam and Eve on the sixth day, the Bible says:

> "Thus the heavens and the earth, and all the host of them, were finished" (Genesis 2:1).

Just six days of work, and creation was done. Such a short time! But not for God! The Bible says:

> "For He spoke, and it was done; He com-manded, and it stood fast" (Psalm 33:9).

Adam and Eve must have gazed in wide-eyed wonder as the blazing sun, in all its glory, began to slip over the western horizon, ending the sixth day of cre-ation. But the Genesis account of creation does not end there. The Bible record continues:

> "On the seventh day God ended His work which He had done, and He rested" (Genesis 2:2).

God rested! Why? Not because He was weary, for the

prophet Isaiah tells us that God never gets weary (Isaiah 40:28). The Creator of the universe permitted Himself the satisfaction of enjoying His completed creation. And then, pleased with His accomplishments over Earth's first six days, God did something especially significant:

> "Then God blessed the seventh day and sanc-
> tified it, because in it He rested from all His
> work of creating" (Genesis 2:3).

A REMINDER OF OUR ROOTS

God blessed the seventh day! He made the seventh day an endless fountain of spiritual refreshing for His people, for all time to come. Next, He sanctified the seventh day! He set it apart as a holy day, a special time every seven days to continually remind us of our beginnings—our roots!

As long as you and I set aside the seventh day to worship our Creator, we will never lose sight of who we are, where we came from, or what our eternal destiny may be. Every seventh day, we are forever linked with our Creator.

Could it be that God, looking down through the centuries, saw that mankind would forget their roots? Could it be that God perceived the great gulf that sin would create as it broke communion between creatures and Creator, well-nigh obliterating the truth of man's divine creation?

Bible history reveals the sad truth that by the time of Moses, God's people, who were in Egyptian bondage, had forgotten their roots and God's special day of fellowship. But God had a plan to remind His people of His special day. As Moses led the Israelites from Egypt to Palestine, the promised land, food rations ran out in the

Sinai wilderness. Here, God miraculously provided bread from heaven, called "manna," for forty years.

But the story is about more than receiving a daily bread supply for forty years! The manna appeared on the ground only six days a week—Sunday through Friday! But on Friday, the sixth day, the Israelites were instructed to gather up enough manna for the seventh day! The manna never fell on the seventh day, and if extra was gathered in advance on any day other than the sixth, it would spoil.

Why? God wanted His people to know that the One who had led them out of Egypt was also their Creator. God wanted to point His creatures back to their creation. Signifying the importance of the seventh day through the way He supplied the manna, God wanted His people to know that His day was very special—that it had in no way faded in significance with the passing of time.

God linked the manna experience with the Sabbath:

> "Six days you shall gather it, but on the seventh day, which is the Sabbath, there will be none" (Exodus 16:26).

Some of the people, refusing to follow God's advice to gather an extra portion on the sixth day, went out on the Sabbath to gather manna. But they did not find any. And our patient Lord asked:

> "How long do you refuse to keep My commandments and My laws" (Exodus 16:28)?

From Genesis to Revelation, the Bible speaks with one voice regarding the importance of the seventh day, the weekly Sabbath. Several weeks after the beginning of the manna experience, God again came close to men and women when He etched on tablets of stone, with His own finger, the great truths He had spoken in the Garden of Eden.

The Israelites were emphatically reminded of how God felt about the seventh day—the Sabbath—when Moses came down from Mount Sinai carrying God's hand-written message:

> "Remember the Sabbath day, to keep it holy. Six days shalt thou labor, and do all thy work: but the seventh day is the Sabbath of the Lord thy God: in it thou shalt not do any work . . . for in six days the Lord made heaven and earth, the sea and all that in them is, and rested the seventh day: wherefore the Lord blessed the Sabbath day, and hallowed it" (Exodus 20:8-10, KJV).

In these immortal words, God asks men and women to remember the weekly memorial of creation—the seventh-day Sabbath. And He promises His people many blessings in connection with this special day:

> "If you turn away your foot from the Sabbath, from doing your pleasure on My holy day, and call the Sabbath a delight, the holy day of the Lord honorable, and shall honor Him, not doing your own ways, nor finding your own pleasure, nor speaking your own words, then you shall delight yourself in the Lord" (Isaiah 58:13,14).

THE HIGH COST OF FORGETTING

Had men and women always remembered this memorial of God's creation, the problems so prevalent today—lack of meaning in life, identity crises, loss of self-worth—would never have arisen. There would be no evolutionists, no skeptics, no agnostics!

Nowhere in the Bible is the Sabbath called "The Sabbath of the Jews." Jesus made it clear that it was a day for all mankind when He said:

> "The Sabbath was made for man, and not man for the Sabbath" (Mark 2:27).

Jesus also said that He is:

> "Lord even of the Sabbath" (Matthew 12:8).

The Sabbath is more than a memorial of creation. It is a weekly reminder of the profound relationship between God and man, an acknowledgment of God's divinity:

> "That you may know that I am the Lord your God" (Ezekiel 20:20).

The creative power used in sanctifying the Sabbath is the same power God uses today in sanctifying sinful men and women. That promise means that our Creator is also our Savior:

> "Moreover I also gave them My Sabbaths, to be a sign between them and Me, that they might know that I am the LORD who sanctifies them" (Ezekiel 20:12).

To observe the Sabbath is to recognize and receive God's creative, sanctifying power in our lives today.

Throughout the New Testament we find that our friendly example, Jesus Christ, did not forget this special memorial of creation while He was on this earth. Luke tells us:

> "So He came to Nazareth, where He had been brought up. And as His custom was, He went into the synagogue on the Sabbath day, and stood up to read" (Luke 4:16).

Jesus' custom, then, was to go to the synagogue on Sabbath. But, you might ask, which day is the Sabbath? How can we be certain on which day Jesus worshipped? How do we know that somewhere between the time of Moses and Jesus, God might have changed the day?

Think about it for a moment. If the day had been changed or forgotten between Adam's time and Moses' time, God would have rectified it when He wrote the Ten Commandments at Sinai. If the Sabbath day had been lost between Moses' time and Jesus' time, Christ would surely have set the record straight.

If God were to make such a major change involving one of His finger-etched commandments, surely somewhere in the Bible we could find a record of it! The issue of which day was the Sabbath never arose while Jesus was on Earth. The only controversy arose over *how* He kept it.

PILING ON THE RULES

Ever since their return from captivity in Babylon, Jewish leaders were determined that never again would their nation forget their Lord or the importance of the weekly Sabbath. In this dedication to "remembering" the Sabbath day to "keep it holy," Jewish leaders, in spite of their good intentions, made the Sabbath a cruel burden. They distorted Sabbath observance by heaping upon it austere, cumbersome regulations. For example, they would not allow a man to spit on the Sabbath, for fear he would irrigate the grass! A man could not travel more than a certain number of miles from his home on the Sabbath. If he had plans to do so, he could travel part way the day before and leave some token—a handkerchief, a piece of cloth—to set up a temporary "home" and thus justify the additional miles.

Jesus tried to eliminate such meaningless man-made requirements and show the true beauty and significance of Sabbath observance. When He was accused of breaking the Sabbath because He healed people on that day, He answered:

> "It is lawful to do good on the Sabbath" (Matthew 12:12).

As we look at Calvary, the true meaning of Sabbath observance is demonstrated by the devoted followers of Jesus. On Friday, the day before the Sabbath, the disciples' hopes in Jesus had been crushed. They witnessed Him dying a cruel death on the cross. Their dreams and hopes lay in a darkened tomb. As a last act of devotion, they wanted to anoint His dead body. But first they paused to give honor and glory to God during the Sabbath hours.

Under the shadow of the world's greatest crisis, Jesus' friends rested according to God's command. Note carefully the sequence of events in these texts:

> "That day was the Preparation, and the Sabbath drew near. And the women who had come with Him from Galilee followed after, and they observed the tomb and how His body was laid. Then they returned and prepared spices and fragrant oils. And they rested on the Sabbath according to the commandment. Now on the first day of the week, very early in the morning, they, and certain other women with them, came to the tomb bringing the spices which they had prepared" (Luke 23:54-24:1).

Let us review the order of events. On the Preparation Day (now called Friday), Jesus died, and the women prepared spices and ointments. On the Sabbath day (now called Saturday), the women rested according to the commandment (the fourth commandment), and Jesus rested in the tomb. On the first day of the week (now called Sunday), the women came to anoint Jesus, but found the tomb empty because Christ had risen!

Here three consecutive days are mentioned in the Bible. The Preparation Day, or Good Friday; the first day of the week, or Easter Sunday; and the day in between, or Saturday, which the Bible calls the Sabbath.

The closer we get to the cross today, the more we realize that just any day in seven will not do! To tamper with the Sabbath is to tamper with creation, Sinai, and Calvary itself!

Our Creator asks us to "remember!" Yet so many have forgotten! This blurring of God's special memorial also blurs our relationship with our Creator.

Jesus expected that Christians would keep the Sabbath for all time. Note His words of instruction given on an earlier occasion, referring to events yet to come to the Jewish people after He had departed:

> "And pray that your flight may not be in winter or on the Sabbath" (Matthew 24:20).

Jesus expected that about forty years after His death, when Jerusalem was destroyed, Christians would still be keeping the Sabbath.

The New Testament reveals that Jesus' followers did keep the Sabbath after the resurrection. In fact, the book of Acts records eighty-four meetings that Paul held on the Sabbath. For example:

> "They came to Thessalonica, where there was a synagogue of the Jews. Then Paul, as his custom was,

went in to them, and for three Sabbaths reasoned with them from the Scriptures" (Acts 17:1, 2).

On another occasion, as Paul preached in the synagogue, a group of visitors approached him and requested that he speak the following Sabbath:

> "The Gentiles begged that these words might be preached to them the next Sabbath . . . And the next Sabbath almost the whole city came together to hear the word of God" (Acts 13:42, 44).

A GOLDEN THREAD

The Sabbath runs like a golden thread from Genesis to Revelation. The book of Revelation describes those who are prepared to meet Jesus when He comes:

> "Here is the patience of the saints; here are those who keep the commandments of God and the faith of Jesus" (Revelation 14:12).

And one of those commandments tells us to "remember" the Sabbath day—a sign between God and man forever!

This Biblical truth about the Sabbath may be new to you. You may never have realized before that God's Sabbath is for all mankind.

But we all have an appointment with God each Sabbath day, every week. Established at creation, given in the heart of the Ten Commandments, kept by Jesus, and honored by the disciples, the Sabbath is God's sign of eternal loyalty. He personally invites you to experience the rewards of Sabbath-keeping.

The Sabbath provides rich opportunities for spiritual renewal, physical rejuvenation, and mental relaxation. It is God's own treasure. It is a precious, priceless gift which He has given to us.

Not long ago I visited the beautiful island of Cuba. I well remember walking down the cobblestone path past the ramparts of Moreau Castle. Moreau Castle was built from 1589 to 1630 to serve as a fortress to guard Havana Harbor.

Treasure fleets from all over the Americas gathered there before setting sail to Spain, laden with vast treasures.

These treasure ships sailed for two centuries from mareau Castle in 70 flotillas at a time, carrying emeralds from Columbia and glittering silver from Bolivia, as well as Inca treasures from Peru and gold from the Aztecs. Some of them made it to Spain. Others did not.

In 1662, the Nuestra Senora de Atoche, the 550-ton flagship of the Spanish fleet, laden with treasurers of gold for Spain, sank in a hurricane off the Cuban Coast.

The vessel had sunk, its treasure lost and neglected for centuries. Century after century passed by. Some explorers tried to find it through the centuries, but nobody really knew the precise spot where the Senora de Atoche went down.

Then in 1985, on speculation, a diving company gathered some investors who invested a few thousand dollars in the expedition. They thought by examining ancient Spanish records they might know where the Atoche went down. And so they began plumbing the depths.

Then to their surprise, they discovered precisely where the sailing ship went down. As they began to bring up the treasures, they discovered far more than they imagined possible. Far more than they ever dreamed could be true.

Marvelous treasures of gold, in fact 47 tons, were brought up out of the ocean valued at 400 million dollars.

What a treasure! A treasure that was neglected. A treasure hidden for centuries, but a treasure that was so near. Some people who had invested just a few thousand dollars ended up as millionaires.

Could it be that in your life a treasure is very near, a treasure that's been hidden, or a treasure that's been neglected?

In this age of evolution, at a time of stress and tension, with nerves jangling, God is calling us to discover the hidden treasure of the Sabbath. You can find a new peace, joy and meaning in your life as you open your heart to follow Him.

Tell Him today, "Jesus, thank you for your wonderful gift of the Sabbath. Jesus, you set the example, and I want to follow you." ❏

12
REVELATION EXPOSES HISTORY'S GREATEST HOAX

A fascinating story comes to us out of Greek mythology and warns against deception dressed in religious clothes. Helen, a Greek princess was kidnapped. Her kidnapper, Paris, brought her to Troy. The Greeks battled the Trojans to get Helen back. The war continued for ten long, bloody years. The Greeks began to think they would never capture the city of Troy.

The Greek patriot Ulysses thought of a trick which might succeed. The Greeks pretended to give up the fight for the city and some of their ships sailed away. Then they built a huge wooden horse and delivered it to the gates of the city. They declared it was an offering to the goddess Athena. But the inside of the huge wooden horse was filled with armed Greek soldiers. The Greeks left the horse outside the walls of Troy and sailed away.

The Trojans were happy. The battle was over. Who could possibly resist something set aside for the gods. Although some of the wise elders raised their voices in caution, the majority clamored to accept this offering to their gods. They argued that the entire nation would be cursed if they refused something so sacred. With rejoicing they brought the wooden horse into the city. They accepted it as a token of divine favor, a symbol of victory from the gods.

But that night, once the horse was inside the city, Greek soldiers jumped out of a secret door. These warriors opened the gates to other Greeks soldiers who had quietly returned. The city was set afire. The Trojans were defeated from within.

They were defeated through deception.

An offering to the gods, a religious symbol, which they at first rejoiced over, was actually part of the enemy's deceptive plan.

Could it be that there is a Trojan horse within the Christian Church? Is it possible that millions are deceived and they don't know it? Maybe we have accepted a so-called "offering to God," but we have actually accepted falsehood under a religious guise.

Let me speak to you plainly. Revelation predicts Satan's greatest deceptions would be religious. Satan disguises error as truth. Satan counterfeits the truth. Satan substitutes falsehood for truth. He is a cunning, deceptive foe and will do anything to mislead us.

Here's how Revelation puts it:

> "And the light of a lamp shall not shine in you anymore. And the voice of bridegroom and bride shall not be heard in you anymore. For your merchants were the great men of the earth, for by your sorcery all the nations were deceived" (Revelation 18:23).

Falsehood would replace truth. Satan's deceptions would deceive millions. Revelation describes the religious state as Babylon—symbolic of total religious confusion.

Error would slip into the Christian church. A counterfeit religious day of worship would be accepted in place of the Sabbath of the Ten Commandments. The central issue in the battle between truth and error is worship. Satan's master deception, his Trojan horse, under the guise of religion, is a counterfeit day of worship. The devil knows if he can initiate the change of the Ten Commandments written with God's own finger on tables of stone, he can open the floodgates for every other species of falsehood to flow into the Christian Church. How did this incredible deception enter the Christian Church? Who changed the true Bible?

The prophet Daniel, our companion book to Revelation, reveals who changed the Sabbath.

In order to answer this vital question, I want to take you on a journey into the prophecies of the Book of Daniel. In an earlier chapter we learned in Daniel how God unlocked a puzzling dream that Nebuchadnezzar, the king of Babylon, had. Now we're going to learn in Daniel's seventh chapter that one night, the prophet Daniel himself went to sleep and had a dream. And in that dream he saw "beasts" rise up out of the sea. This dream deals with events in Daniel's day, in the days of Babylon, but takes us through the days of Babylon, Medo-Persia, Greece, and Rome—the four world empires. It takes us through Christianity's early days and shows how, *after* the death of Christ and His disciples in the first few century, A.D., *a power would arise that would attempt to change the Sabbath.*

DANIEL'S AMAZING DREAM

Daniel woke up troubled, thinking about what he had dreamed. He knew his dream was of great importance and significance. He says: "In the first year of Belshazzar, king of Babylon, Daniel had a dream and visions of his head while on his bed. Then he wrote down the dream, telling the main facts" (Daniel 7:1).

In his dream, Daniel saw *four* great beasts rise up out

of the sea. The *first* was like a lion and had eagle's wings. A *second* beast was like a bear raised up on one side, with three ribs in its mouth. The *third* was like a leopard with four wings on its back and four heads.

Daniel continued:

> "After this I saw in the night visions, and behold, a *fourth* beast, dreadful and terrible, and exceedingly strong. It had huge iron teeth; it was devouring, breaking in pieces, and trampling the residue with its feet. It was different from all the beasts that were before it, and it had ten horns" (Daniel 7:7).

The beasts that were before it were strange enough, but the fourth one was indescribable—not like a lion, a leopard, a bear, or *anything* Daniel had ever seen before! The fourth was a dreadful, powerful beast with iron teeth, brass claws (verse 19), and ten horns.

Next, among those ten horns, Daniel saw *another* horn come up. This horn was little at first, but it became a great power: "In this horn were eyes like the eyes of *a man,* and a *mouth speaking pompous words"* (Daniel 7:8). And this little horn we shall soon learn, tried to change the Law of God! Yes, this little horn spoke out, saying that God's Law *could* be changed and *should* be changed. What could this prophecy mean?

"Oh," somebody says, "prophecy is just guesswork. You have to guess who the lion is and who the bear is. You have to guess about the other beasts Daniel saw coming up out of the sea, and you have to guess what the sea represents. He saw the wind blowing on the sea, so you guess what the wind represents. He saw all those things in his dream, and you have to guess what they all represent."

Let's pause a moment. *Who gave* Daniel the dream? God did. And if God gave Daniel the dream, isn't God smart enough to interpret it? Do you think that when it comes to interpreting prophecy, it's "every man for himself" Peter reminds us: "No prophecy of Scripture is of any private interpretation" (2 Peter 1:20). That means I shouldn't depend on what I personally think the prophecy means—I shouldn't give my own private interpretation.

THE BIBLE EXPLAINS ITSELF

The Word of God explains itself. Let's go to God's Word and discover the meaning of each of the symbols. Daniel wrote that this Little Horn power would "speak great words against the most High, and shall wear out the saints of the most High, and *think to change times and laws"* (Daniel 7:25 Emphasis supplied). This prophecy must pertain to *divine* laws, since legislatures all over the country and all over the world change *man's* laws so often that it's hardly worthy of notice. So we can be sure, first of all, that the Little Horn power intends to "change the times and the law" (RSV).

The only law—the only one of God's Ten commandments—that has to do with *time* is the *fourth* commandment regarding the *Sabbath.* So this Little Horn would "think to change times and laws." Note that the prophecy said the Little Horn would *"think"* to change the law? Can any earthly power *really* change that Law written with God's own finger? No, no human being can change it, but the Little Horn would dare to "think" to change God's Law!

Let's take a careful look at the prophecy. Who's the lion, the bear, the leopard? Who's the dreadful and terrible fourth beast? Who's the Little Horn? Did the Little

Horn try to change God's law? And did the Little Horn *admit* that he tried to change God's law?

Let's let Daniel, under the inspiration of the Holy Spirit, explain the meaning of his dream. Daniel said: "Four great beasts came up from the sea" (Daniel 7:3). Symbol number one is the sea. What does the "sea" represent?

Here's a *free clue:* Bible scholars have recognized for a long time that the prophetic Books of Daniel and Revelation are to be studied together. So let's read Revelation 17:15: "The *waters* which you saw . . . are peoples and multitudes and nations and tongues" (Emphasis supplied). So waters represent people, many people. Now you know that because I told you, right? No! How do you know it? Because the Bible says it: the waters represent people. We use that term ourselves: the great *sea of humanity.* In symbolic prophecy "waters" mean people!

Please don't misunderstand. When you read "water" in the Bible, it's usuallly literal, wet water. But when Jesus says, "Drink the water of life," He's speaking figuratively. When a word is obviously literal, Bible students should stick to the literal meaning unless there's a compelling reason for adopting a figurative or symbolic meaning. But in the *prophecies* of Daniel and Revelation, where it talks about beasts coming out of the sea—a lion with eagle's wings or a leopard with four heads or an indescribable beast with ten horns, we can be sure we're reading a passage with all kinds of *symbols!* So we look for the symbolic meaning. Revelation 17:15 tells us clearly that "the waters" or "the sea" represent people.

What about the winds? Daniel says that in his dream "the four *winds* of heaven were stirring up the great sea.

And four great beasts came up from the sea" (Daniel 7:2, 3). What do winds represent when used as a prophetic Bible symbol? Just as literal winds, like a hurricane or tornado, cause physical destruction, "winds" in prophecy represent political strife and turmoil—as we say, *"the winds of war."*

For instance, God pronounced the doom of the enemy nation of Elam in Jeremiah 49:36, 37, NIV: "I will bring against Elam the four *winds* from the four quarters of the heaven; I will scatter them to the four winds, and there shall not be a nation where Elam's exiles do not go . . . I will pursue them with the sword. . ." In Daniel 11:40 the prophet uses the same metaphor of *winds* to represent *war:* "The king of the north shall come against him *like a whirlwind,* and with chariots, and with horsemen, and with many ships."

UNLOCKING THE SYMBOLS

So far, so good. We've established that the sea represents peoples and the winds represent war. Symbolic prophecy—God's "sign-language"—is easily understood if we let the Bible be its own interpreter. Next, God tells us plainly in Daniel 7:17 and 23 that "Those great *beasts,* which are four, are four kings which arise . . . The fourth beast shall be a fourth *kingdom* on earth." So these beasts are not four individual kings but rather four successive kingdoms or world empires. In fact, *The Living Bible* is more explicit in calling the fourth beast, "the fourth *world empire* that will rule the earth." Therefore, when the Bible talks about *beasts* coming up out of a windy sea, it's talking about kingdoms rising through the bloodshed of war among the peopled nations of the earth. There's no guesswork about this conclusion, for the Bible explains itself.

Even today we use beasts or animals as symbols, don't we? We say the *elephant* is a symbol of the Republican Party, and the *donkey* symbolizes the Democrats. We use the *eagle* as a symbol of the United States. England's symbol is the regal *lion.* We recognize the Russian *bear* as a symbol of that country. Just as we still use animals as symbols to represent nations today, God uses them, too. But which kingdoms or nations do the beasts in Daniel's dream specifically represent?

As if to *underline* the great lessons presented in Daniel 2, God gives an "instant replay" in chapter 7. Using the principle of repetition the Master Teacher goes over the same ground more than once when something is of supreme importance. (Witness the way Christ's life story is told over and over again in the four gospels.)

Chapters 2 and 7 of Daniel's wonderful book contain some *remarkable parallels.* Both chapters are clearly *prophetic,* rather than being historical or narrative in nature. Each chapter features a *God-given dream* filled with vital information. You'll recall from earlier chapters that God inspired the prophet Daniel to interpret King Nebuchadnezzar's dream of a great image. Daniel 2 focuse on four symbolic *metals*—gold, silver, brass, and iron. Daniel 7 focuses on four symbolic *animals*—a lion, a bear, a leopard, and a monstrous beast. In Daniel 2 the *last* part of the image had *ten toes.* In Daniel 7 the last beast had ten horns.

In Daniel 2, the image, with its head of gold, breast and arms of silver, belly and thighs of brass, legs of iron, and feet of iron and clay, represents the four kingdoms that would rule the world: Babylon, Medo-Persia, Greece and Rome. In Daniel 7, the four beasts symbolize the same four world empires, as we shall see.

In Daniel 2, the prophet declared that the image's head of gold represented Babylon. In Daniel 7, the first beast was a lion with eagle's wings which *also* represented Babylon. Babylon ruled the world from 605 to 539 BC. It's incredible but true that archaeologists have uncovered in the ruins of Babylon, the symbol of the lion with eagle's wings! They unearthed a monumental sculpture of a huge lion weighing several tons. The lion with eagle's wings was on Babylonian coins. Countless lions with eagle's wings were all over the tiled walls of Babylon. The *eagle's wings* on the lion denote *speed* of conquest. Speaking of the Chaldeans or Babylonians, Habakkuk 1:6-11 says they are *"swifter* than the leopards . . . and their cavalry . . . *fly as the eagle* that hastens to eat." Jeremiah 4:7 and 13 speak of Babylon, God's instrument to punish Israel for its sins, as a *"lion"* and says, "his chariots shall be as a whirlwind: his horses are *swifter than eagles."* The lion with eagle's wings was the common symbol of Babylon.

But Babylon fell to the Medes and Persians. In Daniel 2 the second metal, silver, represented Medo-Persia. In Daniel 7 the second beast was a bear raised up on one side, with three ribs in its mouth. Notice the accuracy of God's prophecy—don't miss this! Scripture says the bear "was raised up on one side." The Medes and Persians were a joint nation, a dual kingdom, but the Persians were decidedly the more powerful of the two. So the Persians "raised themselves up" over the Medes.

Furthermore, the Bible says the bear "had three ribs in its mouth." Medo-Persia ruled the world from 539 to 331 BC, but in order to gain world dominion it had to conquer three great nations. First it attacked and conquered Babylon. Then it moved north to conquer Lydia, the land of the fabulously wealthy King Croesus, located where Turkey lies today. Then it set out to attack and take Egypt. The Medo-Persians were ferocious like a bear, and the three ribs in its mouth represented its three great conquests of Babylon, Lydia, and Egypt—three major nations, exactly as the Bible predicted.

In Daniel 2 a third metal, brass or bronze, represents a third world power, Greece. The Greek Empire ruled from 331 to 168 BC. In Daniel 7 the third animal was a leopard—but with *four wings* and *four heads!* If wings upon the Babylonian lion signified rapidity of conquest, they'd signify the same here. The leopard is naturally a swift beast, so if you want to depict speed, you might choose a leopard. But if you wanted to depict *rapid speed,* what would you do to your leopard? You'd put *wings* on him. The *two wings* the lion had are not sufficient here—the leopard must have *four,* denoting the rapid conquests of Greek leader, Alexander the Great, who conquered the then-known world by the time he was thirty-three.

PROPHECY PRECISELY FULFILLED

How many heads does the leopard have? Four. Why four? Because after Alexander died in a drunken stupor without appointing an heir to his throne, his four generals divided the empire. Their names were Cassander, Lysimachus, Ptolemy, and Seleucus. *How did the Bible* know Alexander would conquer so quickly? *How did the Bible know* he would die and his empire would be split among four successors? Why don't we have four heads on the *bear*—or on the *lion?* Bible prophecy is history told in advance and carries its own credentials of divine accuracy.

Finally, Daniel 2 tells of the fourth metal, iron, in the legs of the image, representing the *iron monarchy of Rome.*

So very fittingly Daniel 7 describes "a fourth beast, dreadful and terrible, exceedingly strong. It had huge *iron* teeth. . . . and it had ten horns" (verse 7). The iron legs had ten toes. The iron-toothed beast had *ten horns.* Rome ruled the world from 168 BC to 476 AD. But Rome wouldn't be conquered by another kingdom, a fifth world power—the *ten toes* and the ten horns indicate that Rome would be *divided* and remain divided.

At this point in Daniel 2, we've come to the end of the image with the ten toes, and the dream jumps ahead to the Rock that smites the image with the coming of Jesus and the end of the world. But Daniel 7, with the ten horns, gives us more information! God covers the same ground in both chapters, but here in Daniel 7 He adds details because He wants to get *past* the breakup of the Roman Empire to *who changed the Sabbath.* And this is the part we're interested in.

Rome ruled from 168 B.C. to 476 A.D. Daniel 7:24 tells us: "The ten horns are ten kings who shall arise from this kingdom." So Rome would fall and would be divided into ten smaller kingdoms. Indeed there was such a fall and such a division. Bible prophecy is accurate. Like the ten toes, so there'd be the ten horns. Barbarian tribes— like the Huns—came down and divided up the once-great Roman Empire. Those barbarian tribes settled in different places. For example, the Franks settled in the area we know as France. As the Empire fell apart, the Anglo-Saxons settled in what is now England, the Visigoths in Spain, the Suevi in Portugal, the Lombards in Italy, and so forth. Europe was divided.

Now, at this point in the prophetical story, when the Roman Empire was divided, *where are we* in the stream of time? Are we in the days of Babylon, or of the Medes and

Persians, or Greece? No! The days of the pagan Roman Empire? No! At this point in Daniel 7, we're in the early centuries of the church, after the death of Christ, after the death of the disciples. In the days of the Roman Empire when Rome is being divided, *something astonishing* would *happen* in Rome:

> "I considered the horns [he's looking at those ten horns, at the ten divisions of Rome] and behold, there came up among them another horn, a little one, before which three of the first horns were plucked up by the roots; and behold, in this horn were eyes like the eyes of a man, and a mouth speaking great things" (Daniel 7:8, RSV).

THE MYSTERIOUS LITTLE HORN

What can God be telling us in prophesying about this Little Horn power—what can it all mean? In the Bible a *horn* represents a kingdom or power—religious or political. Daniel says a Little Horn would become prominant in the days of those ten horns—those ten European nations. It would be a power small at first, but this Little Horn would grow "exceedingly great" (Daniel 8:9). Let's try to learn all we can about this mysterious power.

The prophet saw some *differences* between this Little Horn and the ten horns already noted. The first thing Daniel noticed that was different about this Little Horn was that it came up *after* Rome was divided into ten parts. Daniel 7:24 says, "The ten horns are ten kings who shall arise from this kingdom [of Rome]. And another [the Little Horn] shall arise *after* them." So to answer the "when?" question about the *time of origin* of this Little Horn power, we can say with certainty that *chronologi-*

cally it became prominent *after* the ten kindoms were established—after Rome's fall and subsequent breakup.

Next, to answer the "where?" question about the *location* of this Little Horn power, we can say with certainty that *geographically* it had to arise within the area of old Rome. Daniel 7:8 says that as Daniel considered the *ten horns* of the divided Roman Empire, "a little horn" came up "among them." So does this Little Horn come up in *South America?* No! Does it come up in *Africa?* No! Does it come up in *Asia?* No! It comes up *"among"* the ten horns, which means out of the Roman Empire, out of Rome.

The differences between the Little Horn and the other horns were very interesting, but there is something else, something very basic about the Little Horn that made it *fundamentally* different from the first ten horns. In fact, Daniel 7:24 specifically says that the Little Horn power would be *"different"* from the former ten. The first ten horns were the ten divisions of the Roman Empire, which became the modern nations of Western Europe. Those were and are all *political* in nature. This Little Horn power would be different in that it proved to be a religious power (or at least a hybrid, being part *religious* and part *political*—a religio-political entity).

Daniel 7:8 emphasizes that this Little Horn had "a mouth speaking *pompous words.*"

Furthermore, Daniel 7:11 tells us that the prophet was fascinated because of "the *words* which the horn was speaking." Finally, Daniel 7:25 says that "He [the Little Horn power] shall speak *pompous words against the most High.*" Clearly, then, God is telling us that this power— this religious power which was "different" from all the political powers of Europe, this power that arose in Rome after the breakup of the Roman Empire—would make great claims, and issue great decrees. It would speak pompously, boastfully, even claiming infallible power to change God's Law and the day of worship!

Sadly, Daniel testifies: "I was watching, and the same horn was making war against the saints, and prevailing against them" (Daniel 7:21). The Bible here foretells religious persecution, for "the saints" are God's faithful people! The Little Horn that changed the Sabbath, persecuted those that didn't go along, and he prevailed against them. The Middle Ages saw many faithful Christians suffer and die for the true faith, some languishing in dungeons, some burning at the stake. Daniel 7:25 predicted that the Little Horn "shall persecute the saints of the Most High," and history tragically verifies that it happened!

GOD WANTS YOU TO KNOW

Evidently God thinks it's important for us to understand these things, for He gives many clues to help us identify this mysterious power—more, in fact, than we even have time to cover in a lecture like this. But let's review briefly the clues we have covered:

1. This power would arise *"after"* the breakup of the Roman Empire into its ten divisions symbolized by the ten toes and ten horns. This point is important, for it means that the attempted change of the Sabbath and God's Law would come long after the death of Christ, even *after* the deaths of all His apostle.

2. The Little Horn arises *"among"* the first ten horns—that is to say, out of the divisions of the Roman Empire.

3. It had *"eyes"* like the eyes of a *"man"*—the symbol of *human intelligence.*

4. The Little Horn would be *"different"* from the first ten horns. The first ten horns were all *political* powers, but this power shall be different, different because it's a *religious* power.

5. The Little Horn power had not only "eyes like the eyes of a man" but also a *"mouth"* that spoke *"very great things"*—even *"great words against the most High."*

6. At times the Little Horn used its power to persecute God's people. It *"made war"* with the saints and would *"wear out"* the saints of the most High, prevailing against them.

When you line up all the identifying features of the Little Horn power, the identity of the Little Horn becomes remarkably clear. The Bible says the attempted change of God's Law would come *not* from the disciples in Jerusalem but come from the early church in Rome.

WITH MALICE TOWARD NONE ...

I was brought up in a very warm Roman Catholic home. I was educated by the priests and nuns for much of my education in early life. Today, the majority of my relatives are wonderful Roman Catholics. I studied with the priest for many years. But as I began studying the Bible, I began to see some things that I never understood before. And I said to myself, "I have to get to the bottom of this. I have to go to the libraries and research this for myself." And now I want to open those libraries to you. I would love to show you photographs of pages in history book after history book, because I want you to see for yourself.

Many people say to me, "Pastor, it's so obvious in the Bible that the seventh-day Sabbath is Saturday. How did it get changed?" We will trace that change—which the Bible *predicted* would happen. The Bible wouldn't allow untold millions of people to *remain* uninformed—to be misled without predicting the change. And the Bible clearly predicted that this change would come out of Rome! I want to show you how history records this change.

Come with me now on that journey to learn how Daniel 7:25 was fulfilled. *Why* and *how* did the church do it? Daniel 7:25 says there would be a power that would dare to *think* to change the times and the laws, or the time in the law. The Bible told us very plainly that after the death of Christ and His apostles there'd be a departure from true Biblical faith. In Acts 20:28-30 the apostle Paul warns Christian leaders, "Therefore take heed to yourselves, and to all the flock . . . to shepherd the church of God. . . . For I know this, that *after my departure* [that is, Paul says, *after my death*] savage *wolves* will come in among you."

The "wolves" would include the pagans who would burn Christian believers at the stake and send them to a martyr's death in those first centuries after Christ. But the "wolves" include others that Paul warned about: "Wolves" would enter among you, "not sparing the flock. Also from among yourselves men will rise up, speaking perverse things, to draw away the disciples after themselves" (Acts 20:30). Paul was saying, "Beware of *leaders in the church!* Leaders will rise up and wander from Scriptural teaching. Paul appealed to these early Christians to remain Biblically centered, to stay by what Jesus taught.

Notice how concerned Paul was in 2 Thessalonians 2:7, where he warned: "The mystery of lawlessness is already at work." He's saying, "I *already* see a trend in the church to drift away from the commandments—to drift away from the Law of God."

The "mystery of lawlessness" arose in heaven, as we

studied earlier when Lucifer rebelled. Ever since he has been leading the rebellion against God's law.

WORSHIPING THE SUN, NOT THE SON

In the very early centuries of this world's history, Satan had a plan. He knew God had established the Sabbath as a sign, as a memorial of creation, to keep men's minds turned toward Him week by week. God said, *"Remember* the Sabbath to keep it holy." But back in Old Testament times Satan said to himself, "If I can get people to think of the sun as a god, as an object of worship—if I can lead them away from the Creator to sun worship, I might get them."

Satan's plan was not too difficult to accomplish. After all, if ignorant man would superstitiously bow down to worship images he himself fashioned out of wood and stone, it's not hard to get him to notice and worship the dazzling sun rising high in the sky. Primitive people all over the earth have worshipped the sun in all its glory—the sun which dispels darkness and gives them l*ight,* the sun which heats the air and gives them *warmth,* the sun which makes crops grow and gives them *food.*

Once you understand this history, you'll understand what happened to God's truth. I've traveled on horseback through deep ravines, into Petra, capital of the Edomites, one of the early pagan tribes. They built great altars to the sun god, especially on their mountain tops where they worshipped the sun and offered human sacrifices. From the very earliest days, the sun has been worshipped. That's where we get the name Sunday—the day of the sun. In Egypt, the pyramids were part of their worship of the sun god. Egypt was a pagan land completely *saturated* with the worship of the sun god!

Go to old Babylon in modern Iraq. Look at the immense archeological displays in Berlin and London. Sun worship is featured in many way. The day of the sun was very, very important for the pagans.

Not only ancient Babylon but throughout the pagan civilizations on most all continents, the evidence of sun worship is everywhere.

Satan led all the pagans—the Babylonians, the Egyptians, other far-flung heathen people—to worship the sun god, anything to lead men and women away from remembering the Sabbath day and the Lord of Creation.

The contrast is clear: You have Lucifer leading Adam and Eve into rebellion. You have the children of Esau, the Edomites, launching pagan sun worship. Egyptian civilization and the Babylonian Empire featured sun worship, and many of the Romans followed Mithraism, which was a form of sun worship. In fact, Roman Emperor Constantine had a coin minted with his picture on one side of the coin and that of the sun god on the other. So you have a division here: a straight line of *Sabbath keeping* among the faithful from the Garden of Eden, and a straight line of *sun worship* among the pagans after the fall. Clearly different also is the *ancestry* of those two practices: the Father of one is God, the Creator of all things, whereas the father of the other is Satan, the Great Deceiver.

What was happening in those last days of the Roman Empire? Politically, it was disintegrating. Constantine knew that he was losing it. And Constantine knew he had only one hope to end the fragmentation of his empire. And that would be, if church and state would unite and the Christians could evangelize the pagans.

There were three problems: 1) Many of the Jews had been revolting against the Romans, thus generating upon themselves hatred and persecution. 2) The early Christians were keeping the seventh-day Sabbath and thus were mistakenly being persecuted as a Jewish sect. And 3), How could the Christian church convert the pagans who were worshipping the sun god on the first day of the week?

These problems confronted Constantine as he struggled desperately to save his empire. Church and state united with a plan: If Christians would stop worshipping on the Sabbath but worship on Sunday instead, they would disassociate themselves from the Jews whom the Romans were persecuting. And if the Christians *accepted* Sunday, let's say in honor of the resurrection, the pagans would be content to join the Christians and worship on Sunday because they already worshipped on the day of the sun.

THE FIRST SUNDAY LAW

So church and state united in a compromise measure in the early centuries. Church leaders took the solemnity from the seventh-day Sabbath and transferred it to Sunday, piously declaring that they had the authority to change even *divine laws* because, after all, they were the church leaders. In AD 321 Emperor Constantine proclaimed: "On the venerable Day of the Sun, let the magistrates and people residing in cities *rest,* and let all the workshops be *closed"* (Emphasis supplied).

Constantine's *civil* legislation was ratified by, and incorporated into, the Catholic Church—first by the Council of Laodicea and later by countless ecclesiastical councils, synods, and Papal pronouncements. Church and state conspired for convenience. Church and politcal leaders united in compromise. Remember, the prophet Daniel said they would "think" to change God's law.

Someone may say, "Mark, this is just a wild idea.

Where do you find such things in the Catholic Church?" We don't have to go to the voluminous record of the historians for the answer. The Catholic Church freely admits that the change of the day of worship, from Saturday to Sunday, is a sign of their authority.

Let's look at one of the Church's catechisms (a set of questions-and-answers used to instruct new church members):

Q. Which is the Sabbath day?

A. Saturday is the Sabbath day.

Q. Why do we observe Sunday instead of Saturday?

A. We observe Sunday instead of Saturday because the Catholic Church transferred the solemnity from Saturday to Sunday."—Peter Geiermann, *The Convert's Catechism of Catholic Doctrine* (1937 ed.), Page 50.

A Catholic periodical, taunts Protestants for observing Sunday as the Biblical Sabbath:

"By what authority did the Church change the observance of the Sabbath from Saturday to Sunday?

The Church changed the observance of the Sabbath to Sunday. . . .the Protestants claiming the Bible to be the only guide of faith, have no warrant for observing Sunday. In this matter the Seventh-day Adventist is the only consistent Protestant. Sunday as the day of rest to honor our Lord's Resurrection dates to Apostolic time and was so established among other reasons to mark off the Jew from the Christian."—"The Question Box," *The Catholic Universe Bulletin,* 69 (Aug. 14, 1942).

Cardinal James Gibons, a brilliant writer, was always one of my heroes as I grew up in the Catholic Church. He put the Saturday-Sunday issue this way:

> "Reason and sense demand the acceptance of one or the other of these alternatives: either Protestantism or Catholicity and keeping holy of Sunday. Compromise is impossible."— *Catholic Mirror,* Dec. 23, 1893.

On this point I agree with the Cardinal 100 percent! These issues are too clear. They demand a choice.

DON'T LET THE DEVIL CONFUSE THE ISSUE

Behind all our discussion of choice of days, the real issue is the choice of masters. We are not talking about mere days. In the final analysis, the question is, Who is our master? Jesus, or church leaders? Man's traditions, or God's will?

Now you can understand why my heart was being torn apart while I was alter boy serving the priests in the Mass! These statements about the origin of Sunday worship were slowly breaking through my own traditions! And I was asking, "Where is my loyalty?"

Tradition carries a lot of weight in the minds of some people. The devil knows that even an empty, meaningless tradition can become a deeply ingrained cultural habit. In fact, popular thinking says that tradition—if old and long-standing—should be honored. If that were so, then *prostitution,* as "the world's oldest profession," deserves great respect from all of us! But *how old* a practice is has no bearing at all on *how valid* it is. Antiquity of error proves only that we've been going wrong for a long time!

What is Heaven's view of tradition? In Matthew 15, Jesus had to deal with religious leaders who accused His disciples of their man-made traditions: "Why do you also transgress the commandment of God because of your tradition? . . . Thus you have made the commandment of God of no effect by your tradition. . . . And in vain they worship Me, teaching as doctrines the commandments of men" (Matthew 15: 3,6,9).

I think it's time to get back to the Bible, don't you? We have the *Word of God* on the one hand, the *teachings of men* on the other. We have the commandments of God on the one hand, the traditions of men on the other. And the issue is, Who is your *Master?*

Some time ago scientists were studying caterpillars. This particular caterpillar was different from others because this particular caterpillar, believe it or not, *always* follows its leader! The caterpillar fed upon a type of aloe plant, and scientists wanted to find out which was the stronger drive —to follow its leader, or to eat this aloe plant. So they took those caterpillars, put them on a ring all around an aloe plant, and let the first "lead" caterpillar go. And those caterpillars just kept following the leader round and round. The aloe plant was there. They could have eaten it at any time. But they kept going round and round and round—one day, two days, three days. After a while, they began dropping from starvation. They died following their leader.

Friend of mine, if you're following some leader when you could be feeding on God's Word, it could lead you to eternal death. But friend of mine, if that Leader is Jesus Christ, it's worth any sacrifice, any hardship to follow Him. Friend of mine, where is *your* allegiance? ❏

13
REVELATION UNMASKS THE CULT DECEPTION

An anonymous caller tipped off police on an otherwise typical Wednesday afternoon. "You might want to check on the welfare of the residents," he said and gave an address.

A squad car rolled up to a palatial mansion in Rancho Santa Fe, California on that March day in 1997. An exclusive neighborhood, with tennis courts and swimming pools everywhere. Set on three hill-top acres this mansion had nine bedrooms.

What sheriff's deputies and investigators discovered when they opened the door made headlines around the world. Thirty-nine bodies were lying on their backs on bunk beds, cots or mattresses. They wore identical black shirts and pants. Both men and women had buzz-cut hairdos. Each had a passport, birth certificate and driver's license in his or her pocket. Some had been dead for three days.

Beside each body stood a suitcase, packed with personal effects. Some also had hand-written notes with instructions on how to mix the combination of vodka and Phenobarbital that killed them. After drinking the mixture, the note read, "lay back and rest." Apparently they had.

This was the tragedy of the Heaven's Gate cult. All thirty-nine had shared a final meal together at a local restaurant. Then they split into three groups and killed themselves in shifts over three days.

These people had come to believe that a special spaceship following the Hale-Bopp comet would stop for them, transporting them to a higher level of existence after their suicides.

Who were these individuals in Heaven's Gate? What led them there? No one, after all, wakes up one day and says, "I think I'll join a cult and commit suicide."

Most seemed very ordinary. Some had been with the cult since it's beginning in the seventies—a 42-year-old former English teacher and a 72-year-old grandmother. Among the newcomers were a 26-year-old animal lover and a 29-year-old postal worker and mother of five. This woman had left her children seven months earlier to join the cult.

These individuals had once led normal lives. But something made them very vulnerable, very needy. They were searching for something to fill the holes in their lives. And they had the misfortune of meeting a charismatic cult leader and falling under his influence. Gradually they were more and more isolated. Gradually they were indoctrinated into the mind-set of the cult.

A lot of people are searching today. A lot of people want to belong to something they find meaningful. Countless individuals have become disillusioned with organized religion and Christianity itself. They're looking for something new, something different, something fulfilling.

The American Bookseller's Association recently reported a 73 percent increase in the sale of New Age books over a two-year period. According to Forbes magazine, close to two billion dollars is spent each year in the United States on channelers, aromatherapists, macrobiotic foods and countless other aids to spiritual and physical well being. People wear crystals around their necks. People invoke the spirits of north, south, east and west. People chant and shake rattles and try to connect with their past lives. People light incense and try to detect the color of their aura.

Beliefs within the New Age movement are like entrees in a long cafeteria line. There's something for just about every taste. But New Agers have this in common: they're all searching for knowledge *within* themselves or that can be verified by their deepest feelings.. They believe that self-knowledge is God-knowledge, that to know themselves is to know God.

Of course, there's nothing wrong with figuring out what makes you tick. It's good to look within and discover what God has planted inside. But what you find there—inside—should make you look up—outside. Look up to the One who created you. If you don't move from the creation to the Creator, then you'll never get a very good picture of God or yourself. You'll just keep making him up out of available materials—within yourself.

Do you realize that there are between 3000 and 5000 "new religious movements" in North America? Many of them are connected to established churches. But that's still 2000 more than what existed ten years ago. How would you sort through them all? It would take more than a lifetime.

Many people are being deceived while trying to sort all this out. They assume that all belief systems are more-or-less created equal. They assume they can just pick and choose according to their personal preference.

But some beliefs can take us right off a cliff. Heaven's Gate is just one example. It makes a big difference who you follow and what you choose to believe.

A belief system is a lens by which you see God. And distortions in that lens result in a distortion of your picture of God. Some religious groups will help you develop a healthy relationship with your Heavenly Father. Other religious groups will exploit you and leave you deeply disillusioned.

How do you tell the difference? How do you find the truth? Are there clear ways in which to identify false religious teachers. I believe there are.

Do you remember those cowboy TV shows of the fifties and sixties? The Lone Ranger, Roy Rogers, and Hop-a-long Cassidy. How did you tell the good guys from the bad guys? As soon as someone came galloping up on his horse you knew. How? The good guys wore the white hats, the bad guys wore black. Simple!

Unfortunatly, identifying false religious teachers isn't quite that easy. More often than not, the bad guys come galloping up with their black hats whitewashed.

But there is a way to know right from wrong, healthy from unhealthy. Knowing what is true and good, will help you identify the counterfeit. Now I'm going to show you five clear features that separate a cult from a healthy religious group. And we're going to see that the book of Revelation highlights these same features. Revelation identifies them as Satan's ways of working—especially in the end-times.

1. Cults have a single powerful leader who becomes the cult's messiah. The leader is a charismatic individual who focuses attention on himself. He becomes more of a source for truth than God's Word, making it difficult for cult members to separate what he says from what God says.

Cult leader Marshall Applewhite believed that he and

his co-leader, Bonnie Nettles, came from "an evolutionary level above human (the Kingdom of Heaven) incarnated in two human bodies." Applewhite believed he'd been temporarily placed in a human body in order to show people how to get to "the next evolutionary level."

Applewhite went further. In September of 1995 he issued an online statement which was entitled, "Undercover 'Jesus' Surfaces Before Departure." This man began to refer to himself as Jesus. He was a messenger from God, just like Jesus, on the same level with Jesus.

The leader of the Solar Temple cult did the same thing. Luc Joret believed he was Christ. He managed to persuade people that, through death, they could journey to a new life on the star Sirius. Nearly one hundred Solar Temple members have committed suicide over the past few years.

Read what the book of Revelation says about Satan's activity in the end-times:

> "These are of one mind, and they will give their power and authority to the beast" (Revelation 17:13).

This is a fearful union of minds. It's not about fellowship and mutual support; it's about giving up your mind to follow that of another. It's about allowing this other person to have complete power and authority over you. Satan makes this happen through false messiahs.

Jesus warned, in Matthew 24, that false messiahs would come. Paul warned in 2 Thessalonians that the Man of Sin would come. John warned in his first epistle that the Antichrist would come, and that many antichrists had already come.

2. The cult leader's word, his teachings, become absolute truth. They overshadow the teachings of the Bible.

Look at Marshall Applewhite and the Heaven's Gate cult again. This man concocted a theology that has very little relation to what is taught in Scripture. He made up his own little world—which included bodies called vehicles, souls called deposits, and a metamorphosis from one evolutionary level to the one above it.

Ho-Ming Chen did something very similar. He was the leader of a cult in Garland, Texas. This man told his 140 followers that God was going to be reincarnated in his body. It would happen at precisely 10 a.m. on March 31, 1998. And they believed him. Chen stated that, as a sign of God's approach, the sky would be filled with UFOs.

What happened when God didn't show up? Chen had to renounce his own prediction. He said, "I would rather you don't believe what I say any more." That's extremely unusual for a cult leader.

Let's look at what Revelation says will happen in the end-times. In Revelation 18:23 John is talking about Babylon, the power that rises up against God: "By your sorcery all the nations were deceived."

Satan will attempt to counterfeit truth in the last days. He will try to dazzle us. He will try signs and wonders. He will try sorcery, a word that describes powers gained when controlled by an evil spirit. Revelation 13:12, 13 tells us the beast will perform great signs and that he deceives those who dwell on the earth by those signs.

Only those who know the truth will turn away from this last-day counterfeit. Only those who are grounded in God's principles will reject the counterfeit.

Don't be deceived in your search for truth. Check everything you hear against the clear teachings of Scripture. Don't take somebody else's word for it. Put the Word of God on it. Study it for yourself. Don't put anyone else's teaching higher than the principles of the Bible.

3. Cults manipulate. Cults use pressure tactics and deception to recruit members. And they coerce members into staying and into submission.

Last summer the *Christian Science Monitor* published an article entitled, "On Campus, Join Carefully." It revealed that cults are everywhere on college campuses. And many times they use fake names so students won't connect them with a cult. Many who join think it is only a social club. The Heaven's Gate cult is still recruiting on campuses today—using various names.

My sister Sandy has a phobia about people in costumes. The worst kind for her is someone in a gorilla suit. Last summer she was promoting a book at a book sale she'd written. Suddenly two people, who were going to promote the next book, skipped onto the stage in Chip & Dale chipmunk costumes.

Sandy's heart started pounding. She gripped the podium. Her knees started knocking. Something about not knowing who, or what, is inside that costume shakes her up.

I don't have a solution for Sandy's costume phobia. But I can tell you this: Satan puts on costumes. And we need to know what's inside. He's always pretending to be something he's not. And we have to look past the costume to the reality.

Paul saw this problem clearly:

"And no wonder for Satan himself transforms

himself into an angel of ligh" (2 Corinthians 11:14).

Satan uses deception and force. Satan uses coercion.

Revelation tells us tha all this will certainly happen in the last days. John writes:

> "And he causes all, both small and great, rich and poor, free and slave, to receive a mark on their right hand or on their foreheads, and that no one may buy or sell except one who has the mark or the name of the beast" (Revelation 13:16,17).

This is economic coercion. No one can buy or sell unless he has the beast's mark. That is one way Satan coerces. This beast figure, this Antichrist force, is really the ultimate cult. It's the ultimate attempt at mind control. It's the ultimate attempt to deceive.

Look at how Jesus tried to win people to the truth. One day Christ's disciples were very upset because some Samaritans wouldn't let them enter their village. Two indignant disciples asked, "Do you want us to command fire to come down from heaven?"

Jesus' answered:

> "The Son of Man did not come to destroy men's lives but to save them" (Luke 9:56).

What does this tell you about the character of God? He won't use force or coercion to try to persuade people to obey Him. Everyone has been given freedom of choice.

When any church, when any religious leader, modifies the gospel, distorts biblical principles, adds coercive tactics—God is not represented. You have a better place to go to, a place of safety in Jesus Christ, and His written Word.

4. Cults regularly appeal to miracles as a sign of their "divine" credentials. They do this especially when their teachings contradict the truths of the Bible. They hope you will close your eyes to the clear teachings of Scripture and just focus on their razzle-dazzle.

John warns us about placing too much credibility in miracles alone.

> "He performs great signs, so that he even makes fire come down from heaven on the earth in the sight of men. And he deceives those who dwell on the earth by those signs" (Revelation 13:13, 14).

Satan can perform great wonders. He can deceive many through miracles. So be careful.

Don't be persuaded by what appear to be miracles alone. God's truths are what provide a solid foundation for our faith. Check every claim against the principles of the Word of God.

5. Cults isolate. Cults isolate converts from their families, very dangerous thing.

Cult leaders want to immerse you completely in the cult environment. The cult has to become your one source of information. Forget about family and friends, they say, you have to concentrate on this new life.

And that new life often involves every detail of what you do, what you eat, how you sleep. Personal choice is swallowed up within the "group-think."

Cults often foster a fear or hatred of those outside the group. Someone or some force or some organization is always out to get them. Everyone else is conspiring against them. Everyone else is full of error.

Most members of the Heaven's Gate cult only contacted their families once or twice—in a period of twenty years. The cult actually went underground from 1975 to 1992, completely cutting itself off from the world. One member, David Moore, explained it to his mother. He said that associating with family members would drag down the objectivity of the group and "tug at their vibration level." And this is what one father of a cult member said: "There was nothing we could say or do to get her back. We tried everything. It was like they kidnapped her mind."

Cult leaders want total control. That's what Satan seeks as well. And that's what he'll get in the last days. He'll actually persuade his followers to march out into a completely hopeless battle and commit suicide.

John continues:

> "For they are spirits of demons, performing signs, which go out to the kings of the earth and of the whole world, to gather them to the battle of that great day of God Almighty" (Revelation 16:14).

Satan's demonic spirits compel his followers all over the world to gather for battle. They're going to try to fight against the representatives of God Almighty, even against Jesus Christ, who will descend from heaven in the glorious New Jerusalem.

It's hopeless. It's insane. But Satan has kidnapped their minds. Satan has total control. His self-destruction becomes their self-destruction. That's what cult leaders do. But that's not what Jesus does. Jesus doesn't kidnap our minds; He enlightens our minds and widens our hearts. Jesus doesn't cut us off from relationships; He nurtures relationships.

When authorities entered that mansion in Rancho Santa Fe, they at first assumed it was a cult of men only. They all had the identical black shirts and pants, the same buzz cut, the same Nike track shoes. It was only later that they realized there were 21 women in that group of 39.

Cults try to press everyone into the same mold; everyone has to become a passive follower of one individual's ideas. Everyone has to be the same.

That is not God's way! Look at creation and you'll see it. Look at the incredible diversity. God didn't create generic things. He didn't create a bird and then make replicas. God created nearly 10,000 different kinds of birds! Birds with all kinds of different colors, birds with all kinds of different feathers.

Millions of different kinds of insects are in the world. You'd think the Creator might have just come up with one basic bug model, one bug stamp. How important can bugs be? Well, he invested an incredible amount of creativity in bugs, in a mind-boggling array of insects, each with a different function, a different style, a different role to play.

God created individuals, each with a different personality. And He wants to keep it that way. He doesn't want a bunch of clones out there bowing on cue. He wants us to develop as individuals and to freely respond to His love.

So, when someone tries to squeeze you into a box, it's time to break out. When someone tries to make you a robot, leave the factory. Cults want their members to be all alike. God expects diversity. Do you know why? Because that glorifies Him. It takes all of our personalities to paint the image of God. We're all like pieces of a giant puzzle, many different pieces with many different shapes. And in our individuality we're part of a wonderful picture.

Scripture asks us to evaluate all religious claims critically. John tells us:

> "Beloved, do not believe every spirit, but tests the spirits, whether they are of God; because many false prophets have gone out into the world" (1 John 4:1).

You must not give away your judgment. You shouldn't accept the word of someone else, without some kind of test. Each one of us is asked to evaluate the truth for ourselves. It doesn't have to be complicated. There are clear, plain teachings of Scripture which no one should contradict.

Paul wrote that we will be accountable for our life's decisions:

> "So then each of us shall give account of himself to God" (Romans 14:12).

On that judgment day, when you stand before your Heavenly Father, he's not going to ask, "Did you do what Mark Finley said you were supposed to do? He's not going to ask, "Did you do what your pastor said?" or "Did you follow the teachings of your parents."

No, we can't just blindly follow another human being, no matter how noble they might seem, no matter how convincing they might sound. We need to go directly to the Source of truth, to the Word of God. And we need to base our beliefs, and our life, on those teachings.

Do you know who *you* are following and why? Sometimes we may not even realize that we are depending too much on the teachings of another individual. It's best to become grounded in the Word. It's best to focus on the life of Jesus Christ. It's best to get on our knees and ask Him for guidance.

Are you searching for a place to belong? You already belong to the heart of God. Trust him enough to show you what to do next.

Are you looking for a sense of purpose? You already have a sense of purpose—to show the world something about what God is like, to share God's love, to share his goodness.

Are you hungry for knowledge? Go directly to the one whose mind is infinite. Cut through the confusion of man-made religion. Go to the heart of the matter. Go to the heart of God. ❏

14
REVELATION'S SEVEN LAST PLAGUES UNLEASHED

A PREVIEW OF EARTH'S FINAL HEADLINES

What if you had comfortably settled into your favorite lounge chair to watch TV and the announcement came blaring across the screen . . .

"We interrupt this broadcast . . ."

Finally, the world's media are jolted from their endless, narrow preoccupation with the local politics of Earth and forced to report events of truly cosmic significance.

Network anchors ponder the meaning of an unprecedented series of worldwide catastrophes. Newspapers print headlines that signal alert Christians that the Great War has reached its final battle. The cable headline news is about to circle the world for its final half hour.

Those who have thrown in their lot with Satan will reap a harvest of intense suffering as they reel under the impact of serial plagues. But God will miraculously protect and provide for His loyal followers throughout this time of trouble and terror.

Then, just as headline writers are searching their dictionaries for the spelling of "Armageddon," the battle is interrupted by what would be history's greatest headline ever—if anyone were around to read it!

Which astronomer will be the first to sight the cloud

closing in on Earth and growing brighter by the second, a mysterious light racing Earthward through the yawning vault of Orion's Great Nebula?

From all indications, we won't be waiting long for the answers.

I was sitting in my living room conducting a Bible study recently, when a young woman related an interesting story. The night before, while driving home from shopping, a meteor shower suddenly lit up the night sky. Unaccustomed to such a starry display, she anxiously pressed down on the accelerator. "All I wanted to do was to get home and be with my son," she told me. "I was sure Jesus was coming that very minute!"

Linda, like many people today, had the mistaken idea that Jesus might come at any moment—something like Russian roulette. Although the Bible teaches that Jesus is coming soon, specific events will take place before He comes. A significant part of being ready for His coming involves an understanding of what the Bible teaches regarding what will occur in Earth's last days.

John writes about the sequence of events—this preview of Earth's final headlines:

> "Then a third angel followed them, saying with a loud voice, 'If anyone worships the beast and his image, and receives his mark on his forehead or on his hand, he himself shall also drink of the wine of the wrath of God, which is poured out full strength into the cup of His indignation. And he shall be tormented with fire and brimstone in the presence of the holy angels and in the presence of the Lamb'" (Revelation 14:9, 10).

Before Jesus comes, the mark of the beast will be enforced upon men and women throughout this world. We read in Revelation 13 that "the mark or the name of the beast, or the number of his name" (verse 17) will be forced upon all classes of people—rich and poor, small and great, free and bond. Only those with the mark will be allowed the privilege of buying and selling.

Those who do not have the mark become the objects of an economic boycott. Ultimately, they will be threatened with death. Before Jesus comes, the whole world will be tested in the area of worshipping the Creator on the true Sabbath.

The entire issue of the great controversy focuses on the question of loyalty. In the days of Daniel, the test of loyalty for the three Hebrew worthies was the second commandment, forbidding the worship of graven images. Since the three Hebrews would not bow down to the image and violate the second commandment, they were threatened with imprisonment and death.

In the last generation, the issue will not be the second commandment, but the fourth. After the mark of the beast is enforced, there will be two classes of people—those who receive the mark of the beast, and those who receive the seal of God; those who are disloyal, and those who are loyal. Each person will be on one side or the other. After each person has made a final, irrevocable decision, God's wrath unmingled with mercy will be "poured out full strength into the cup of His indignation" (Revelation 14:10).

The wrath of God, poured out without mercy! What a picture! We find in Revelation 15 that God's wrath, in earth's last hour, will come in the form of the seven last plagues, reserved for those who receive the mark of the beast. Those who yield to human traditions and human laws, selling out their devotion to Christ, will ultimately experience the unmitigated wrath of God.

But what of God's people during this time of calamity that is unlike any other crisis in human history? God's Word assures us that His children will be alive during this time, protected by His grace. While the plagues will be falling all around them, they will not be touched. God's church will go through the tribulation and emerge triumphant.

Thus the sequence of events in the time of the end is clear: Before Jesus comes, the mark of the beast will be enforced. This will lead to the outpouring of the seven last plagues. At the end of the plagues, Christ will come to deliver His people and take them home.

John tells us:

> "No one was able to enter the temple until the
> seven plagues of the seven angels were com-
> pleted" (Revelation 15:8).

Thus the popular teaching of the "secret rapture" is not supported by Scripture. If God's people were to be raptured or taken to heaven before the plagues were poured out, they would obviously have entered the heavenly temple. But the Bible clearly says that nobody will enter the temple in heaven until the seven last plagues are fulfilled.

Prior to the beginning of the plagues, the solemn announcement will be made:

> "He who is unjust, let him be unjust still; he
> who is filthy, let him be filthy still; he who is
> righteous, let him be righteous still; he who is
> holy, let him be holy still" Revelation 22:11.

Then and only then will Christ's work as our High Priest in heaven be ended. Every case will have been decided for eternal life or eternal death. The door of God's mercy will be shut, ushering in the "time of trouble" spoken of by the prophet Daniel (see Daniel 12:1).

The most vivid description of this period of earth's history cannot match its reality as the wicked drink the cup of God's wrath unmixed with mercy. John was given a preview of this terrible time of trouble that would take place just before the coming of Jesus and the deliverance of His people:

> "Then I heard a loud voice from the temple saying to the seven angels, 'Go and pour out the bowls of the wrath of God on the earth'" (Revelation 16:1).

PLAGUE ONE

In John's description of the plagues, we find a striking similarity between the plagues of the last days and those that fell upon Egypt. The first plague to fall upon the wicked is "a foul and loathsome sore" (verse 2), possibly resembling the boils and blains suffered by the Egyptians during their plagues. Many scholars believe them to have been some type of cancerous lesion. But whatever the diagnosis, we do know that the sores under the first plague will be painful, and they will fall on all those who have chosen to follow the dictates of man instead of the commands of God.

Can you imagine the impact such a plague would have? Schools would close. Factories would shut down. Stores would not open. Hospitals would be overflowing with people seeking emergency treatment, but most of the doctors and nurses would be suffering from the same affliction.

PLAGUE TWO

And then, while people are still suffering from their sores, another calamity strikes! "Then the second angel poured out his bowl on the sea, and it became blood as of a dead man; and every living creature in the sea died" (verse 3). What a sight—and what a stench, as the creatures of the sea wash ashore.

PLAGUE THREE

The third plague is closely associated with the second: "Then the third angel poured out his bowl on the rivers and springs of water, and they became blood" (verse 4).

Just think! A person turns on the faucet to get a drink—and instead of water, blood flows! What havoc! Could anything be worse?

But, ghastly and frightening as the seven last plagues may be, God's justice is fully vindicated. For the angel declares, "You are righteous, O Lord, The One who is and who was and who is to be, Because You have judged these things. For they have shed the blood of saints and prophets, And You have given them blood to drink. For it is their just due" (verses 5, 6).

At this time, when the wicked are perishing of thirst and have nothing to drink but blood, the promise is made to those who walk righteously that "Bread will be given him, His water will be sure" (Isaiah 33:16). This promise may sound like poetry now, but then it will be worth more than the wealth of all the world's banks.

PLAGUES FOUR AND FIVE

Then the fourth angel pours out his bowl, scorching men with fire and great heat. The fifth angel follows, spreading darkness throughout the land, while men continue to suffer from the earlier plagues, gnawing their tongues in pain. This text indicates that the plagues are not all universal, nor are they all immediately fatal, since those under the fifth plague are still suffering from the sores of the first plague.

Apparently the plagues fall successively, instead of simultaneously, as their effects overlap; the accumulation of dreary trouble becomes unspeakable!

PLAGUE SIX

The sixth plague includes the great final battle, Armageddon.

Revelation 16 describes "three unclean spirits like frogs coming out of the mouth of the dragon, out of the mouth of the beast, and out of the mouth of the false prophet" (verse 13). These unclean spirits, symbolizing "spirits of demons," will "go out to the kings of the earth and of the whole world, to gather them to the battle of that great day of God Almighty" (verse 14).

The whole world is to be involved in this final conflict.

The Battle of Armageddon focuses on the final offensive of the combined forces of rebel religious powers, as they mobilize against God's people. The aim of these rebel forces is to completely destroy those loyal to God. All of us will be involved in the Battle of Armageddon.

In the last moment of time, when it looks as if God's people will be annihilated, the last phase of the battle occurs. Christ returns, accompanied by His armies from the sky. The wicked are themselves slain under the artillery from heaven. This is Armageddon!

PLAGUE SEVEN

> "Then the seventh angel poured out his bowl into the air, and a loud voice came out of the temple of heaven, from the throne, saying, 'It is done!' And there were noises and thunderings and lightnings; and there was a great earthquake, such a mighty and great earthquake as had not occurred since men were on the earth ... Then every island fled away, and the mountains were not found" (Revelation 16:17, 18, 20).

This catastrophic convulsion of the earth levels the cities as well as the mountains. Next comes a "great hail" out of heaven, "each hailstone about the weight of a talent" (verse 21). Most scholars place the weight of a talent at about fifty-seven pounds. The devastation from such a hailstorm is beyond human comprehension. But the Bible tells us that the Lord Himself will interrupt the conflict as He rides forth with the armies of heaven to deliver His people from a planet in rebellion.

We can learn a lesson for the future from the past. After the children of Israel had been captives by the Egyptians for many years, the time arrived for God to fulfill His promise to deliver them from bondage. Sending Moses and Aaron to Pharaoh with the message, "Let my people go" (Exodus 5:1). God's wrath was kindled with the response of this haughty earthly official: "Who is the Lord, that I should obey His voice?" (Verse 2).

In the ten plagues that fell on Egypt just before God's people were delivered, God answered Pharaoh's question in a graphic way.

In the final chilling plague, all the firstborn in Egypt were slain, beginning with the Pharaoh's family. With an aching heart, Pharaoh learned too late, to take the warnings of God seriously.

But what was happening to the children of Israel during this time of great suffering and turmoil throughout Egypt? While Moses and Aaron had requested Pharaoh to deliver God's people from bondage, they had also instructed their fellow Israelites as to how they should respond to this remarkable intervention by the Lord. On the fourteenth day of the first month, the Israelites were to slaughter a lamb and sprinkle its blood on the door posts of their houses. Such a sign was not done lightly. It clearly differentiated between those willing to trust the God of Israel and those who were either hesitant or afraid to declare themselves, fearing Egyptian reprisals. It was a night of testing for Israel as well as for the Pharaoh.

Just as God had warned, at midnight the destroying angel passed through the land, visiting death upon the homes of all those without God's identifying mark—the blood on the door post—and sparing those families who had declared their loyalty to the God of Israel, regardless of the consequences. That night the children of Israel left for the promised land under God's direction.

Just so in earth's last hours, the final plagues will fall on those who have rejected or neglected God's deliverance and salvation. But those who have chosen the blood of the Lamb for forgiveness and cleansing from their sins will be delivered.

By our lives we are choosing today which side we will be on—God's side or the side of a rebel angel. When the destroying angels begin their work, it will be too late to change sides! Probation's door will have already closed forever.

UNDER THE WINGS OF SAFETY

The story is told of an Australian lumberman who built a simple cabin at the edge of a forest. One day, returning home from work, he was stunned and heart-broken to find his home reduced to a heap of smoldering ruins. All that remained were a few pieces of charred lumber and blackened metal. Walking out to where his old chicken coop had stood, the lumberman discovered only a mound of ashes and some burned wire. Aimlessly, he shuffled through the debris. Then, glancing down at his feet, his eye caught a curious sight—a mound of charred feathers. Idly he kicked it over. Four little fuzzy baby chicks scrambled out, miraculously protected by the wings of a loving mother.

In the most beautiful and meaningful language of Scripture, God describes what He longs to do for every one of His children on earth when the plagues fall:

> "He shall cover you with His feathers, And under His wings you shall take refuge" (Psalm 91:4).

God has given wonderful assurance to those who choose to follow Him. Down through the ages, Christians have memorized the words of Psalm 91, taking courage in God's promise: "A thousand may fall at your side, And ten thousand at your right hand; But it shall not come near you . . . No evil shall befall you" (Psalm 91:7, 10). The good news of the Bible is that while the plagues will be falling all around those loyal to God, He will give His angels charge over them (see verse 11).

We already know how the Battle of Armageddon will turn out. We know who will walk away, shaken perhaps, but with a song on their lips. John the Revelator names the song, "The Song of Moses and the Lamb." See Revelation 15:3.

The valiant heroes of earth's final conflict—those qualified to sing this victory song—are described as "those who keep the commandments of God and the faith of Jesus" (Revelation 14:12). What a group to belong to! The invitation to join that group is ringing around the world today. And you are invited!

Armageddon is cut short by Christ's return. But it will be another thousand years before the Great War is forever over. Yet for God's people, it will be the first thousand years of eternity—a millennium spent with the King in Heaven.

Satan, on the other hand, will spend ten centuries confined to the hell he has made of Earth. ❏

15
REVELATION REVEALS
DEADLY DELUSIONS

I t's sometimes said that you never really feel alone in the world until you stand at your parent's grave. It leaves you without a lifelong cheerleader. It makes you realize you're next in line. And it haunts you with a question— "Can I find hope that goes beyond the grave?"

Take a woman named Tina, for example. She sat in the hospital at 3 a.m. listening to her father's painful gasps. This was the man who'd helped change her diapers and taught her to ride a bike. He'd been a dock worker most of his life. But now cancer had reduced him to a frail, disoriented fragment of himself.

Dad was dying. He couldn't fight any longer.

After the funeral, Tina thought she'd be able to just go on with her life. But nothing was quite the same. She's haunted by the parent who isn't there. She may catch a scent of Old Spice after shave, or hear a Sinatra song he loved, and be overcome with tears. Tina says, "I know I'm an adult and I'm supposed to be strong. But there are some days I feel like I'm four years old and all I want is my dad."

Millions of people like Tina are facing one of life's toughest rites of passage—watching a parent die. It's an experience that's going to hit many of us hard as we journey into the next few years. The generation born after World War II, the baby boomers, are well into middle-age. Statistics tell us that by the time they turn 50, a quarter of the population typically lose their mothers and half lose their fathers.

Have you ever looked death squarely in the face and wondered, "What happens five minutes after death?" Is it heaven, hell or nothingness? It seems so confusing at times. Many varied beliefs abound about the subject of death.

Let's suppose each one of us surveyed some of the people living in our own community on their beliefs regarding the after life. Our survey has only one question—What happens when you die?

1. My Hindu neighbor says: "Your immortal soul leaves your body and eventually you are reincarnated as something or someone else. You may be a cow, a servant, a wealthy businessman or an insect depending on how you treated people in this life."

2. My Catholic neighbor says: "There is an immortal soul that leaves the body at death which ascends to heaven if you have been good, purgatory if you're not so good, and hell if you have been really bad."

3. My Protestant neighbor may say something similar but leave out the idea about purgatory.

4. My secular, humanist neighbor might say: "Death is the end. You have lived once and that's it. It is over—finished."

5. Other Bible-believing Christians believe death is merely a sleep until the resurrection day when Christ finally returns.

Where can we find credible information on the subject of death?

We all have seen an amazing upsurge of interest in spiritualism and communication with the dead in the past

30 years. If, as so many believe, the soul is immortal, can the dead communicate with the living? Is the assumption of so many people really true that there is an immortal soul which survives bodily death?

The Bible gives us rock-solid answers to the question—"What happens when you die?" It reveals not only what happens when you die, but also how to face death with new hope and confidence.

Let's start with the book of Revelation. Let me tell you what happens at the very beginning of Revelation that reveals our ultimate human destiny.

In the very first chapter Revelation introduces us to a glorious person, the person of Jesus Christ. He is dressed in a glowing white robe and His eyes are flames of fire. And Jesus identifies Himself in this way:

> "I am He who lives, and was dead, and behold,
> I am alive forevermore. Amen. And I have the
> keys of Hades and of Death" (Revelation 1:18).

Jesus Christ is the man who was dead and who was resurrected from the dead to eternal life. He is the one who has penetrated the mystery of death. He has broken the jaws of death. And that's why He has the keys of hell and of death.

Jesus holds the key that unlocks the mystery of death. He is also our key to *our* hope for life beyond the grave. Because of Christ's resurrection we can have hope in the same kind of bodily resurrection. It will happen at the second coming of Jesus Christ:

> "Blessed and holy is he who has part in the
> first resurrection. Over such the second death
> has no power" (Revelation 20:6).

The first resurrection is the resurrection of the righteous. The second death refers to final death, to eternal death.

Believers are said to "reign forever and ever" (Revelation 22:5). And this is God's promise in Revelation 21:4:

> "And God will wipe away every tear from their eyes; there shall be no more death, nor sorrow, nor crying; and there shall be no more pain, for the former things have passed away."

No more death! Revelation tells us that God will bring about a final, permanent solution to the death problem. And it tells us that this solution centers on the person of Jesus Christ Who has the keys of hell and death.

That's the great hope of the book of Revelation. Now let's see exactly how this hope plays out in the rest of the Bible. The evidence of scripture may surprise you.

SOUL IS A KEY WORD

Let's go back to creation week to find a clue as to what happens when a person dies. Maybe if we understand what happened at man's creation, we can understand something about what happens at death. The Bible says in Genesis 2:7:

> "The Lord God formed man of the dust of the ground, and breathed into his nostrils the breath of life; and man *became* a living soul."

Notice, God formed man out of the *dust of the ground.* That's his body, right? Then He breathed into his nostrils the *breath of life*—the power of God—and man *became* a living soul.

Does it say that God *put* an immortal soul *into* man? No, it says that God formed man out of the dust of the ground, breathed into his nostrils the breath of life, and man became a living soul, a living being, a living person. In fact, virtually all modern Bible translations translate the Hebrew text most accurately with "a living being" or "a living person." So the formula reads:

Dust + Spirit = Living Being

Adam *became* a living being or a living person. You see, a living soul *is* a living person.

Suppose you went to the supermarket, and when you came home you said to your spouse, "There wasn't a *soul* there." And your spouse jokingly replies, "Oh, I'm glad there wasn't any soul there, because that would have scared me!" He knows, when you say "soul," you mean "There wasn't a *person* there."

The Bible never says a person "has" a soul—as if it were a *separate entity* we possess. I don't *have* a soul, I *am* a soul, a living creature, a person—and so are you.

But someone says, "Wait a minute—I don't want to get caught up in mere words! Just answer me one thing: Our physical *bodies* die, but our *souls* can never, ever die, can they?"

God says quite plainly that they can and do:

"The soul who sins shall die" (Ezekiel 18:4, 20).

The *pagan Greeks*—especially the philosopher Plato—asserted that the soul of man is "imperishable." If that pagan idea were true, *why* did the Holy Spirit inspire Ezekiel to write those words—twice in one chapter?

A soul is a person, and if a person sins, he or she will die. Modern Bible versions render Ezekiel 18:4 as follows:

"The *person* who sins is the one who will *die*."
(*Today's English Version*)

"It is for a man's own sins that *he* will *die.*"
(The Living Bible)

"The *soul* who sins will *die.*" *(New American
Standard Bible.* A footnote on the word *soul*
says *"person."*)

The Bible word "soul" may also mean "life." For
instance, Jesus taught that:

"Whosoever will save his *life* shall lose it; and
whosoever will lose his *life* for My sake shall
find it. For what is a man profited, if he shall
gain the whole world, and lose his own *soul?*
Or what shall a man give in exchange for his
soul" (Matthew 16:25, 26, similarly translated
in Mark 8:35-37)?

In this passage, Matthew wrote the same Greek
word "psyche" four times, but the King James translators twice rendered it "life" and twice "soul." You can
see for yourself that the two words are interchangeable.
And you can see, further, that "life" is not something
naturally and irrevocably ours—we can lose it, for we're
not inherently immortal.

ONLY GOD IS IMMORTAL

The word *mortal* means "subject to death," and
immortal means the opposite—imperishable. You don't
find the term "immortal soul" or "immortality of the soul"
even once in the entire Bible! The Word of God doesn't
teach such a concept. The King James Version uses the
expressions "soul" and "spirit" but never once attaches the
term "immortal" to either word. If human beings really
had an immortal soul or immortal spirit, don't you think
the Bible would use that term at lease once?

Mankind has the *promise* of immortality—to be given to the faithful as a gift when Jesus returns. Paul writes:

> "Behold, I tell you a mystery; we shall not all sleep, but we shall all be changed, in a moment, in the twinkling of an eye, at the last trumpet: for the trumpet will sound . . . and this mortal must *put on* immortality" (1 Corinthians 15:51-53).

We mortals, who are subject to death and decay, have to "put on" immortality at Christ's second coming. But man is *not* inherently or naturally immortal now.

In fact, the very word immortal is used only once in scripture, and in that sole instance—1 Timothy 1:17—the word applies not to man but to "the only wise God."

To clinch this point, Paul explicitly declares that:

> "The King of kings and Lord of lords . . . only has immortality" (1Timothy 6:15,16).

When the Bible plainly declares that God alone is immortal, that "[He] only has immortality," we needn't waste our time trying to find verses that say man is immortal or has an immortal soul—for we won't find them. The Holy Spirit does not contradict Himself.

Furthermore, the Bible never says a person "has" a soul that leaves the body at death—a conscious, feeling, thinking kind of an ethereal thing that floats away—that's man's idea.

Psalm 22:20 prays, "Deliver my soul from the sword." But if a soul were our non-material "essence," a sword couldn't hurt it.

"SPIRIT" IS A KEY WORD

Now, what happens when we die? When Adam was

created, God formed his body from the dust of the ground, breathed the breath of life or spirit into his nostrils, and he became a living person. According to the Bible the opposite occurs at death:

> "Then the dust will return to the earth as it was, and the spirit will return to God who gave it" (Ecclesiastes 12:7).

So the body goes to the earth and the spirit returns to God who gave it. What goes back to God? The spirit or the breath? The Bible never once says the soul goes back to God.

Here's where people make a mistake: They don't understand what the "spirit" is. Is the spirit something that thinks? Is it something that's conscious? The word "spirit" itself comes from the same root as other words pertaining to "breath" or "breathing," such as inspire or respiration.

The New Testament Greek word for "spirit" is *pneuma,* which gives us words like pneumonia, the respiratory disease, and pneumatic, a description of tires we blow up with air.

But let's listen to the Bible define what the spirit is that goes back to God. In the Hebrew language of the Old Testament there's a literary device called *parallelism* in which the first phrase says something and the second phrase defines it. Job tells us what the spirit of God is:

> "As long as my breath is in me, and the breath of God in my nostrils" (Job 27:3).

So the spirit is equal to, or the same as the breath. God breathed into man the breath of life—God breathed into man His life-giving spirit. When a man dies, what goes back to God? The breath of God, or the power of God—that spark of life—returns to God.

James 2:26 says: "The body without the spirit is dead."

That's how we describe death even today. We say, "He died" or "He expired" or "He breathed his last." So the body without God's breath is dead, because at death God's spirit or His breath goes back to Him.

THE UNCONSCIOUS DEAD CANNOT THINK

But that breath is *not* a thinking, conscious entity which survives death. Since the Bible says the dust returns to earth "as it was," we can assume that the breath or spirit returns to God the same "as it was." Adam's breath was not conscious before God created him by breathing into his nostrils, so why should we assume that it's conscious after death? No Bible student should believe in the pre-existence of the human soul or person before life on earth. That's a pagan concept.

The Word of God specifically forbids any idea of consciousness after death. What happens to us when our breath goes back to God? The Psalmist wrote:

> "His spirit departs, he returns to his earth; in that very day his plans perish" (Psalm 146:4).

So is a dead man able to think? No! The Bible says that on the day he dies, his thoughts perish. Soloman says plainly:

> "The living know that they will die: but the dead know nothing. . . . and they have no more reward, for the memory of them is forgotten" (Ecclesiastes 9:5).

Friends, no matter what we've been taught in the past, no matter what the devil said to Eve in that first lie, the dead know not anything!

DEATH IS A DREAMLESS SLEEP

The Bible teaches that death is but a *sleep* that lasts until Christ's second coming. More than fifty times, Bible writers consistently describe death as a sleep. Writing under inspiration, the Psalmist David prayed to God lest he "sleep the sleep of death" Psalm 13:3.

Later, the writer of 1 Kings says:

> "Now the days of David drew nigh that he should die . . . So David slept with his fathers, and was buried" (1 Kings 2:1, 10).

Jesus Himself spoke of death as a sleep. When His beloved friend Lazarus grew very sick in a nearby town, the Master said:

> "Our friend Lazarus sleeps, but I go that I may wake him up. Then disciples said to Him, 'Lord if he sleeps, he will get well.' However, Jesus spoke of his death, but they thought that He was speaking about taking rest in sleep. Then Jesus said to them plainly, 'Lazarus is dead'" (John 11:11-14).

When people die they go to sleep, awaiting the Voice of Jesus the Lifegiver. No more pain, no more suffering, no more heartache, no more sorrow. It's as if we rest in Jesus' arms until He taps us on the shoulder and says, "Wake up, My child, it's time to go home!"

Someone says, "But, Pastor, I always like to think of my mother up in heaven looking down on me. That makes me feel good." Another says, "I like to think of Daddy looking down at me—he's so proud!"

Oh, dear friends, I know we've been so brainwashed in this culture that it's going to take a conscious effort on our part to say to Jesus, "Dear Lord, I just want to know Your will, Your truth. Teach me the truth about the state of the dead."

Job helps us to understand that the dead do not know whats happening to their friends:

> "If his sons are honored, he does not know it;
> if they are brought low, he does not see it" (Job 14:21, NIV).

God's Way is the Best Way

If we think it through, we'll realize that God's way is the best way. Let's suppose that a mother died and that she does have a conscious, immortal soul in heaven. Let's suppose she can look down and see everything that happens on earth. She sees her son in the Vietnam War flying a combat mission. The enemy turn their guns on him, blow his helicopter apart, and he goes down. He's taken prisoner of war and is tortured. Do you think that mother in heaven would be happy?

Or a little boy six or seven years old is playing ball, and the ball goes into the street. He runs to get it as a car speeds down the street, ready to hit the child. If his mother were consciously aware of all this in heaven, she'd scream, "Oh, please stop!"

Or think of the dead mother whose kid is on drugs and she sees him lying in a back alley. He's destroyed his whole body. Wouldn't that mother weep and cry to see this?

Or a dead husband looks down from heaven and sees his beloved wife suffering terribly from cancer, yet there's nothing he can do. You see, God is so merciful. His way is best.

God's way is—that when you die, you sleep. You sleep soundly. It's a quiet rest in the arms of Jesus. You're secure, and when Jesus comes again to wake you up, earth's heartache and suffering will be all over. Our loved-ones who have gone to their rest are conscious of nothing—not even the passage of time. They don't see that child abused. They don't see the drunk driver who hit those kids. They don't see that man who comes home and beats his wife. Jesus' way is so much better!

Listen to Soloman:

> "The living know that they will die, but the dead know not nothing" (Ecclesiastes 9:5).

Isn't God's way best? It couldn't be any plainer:

> "The dead do not praise the Lord, nor any that go down into silence" (Psalm 115:17).

Yet you know that *if* you died and immediately went to heaven, you'd praise the Lord, wouldn't you? The Bible says, "The dead know not anything." The Bible says, "The dead praise not the Lord."

DEATH AND LIFE MAY BE LIKENED TO A BOX

Let's suppose we let life be represented by building a box. I need nails and boards to construct the box just as I need God's spirit (the nails) breathed into my body (the boards) to construct the box. What happens to the box if I pull the nails out. The box no longer exists because a box is nails and boards.

So when we die, the soul or person does not go anywhere. We simply cease to exist as a conscious personality until the resurrection. God has preserved a record of our lives. We are His. Paul puts it this way in a letter to the Colossians:

> "For you died, and your life is hidden with Christ in God. When Christ who is our life

appears, then you also will appear with Him in glory" (Colossians 3:3, 4).

People who place their faith in Jesus Christ as Savior and Lord are given a new identity. They die to the old life and they find a new life "hidden in Christ in God." Their identity is hidden away, tucked securely away, with Christ in God.

Here Paul is giving us an essential principle. This is why hope is possible. This is what it's based on—our life being "hidden with Christ in God." In the New Testament all kinds of good things happen to human beings because they are "in Christ." And one of those good things is "eternal life."

Paul could not be clearer:

"For the wages of sin is death, but the gift of God is eternal life in Christ Jesus our Lord" (Romans 6:23).

Eternal life comes to us in Christ Jesus. It comes to us because our life is hidden with God in Christ.

NATURAL IMMORTALITY IS A PAGAN CONCEPT

Where did the doctrine of innate, natural immortality come from? From man— but ultimately, of course, from the mind of Satan. The pagans worshiped on the day of the sun—Sunday, the first day of the week—and gave allegiance to the sun god. Long ago, the Greeks came to believe in the natural immortality of the soul. They believed the soul lived on outside the body as a separate, conscious entity—an idea popularized by Plato and other heathen philosophers.

When pagan scholars became Christians and joined the church, they carried with them many of their former heathen beliefs and practices. They brought the images and idols of their pagan gods into the church. They brought Sunday in as a holy day. And they brought the pagan idea of the natural immortality of the soul into the church.

Here's what William E. Gladstone, four-time Prime Minister of Great Britain and a brilliant Bible student, wrote:

> "The doctrine of natural immortality, as dis-
> tinguished from Christian immortality . . .
> crept into the church, by a back door . . . The
> natural immortality of the soul is a doctrine
> wholly unknown to the Holy Scriptures."

According to Revelation, the devil is getting ready to deceive thousands of Christians by impersonating their loved ones, telling them it's not necessary to obey God's Law. We're going to find the greatest spiritualistic decep-tions of all time in these last days.

THE CASE OF THE MISPLACED COMMA

My Bible says, "Follow the teachings of Jesus." What did Jesus Himself teach about death? I'm always asked about the thief on the cross. What did Jesus mean when he spoke to the thief on the cross and promised,

> "Assuredly I say to you, today you will be with
> Me in paradise" (Luke 23:43)?

Did He mean that the thief would go with Him to paradise that day? Obviously not, because when Mary came to Jesus on the resurrection morning, she looked at Jesus through her tears and thought He was the gardener. After Jesus revealed Himself, Mary threw herself at His feet. Then Jesus said:

"Do not cling to Me, for I have not yet ascended
to My Father" (John 20:17)

Jesus' promise to the thief appears, on the surface in
some English translations, to present a strange contradiction. First, it seems to contradict clear Bible teaching on
the subject of death that man sleeps in the grave until
called forth by Jesus. Second, if Jesus had not yet
ascended to His Father on Sunday morning, how could
He have told the thief on Friday that they'd be in paradise
that day? Are we forced to believe either Christ's statement to Mary on Sunday morning or His promise to the
thief on Friday afternoon?

When we encounter an apparent contradiction in the
Bible, we immediately realize that something is wrong—
not with the Word of God, but with our limited understanding or with the translation.

But this particular apparent contradiction instantly dis-
appears with the simple movement of a comma. The place-
ment of a comma can make a world of difference. We must
remember that the punctuation found in the Bible is *not*
inspired. In fact, the original Greek New Testament had *no*
punctuation at all!

Punctuation was not added until about the time of the
Reformation—AD 1500 or so. Even when the King
James Version appeared in 1611 with some punctuation,
it still had no quotation marks around words spoken—
those were added in still later versions.

THISISWHATANCIENTGREEKLOOKEDLIKE
OFCOURSEITISNTGREEKITSENGLISH

You see, those who added the commas and other punctuation marks to scripture had no help from Luke's Greek
manuscript, because Greek was written all in CAPITAL letters, with no breaks between sentences, in fact no breaks

between words, in order to save on costly parchments.

So the comma in this verse was not added until many centuries later. Translators used their best judgment in inserting punctuation, but they were certainly not inspired. If their interpretation of the text was colored by their mistaken belief in the immortality of the soul, they would naturally put the comma in the wrong place, which is exactly what happened.

The comma in this Bible text can be placed either before or after the word "today," or for that matter, not used at all. Where the comma is placed depends on someone's personal choice:

> "Assuredly I say to you, today you will be with Me in paradise."

> "Assuredly I say to you today, you will be with Me in paradise."

What did Jesus really say to the thief? It's very simple. He boldly made this promise—*today,* as I die on the cross and My ministry ends in agony and shame; *today,* as blood runs down My face and nails pierce My hands; *today,* when it doesn't look as if I can save anyone and My claim to be the Son of God appears false; *today,* when My own disciples have forsaken Me, *today,* in my darkest hour, you understand who I am and I assure you *today,* inspite of how things seem to look, you will be with me in paradise.

The Bible is plain that Jesus Himself did not go to paradise on that day. On that Friday, instead, Christ would enter the grave and rest in the tomb. And as the Bible says, He did not ascend to His Father till some time after encountering Mary Magdalene on Sunday morning. All conflict and contradiction disappear when the comma is properly placed.

Because Christ burst the bonds of the tomb, because

Jesus went into the grave and came out the other side triumphant, you and I need not fear death. Paul sings:

> "O Death, where is your sting? O Hades, where is your victory? . . . Thanks be to God, who gives us the victory through our Lord Jesus Christ" (1 Corinthians 15:55-57).

Christ Himself removed the tragic sting from death and gave us victory over the tomb.

TAKE JESUS' HAND

The Christ who conquered death will take our hand and guide us through it. The Christ who resurrected Lazarus from the dead will resurrect us from the dead. Death is but a sleep—a dreamless sleep until the coming of the Lord. We need not weep and mourn our loved ones as others who have no hope. Certainly, there's an emotional loss. Our hearts are broken if a loved one dies, but the Bible says our Lord will come. The Bible says those graves will open, and you and I can have the absolute assurance that though we go into the grave, Christ will take us through death into eternal life.

Paul promises:

> "I do not want you to be ignorant, brethren, concerning those who have fallen asleep, lest you sorrow as others who have no hope" (1 Thessalonians 4:13).

Don't be ignorant—don't be confused by Satan's lie that the soul is immortal. Don't accept the old pagan idea of natural immortality. Don't be ignorant, because if you're ignorant, you'll be deceived. Don't sorrow as others who have no hope.

Then Paul goes on to say in verse 16:

> "For the Lord Himself will descend from
> heaven with a shout, with the voice of an
> archangel, and with the trumpet of God. And
> the dead in Christ will rise first."

The Christ who died, the Christ who offers forgiveness, the Christ who can transform your life, is the Christ who went into the grave and came out victorious, the conqueror of death!

Good news! That little baby's hands can touch your cheeks again.

Good news! You can see the smile on the face of that son or daughter again.

Good news! You can throw your arms around your wife and look into those eyes again.

Good news! You can hear his words again, "Oh, I love you so much!"

DEATH IS NOT THE END

Death is NOT the end of the road—it's a sleep. It's an instant, a twinkling of an eye, for there's absolutely no awareness of the passing of time in death. The Bible says:

> "We who are alive and remain [that is, remain
> alive till Jesus comes] shall be caught up
> together with them [the resurrected dead] in
> the clouds, to meet the Lord in the air" (1
> Thessalonians 4:17).

We go to heaven when Jesus comes, whether alive or resurrected. The Bible's whole focus is on that grand, glorious event of Jesus' second coming.

A REAL HOPE – TANYA'S STORY

I believe the New Testament hope makes all the difference in the world. That came through to me very clearly during a trip to Russia for meetings in Moscow's Olympic Stadium. There I met a woman whom I'll call Tanya who told me about her family. Years before, her parents had emigrated to China and became wealthy in the tea business. After some time, they decided to return to Russia, and they established their tea business in Kazakhstan.

Just as it was beginning to flourish, Stalin began his purges of the elite and wealthy. When Tanya was 17, her father was taken out of the house by the secret police and shot through the head. Later, during the Second World War, her brother, sister and husband were killed. Within two years, she had lost everyone close to her.

Tanya struggled with depression. She attended an English school and eventually became fluent in the English language. Toward the end of the Second World War, the Russians needed translators in the military, so she became a translator for an American General.

Tanya had come from an Orthodox Jewish background, but had little interest in religion because of the horrors of the war. Through the years, she did rather well for herself, advancing in educational and diplomatic circles. Yet she always sensed that something was missing in her life. She could never come to terms with all the suffering her family had experienced, and she couldn't accept the terrible finality of their cruel deaths.

One day, someone on the street handed Tanya a brochure advertising Christian evangelistic meetings. She attended and accepted Christ as her Savior. She found a new peace and meaning in her life.

Tanya was much happier as a believer, but there was still something she couldn't quite grasp. Why would a loving God permit so much suffering? What really happens when we die? Not all the pieces seemed to fit together in the puzzle.

One day as she passed the Olympic Stadium in Moscow, she saw a large sign proclaiming "The Bible Way to New Life" and picked up a brochure. After reading it, she decided to check out the meetings.

Tanya was there night after night, including the night I spoke on the subject of Jesus' soon return. After the meeting, she came up to me and said, "Pastor, I was deeply moved tonight." And she began showing me old photographs of her family and telling me about their tragic deaths.

Her face was beaming as she exclaimed, "Now I can look forward to seeing them again." She wasn't broken-hearted any longer.

Tanya wasn't looking forward to an out-of-body experience. She was looking forward to face-to-face reunions in a very real place with very real people.

Tanya was looking forward to that ultimate reunion. And she was among the 700 individuals who committed their lives to Christ in baptism one unforgettable day in Moscow.

Don't you want to have that kind of assurance in your life? Don't you want to be able to look forward to a face-to-face reunion with family, loved ones, friends and Jesus Christ?

Heaven, eternity, a real city, a real world, a real body and a real Savior is waiting for you. He longs for you to be there with Him through all eternity. ❏

16
REVELATION'S THOUSAND
YEARS OF PEACE

The time was the Roaring Twenties and a young woman from New York City named Rose, did her level best to live up to the times. High-spirited and talented, she attended innumerable parties and shows, and enjoyed the attentions of admiring young men. Rose also loved to fly, and traveled across the U.S. by air several times, quite an unusual adventure in those early days of the airplane.

But suddenly, at the age of 21, Rose was struck down by Sleeping Sickness. The disease began with a series of nightmares which proved prophetic. She dreamed she was imprisoned in an inaccessible castle—shaped like herself. She'd become a statue and she'd fallen into a sleep so deep that nothing could awaken her. The world had come to a stop.

And then Rose awoke immobile, frozen in an awkward position on the bed. The local doctor said this was just a "catatonia" which would go away in a week. But that inaccessible castle did not dissolve as the months and years passed. Rose remained fixed in some incomprehensible state, looking as if she were trying her hardest to remember something.

Eventually her body became rigid and she developed symptoms of Parkinson's disease. Rose was committed to an institution, where she lay in bed or sat in a wheelchair—with a face completely masked and expressionless—as the decades passed.

Then, in June of 1969, Dr. Oliver Sacks began administering a newly-developed drug to the few survivors of the sleeping sickness. L-DOPA was designed to counter a dopamine insufficiency detected in the brains of those who died from Parkinson's disease.

Dr. Sacks injected Rose with 1.5 grams of L-DOPA—and the young woman awakened from her long sleep. During the following days, her eyes brightened up and she lost her rigidity. She began to feel sudden bursts of energy and excitement. Rose asked for the use of a tape-recorder and began composing songs and light verse—all reminiscent of the 1920s. She was full of anecdotes about people she thought of as current public figures—all from the twenties. She didn't want to know about anything happening now, because now was still 1926.

But one day the truth began to dawn on her. Looking anxious and bewildered, she told Dr. Sacks, "Things can't last. Something awful is coming. God knows what it is, but it's bad as they come." Thereafter the old symptoms began to reappear again. And slowly Rose sunk back into her trance. The almost half-century gap was simply too great for her to bridge. Rose still felt like that twenty-year old girl, always the life of the party. She could not fathom who this sixty-four-year-old woman was staring back at her in the mirror. As Dr. Sacks wrote, "she is a Sleeping Beauty whose 'awakening' was unbearable and who will never be awakened again."

It is hard for us, of course, to imagine the kind of shattering experience that such an awakening creates—what it must be like to wake up suddenly in a strange new world, to have lost yourself somewhere far back in time.

But I believe each one of us is going to experience an awakening even more startling than the one Rose went through. We are going to find ourselves suddenly thrust into a whole new world which none of us could begin to imagine.

Paul tells us about this climactic event:

> "For the Lord himself will descend from heaven with a shout, with the voice of an archangel and with the trumpet call of God. And the dead in Christ will rise first. Then we who are alive and remain shall be caught up together with them in the clouds to meet the Lord in the air" (1Thessalonians 4:16 and 17).

The Second Coming of Christ will arrive on this planet like a star bursting in the heavens. The Bible tells us that every human eye will see Jesus Christ when he appears in glory, and every human being, both the living and the resurrected redeemed will suddenly be confronted with the kingdom of God. In the brilliant light of Christ's coming, the history of this planet will seem dark indeed, marred as it has been with cruelty and tragedy. At that moment we will feel, as never before, the loss, the waste, the suffering of our centuries of separation from God.

Christ's coming will bring us new dawning, a new life. Those awakening from the graves will feel as if time had stood still since the day they closed their eyes. Now they're suddenly alive, and more alive than they've ever been before.

But the sad fact is that for some people, their awakening won't be wonderful news. The new day of God's kingdom will seem strange and terrifying.

What many people don't realize is that these two different awakenings, these two different fates, happen as two different events. Revelation confirms what Jesus had said—there are actually *two* general resurrections—the resurrection of life, and the resurrection of damnation. Jesus said:

> "Do not marvel at this for the hour is coming in which all who are in the graves will hear His voice. And come forth—those who have done good to the resurrection of life and those who have done evil to the resurrection of damnation" (John 5:28, 29).

Notice carefully: every human being will be resurrected or awakened from sleep at one of the two resurrections. Jesus' words are clear. "All who are in the graves shall hear His voice." Then our Lord describes the two resurrections: 1) The resurrection of life, 2) The resurrection of condemnation. Revelation 20:6 says, "Blessed and holy is he who has part in the first resurrection."

Two things are taught here. By identifying this as the first resurrection, God lets us know there will be a second one. And, by specifying that those raised in the first resurrection are the faithful dead, the blessed and holy, we also learn that the rest of the dead, the unfaithful, are raised at some later time.

What happens to those who rise in the *first* resurrection? Let's read on in verse 6: "Over such the second death has no power, but they shall be priests of God and of Christ, and shall reign with Him a thousand years."

So, in this first resurrection, the resurrection of life, the dead *in Christ* are caught up to meet Jesus in the sky. They will journey to heaven and reign with him for a thousand years. As we'll see in a moment, the resurrection of damnation takes place at a later time.

What about believers who are living when Christ comes? The Bible tells us that when Jesus returns, the dead in Christ are resurrected first and caught up to meet him in the sky. The living righteous are changed, transformed and they also rise up to meet Christ. Paul gives us a wonderful assurance:

> "We shall all be changed. For this corruptible must put on incorruption, and this mortal must put on immortality" (1 Corinthians 15:51-53).

The word mortal means subject to death—destined to die. Our mortal bodies get tired, get sick, get old. But when we look up and see Jesus coming, we'll be changed in an instant, transformed in a moment. New life will pulsate through our bodies with incredible energy and vitality! We rise up into the air toward a glorious destiny with our Redeemer.

But what about the wicked? What about the unrighteous who rejected God's love?

Those are the people described in Revelation 6:15-17. They pray for the rocks to fall on them. They look up and don't see a Savior; they only see wrath, the face of a disappointed Father, grieving over the fate of rebellious children. That's what fear and guilt and rebellion do to people. They see the Lamb of God coming and think they're seeing a lion.

These are people God wanted to save. These are people for whom Christ died. But they just didn't respond to His appeals. They refused to be rescued. They refused to accept the message of salvation.

Tragically enough, many people find the Good News not to be good news at all. Paul writes:

> "For the message of the cross is foolishness to those who are perishing, but to us who are being saved it is the power of God" (1 Corinthians 1:18).

It's the same message, but it is received very differently depending on a person's response to God's appeals. To some it's just a foolish old myth and fails to awaken their interest. To others it is accepted as the power of God—and becomes just that! It's not that God gives good news to some and bad news to others. No, He presents grace to every human being, just as his sunshine and rain come on the just and the unjust. But unless we accept the gospel, it won't be the good news for us. If we pass it off as a useless fairy tale; the coming reality will be horrible indeed!

Several of those cut down by the sleeping-sickness epidemic and who were suddenly awakened decades later by L-DOPA, experienced moments of insight which only gave them a heart-rending sense of their enormous loss.

One despairing man named Rolando could not escape Parkinson symptoms despite treatment with L-DOPA. He told Dr. Sacks, "I've been shut up in different places with illness since the day I was born. Why couldn't I have died as a kid? What's the sense, what's the use of my life here?"

The sad fact is, of course, that the victims of Sleeping Sickness did not individually bring this tragedy on themselves. The same is not true however for that other deadly slumber of sin. If we do not find a cure for our separation from God, we will become responsible for the final tragedy.

This is what happens at the second coming of Christ: The wicked living are slain. The wicked dead remain in their graves. All the followers of Christ, however, are caught up in the sky to go to heaven with Jesus.

But what about the earth? What's happening here on earth while the righteous are reigning with Christ for a thousand years?

Here is how John described it:

> "Then I saw an angel coming down from heaven, having the key to the bottomless pit and a great chain in his hand. He laid hold of the dragon, that serpent of old, who is the Devil and Satan, and bound him for a thousand years" (Revelation 20:1, 2).

This period is called "the millennium." The word "millennium" comes from the Latin. It literally is "millo" 1000 and "annum" years, or "1000 years." This word is not found in the Bible but used to describe the 1000 years here mentioned in Revelation 20:1. During this time Satan is bound in a bottomless pit.

Why? What does this mean?

The Greek word translated here as "bottomless pit" is *"abussos"*. We get our English word abyss from it. "Abussos" means without form and void. It's what was described in Genesis 1:1, 2:

> "In the beginning the earth was without form and void."

That's the way it will be on earth after the second coming. All human beings are dead. Everything here is devastated. It's a void. And so Satan wanders through the earth, looking at the devastation which his rebellion has caused. The utter destruction of sin stares him in the face.

The prophet Jeremiah uses the very same expression, "without form and void" to describe the earth after Jesus' return:

> "I beheld the earth, and indeed it was without

form, and void; And the heavens, they had no
light. I beheld the mountains, and indeed they
trembled, And all the hills moved back and
forth. I beheld, and indeed there was no man,
And all the birds of the heavens had fled. I
beheld, and indeed the fruitful land was a
wilderness, And all its cities were broken
down at the presence of the Lord, by His fierce
anger. For thus says the Lord: 'The whole land
shall be desolate; yet I will not make a full
end'" (Jeremiah 4:23-27).

Jeremiah adds:

"And the slain of the Lord shall be from one
end of the earth even to the other end of the
earth" (Jeremiah 25:33).

If Satan is alive throughout these 1000 years, how is
he "bound" (Revelation 20:2)? What does that mean?

It's unlikely that he's bound up with a literal chain.
Remember that Revelation is a book of symbols. John is
depicting the earth to be a terrible prison for Satan. He
is bound by a chain of circumstances. That's what ties
him up securely.

All the righteous have gone to heaven. All the
wicked have been struck dead. In other words, no one left
for Satan to tempt! There is no one left for him to manipulate and deceive.

This earth will become like a bottomless pit for
Satan. In the wreckage of the planet, one principle is
echoed over and over: the wages of sin is death. And
looking on, the whole universe will bear witness to the
terrible truth of those words. He is now confronted with
the horrible results of rebellion.

But what will the righteous be doing? Remember Revelation 20:6. Those who rose in the first resurrection will be priests of God and reign with him for a thousand years.

Think about being with Christ during the millennium. It will be inexpressibly wonderful. But you'll also have a lot of questions. You may wonder why a loved one isn't there. You may not understand why a friend—who seemed like such a good person—wasn't saved.

Guess what? Our gracious God is going to answer all of our questions. We'll be able to review God's decisions.

Look at Revelation 20:4, where John is speaking of the redeemed during the millennium:

> "And I saw thrones, and they sat on them, and judgment was committed to them."

We know that God is the ultimate judge. Only the all-knowing God can preside over the heavenly courts. But, in some sense, judgment will also be given to the redeemed. Revelation 20:12 says that "the books were opened." The redeemed now in heaven will then be allowed to look over heaven's records; it's a kind of a judicial review.

Remember how Paul stated it:

> "Do you not know that the saints will judge the world? . . . Do you know that we shall judge angels?" (1 Corinthians 6:2, 3).

We'll be looking over the cases of people who have been lost.

Paul wrote:

> "Therefore judge nothing before the appointed time; wait until the Lord comes. He will bring

to light what is hidden in darkness and will expose the motives of men's hearts" (1 Corinthians 4:5, NIV).

This implies that one day we will fully understand why it was impossible for God to save some people. This happens during the millennium. We may not on our own, understand why this person or that person didn't make it. But God can show us why. He can show us all the ways he tried to win this person, all the ways he tried to enable love to break through. He can show us what was really in people's hearts, things that people kept hidden so well.

At the end of that period of judicial review, we are going to fall at God's feet and proclaim that God is just and fair. The redeemed will sing: "Lord God Almighty, true and righteous are Thy judgments" (Revelation 16:7).

During the millennium all your questions will be answered—questions about other people, questions about your own life. You will come to understand completely why certain things happened. You'll understand the hard times and the good times. You'll see how everything ultimately fits into a wonderful plan.

Now let's look at what happens at the *end* of the millennium, the end of the thousand years.

John wrote:

> "Now when the thousand years have expired, Satan will be released from his prison and will go out to deceive the nations which are in the four corners of the earth" (Revelation 20:7, 8).

I hear you saying, "I thought the wicked were dead. Who is Satan going to deceive?"

Let's look at the big picture. Another great event

takes place at the end of the millennium. It's the second resurrection:

> "But the rest of the dead did not live again until the thousand years were finished" (Revelation 20:5).

As we noted earlier, "the rest of the dead" are the wicked dead. We have a resurrection of life for believers at the beginning of the thousand years, and we have a resurrection of damnation for the wicked at the end of the thousand years.

John describes this scene:

> "The sea gave up the dead who were in it, and death and Hades delivered up the dead who were in them, and each person was judged according to what he had done . . . If anyone's name was not found written in the book of life, he was thrown into the lake of fire" (Revelation 20:13, 15).

This is the earth's final tragedy, an awakening that does not last, a rising from sleep that only leads to eternal slumber. It is difficult for us to imagine the sense of loss of those who look at God in all His love and glory and realize that they will never be a part of life with Him in heaven. They will miss out on eternity! What inexpressible anguish that thought must bring. No wonder Scripture describes it as a time when there will be weeping and gnashing of teeth.

It's almost impossible to conceive of such a tragedy. But those victims of the Sleeping Sickness epidemic who were awakened at last only to be overwhelmed by the realization that their life was gone—they give us some idea, some hint, of that terrible, final awakening. Those who discovered suddenly that they had plummeted from youth into dying old age, that all the years in between had disappeared without a trace—-only they can tell us something of the final tragedy on this planet.

Let's look at the other important events that take place at the end of the millennium.

God is going to make all things new. He's going to remake the earth as it was in the Garden of Eden. John wrote:

> "And I saw a new heaven and a new earth, for the first heaven and the first earth had passed away . . . Then I, John, saw the holy city, New Jerusalem, coming down out of heaven from God, prepared as a bride adorned for her husband" (Revelation 21:1, 2).

Do you know what this is describing? Our return trip, after the millennium, from heaven back to earth. We are in that New Jerusalem. It's like our space ship. And its destination, its destiny, is to reclaim Planet Earth. Let's read on in verse three: "And I heard a loud voice from heaven saying, "Behold the tabernacle of God is with men, and He will dwell with them, and they shall be His people, and God Himself will be with them and be their God.

God is going to live with us in this New Jerusalem! This sin-scarred earth is going to be remade into a spectacular footstool for God's throne.

This is wonderful news. But it's not good news for Satan at that moment. He sees that holy city coming down and he is driven to one last act of defiance, one last act of rebellion. He can't help himself.

Remember, at this time the wicked have been resurrected, the wicked from all ages. As Revelation 20:8 tells us, their "numbers is as the sand of the sea."

Satan gathers his forces from all over the earth into one vast army. He will take as much time as necessary to build his army under the brightest generals of all time and furnished with the most sophisticated killing machines that great minds can devise. Then he attacks the holy city:

> "They went up on the breadth of the earth and surrounded the camp of the saints and the beloved city" (Revelation 20:9).

This is Satan's last gasp. It's the last battle in the long conflict between Christ and Satan for the heart of the universe. It's the final battle of the war called Armageddon. The armies of hell are rushing up against the city from heaven. Let's look at what happens:

> "And fire came down from God out of heaven and devoured them" (Revelation 20:9).

Fire destroys. Fire utterly consumes. That's what will happen to those outside the city. This is the ultimate fate of the wicked. This is what happens when people throw Christ off the throne in their lives. They'll find themselves on the outside looking in.

The fire which consumes the wicked also cleanses the earth. It wipes away all the scars of sin. It removes the ravages of rebellion. And that is how God makes all things new. Now he can create a new heaven and a new earth.

Let me tell you about one of those patients who was given L-DOPA and awakened from a long imprisoning slumber.

Growing up in the early 1900s, Magda was a happy child. She did well in high school, receiving honors both as a scholar and an athlete. But in 1918, while working as a secretary, she contracted the Sleeping Sickness. Magda recovered after a few months but then, in 1923, started showing signs of Parkinson's and slipped into a state of limbo that lasted forty-five years. The woman spent her days in institutions, sitting in a wheelchair, motionless, expressionless, apparently oblivious to anything happening around her. Those who provided nursing care regarded her as a hopeless case.

But then she was administered L-DOPA. Magda gradually awakened. First she found her voice again, then began writing a few sentences. Soon she was able to feed herself and walk a bit. And then a whole person blossomed, where there had been only a shell. Dr. Sacks wrote, Magda "showed an intelligence, a charm, and a humor, which had been almost totally concealed by her disease."

Magda recalled happily her childhood in Vienna and talked nostalgically about school excursions and family holidays. But she did not remain trapped in the past. Somehow this courageous woman found the strength to cope with the forty-five year gap in her life. She renewed emotional ties with her daughters and sons-in-law. She discovered her grandchildren, and enjoyed visits with many other relatives who came to see the miracle of Magda restored to reality.

What an incredible awakening! This is the hope that God offers to each of us even now, no matter how long or deep our slumber in sin has been. But there will be another awakening when the kingdom of God shines down on this planet. We can look up with joy and be taken up in the air with Jesus Christ.

We don't have to remain trapped in the tragedies of

life in a sinful world—unable to bridge the unimaginable gap between life as we've known it and the life God wants to give us today. We don't have to remain numb in the grip of a deadening affliction called sin.

But when the righteous are resurrected they are the opposite of the awakenings of those Sleeping Sickness patients. We won't wake up and suddenly find ourselves old. We will wake up and find ourselves young again, with new bodies, recreated like the glorious resurrected body of Christ. Those who labored with handicaps all their lives, the lame, the blind, the scarred, will awake in perfect health.

What kind of awakening from the long slumber of sin will you experience?

Will it be a rising up in the second resurrection to the horror of God coming in judgment, a final realization of what you have lost? Or will it be a rising up to meet your Savior in the air, a final farewell to that deadly slumber?

It's up to you. You can decide right now. Accept the good news about Jesus as the great Lifegiver. Accept Christ's dying on the cross as the power of God made available to you—-for now and forever. ❏

17

REVELATION'S LAKE OF FIRE

WILL A LOVING GOD BURN SINNERS IN HELL FOR MILLIONS OF YEARS?

It was not a job for the feeble or the faint-hearted. Hundreds of blazing oil-wells in the desert of Kuwait had to be somehow extinguished. Men had to be found who would brave the searing heat and hoist a barrel of dynamite over the exploding oil.

One extraordinary team of oil fire specialists, called "Boots and Coots" took on some of the most dangerous of the wells. Their ordeal has been described as "Six Days in Hell."

Kuwaiti citizens who woke up early on the morning of February 23, 1991, were greeted by a horrifying sight. The desert seemed to have erupted. Clouds of fire had sprung from the ground, and dense black smoke banks were eating up the sky.

Later, the world would learn that on this day, Iraqi engineers had begun igniting Kuwait's vast oil fields. Almost 90 percent of that country's producing wells were turned into roaring blowtorches. Sixty million barrels of crude oil a day was going up in smoke.

This was Saddam Husain's parting shot at a land which he couldn't keep. He seemed to be saying that if he couldn't exploit the oil fields of Kuwait, then no one else would.

What resulted was one of the worst man-made eco-logical disasters of modern times. Aside from the destruction to living things, the smoke from these infernos polluted the air over much of the planet, reaching as far as the islands of Hawaii.

Every war has produced its share of horror and madness. But this act seemed particularly senseless and devastating. As the world looked on, most people were outraged at the black horizons of Kuwait and wondered why? Why would anybody do such a thing—even to people you hate?

And yet there was something strangely familiar in this apocalyptic landscape. For some people it made vivid certain images that had long rested in the back of their minds. Those images come from the book of Revelation, the Biblical book that shows us last-day events.

Speaking of the one who follows and worships the Antichrist, John writes:

> "He shall be tormented with fire and brimstone
> . . . And the smoke of their torment ascends
> forever and ever" (Revelation 14:10, 11).

A little later, in the book of Revelation, when John pictures the burning of wicked Babylon, he uses the same phrase:

> ". . . And her smoke rises up forever and ever"
> (Revelation 19:3).

The burning oil fields of Kuwait have given us a rather stunning preview of earth's final fire. But this raises a very important question: If Kuwait's inferno was such an intolerable disaster, which no one in their right mind wanted to see continue, what about the fires of hell? What about that smoke that ascends forever and ever? Is God's final solution for the wicked to be a ceaseless inferno?

Let's try to get a clear picture from the Bible of what will happen at the end of time.

Revelation, chapter 20 describes this "lake of burning sulfur" into which the wicked are thrown. This is Scripture's graphic picture of hell. Now let's put it in its proper setting.

Revelation 20 is talking about what happens at the *end* of the millennium, the thousand-year period. John tells us that Satan is released from his prison and goes out to deceive the nations that are "in the four corners of the earth." Satan gathers an army, and, verse nine tells us:

> "They went up on the breadth of the earth and surrounded the camp of the saints and the beloved city" (Revelation 20:9).

At this point fire comes down from heaven and devours them; then the devil is thrown into the lake of burning sulfur.

This fire is called "the second death."

Now, it's possible to imagine that there is a lake of fire somewhere out in space. But Scripture tells us that the lake of fire will happen on this earth. This is where the final battle is waged, where the dead come forth to judgment, and where fire from heaven strikes and devours.

We have no hint of any other place of destruction called "hell" other than this earth.

Let's move on to chapter 21:

> "And I saw a new heaven and a new earth, for the first heaven and the first earth had passed away" (Revelation 21:1).

Verse two describes New Jerusalem descending to the earth. John tells us: "Behold, the tabernacle of God is with men" (Revelation 21:3).

Then that wonderful promise in verse four. Speaking of God, John writes:

> "God will wipe away every tear from their eyes; there shall be no more death nor sorrow nor crying and. . . no more pain, for the former things have passed away" (Revelation 21:4).

These words of hope refer to life on the New Earth. No more death, no more pain. The old order has passed away.

Now you'll recall that a lake of fire—on the earth— is described in Revelation 20. Think about it. This presents a big problem. If that smoke of torment is still ascending, forever and ever, there will still be a great deal of mourning and crying and pain. The old order will definitely not have passed away. How is God's promise to be fulfilled?

To put it simply, you can't have hell and heaven in the same place. Some people question whether you can have hell and heaven in the same universe.

How are we to resolve this supposed conflict? To picture an answer, let's take a closer look at those raging infernos in the Kuwait desert.

The "Boots and Coots" team of oil-fire specialists were assigned to B.G. 360, an especially dangerous well. The thunderheads of smoke erupting from it were the size of several football fields. One fire fighter circled the well at some distance, trying to get a glimpse of the wellhead. It thundered like a freight train; he could feel the intense heat through the soles of his boots.

The problem was getting close enough to work on the well with long booms—without becoming incinerated. Fifty thousand gallons of sea water had to be pumped into a nearby pit. Two massive pumps sprayed water on the site at the rate of 8000 gallons a minute. But this did very little to the sea of flame, it only served as protection for the men. Each person had to drink three gallons of ice water during a shift. Otherwise they could be killed by dehydration from the fiery heat.

Everyone had to wear metal hard hats; the plastic kind melted would melt to their heads. Men maneuvering machinery toward the site had to work behind large heat shields of galvanized tin. A discarded two-by-four on the ground instantly burst into flame like a match stick.

Finally the crew was able to position a 55-gallon steel drum, loaded with sticks of dynamite, above the wellhead. The dynamite was touched off and the explosion created a huge vacuum. Sheets of tin flew into the vortex. But the explosion sucked up oxygen and suffocated the fire. B.G. 360 had ceased to be an inferno.

Still there was great danger. The smallest spark or drifting ember could set off fumes, causing a flash fire that would consume everyone. The men had to lower a new capping assembly on the wellhead very carefully, inch by inch. The slightest slip could spark a new inferno.

Fortunately the last bolt slid into place without incident, and the rush of oil stopped. Wiping the soot and oil from his face, one man remarked, "I got one piece of advice. Put a white cross over that [thing] and let a dead well lie."

These men who braved the oil fires of Kuwait have something to tell us about staring into an inferno. It means one thing: total and complete destruction. They'd seen the remains of those who perished in intense fires: there wasn't much left, just a few bone fragments fused to metal. They knew that, to get close to an intense inferno, is to be consumed.

Now let me ask you. What is going to happen to those who are thrown into a lake of fire? How long will they survive? Isn't it true that, the bigger the fire, the quicker the death? If you want to torture someone for a long time you need a very small flame, not a great conflagration. Could the Bible be trying to tell us something by calling this lake of fire the second death?

Let's let the Bible speak for itself. Here's what Scripture declares about the final destruction of the wicked: "'For behold the day is coming, burning like an oven. And all the proud, yes all who do wickedly will be stubble. And the day which is coming shall burn them up,' says the Lord of hosts, 'that will leave them neither root nor branch'" (Malachi 4:1).

Notice these two clear facts:

1. The wicked will be burned in the future. Hell is not a hot spot burning in the center of the earth today. According to 2 Peter 2:4, they are "reserved for judgment."

2. The wicked will be consumed, burned up and turned to ashes.

This is a consistent teaching of the Bible:

> "But the wicked shall perish; and the enemies of the Lord, like the splendor of the meadows, shall vanish. Into smoke they shall vanish away" (Psalm 37:20).

But if the wicked are going to perish, what about that smoke of torment that goes up forever and ever?

Let's look at some other verses in the Bible which shed light on this:

Hebrews 9:12 states that Jesus obtained "eternal redemption" for us.

Hebrews 6:2 speaks of "eternal judgment."

Now we know that Christ's great act of redemption took place at one specific time. And we know that the final judgment takes place at one specific time, that is, it won't go on forever. But still they are referred to as "eternal redemption" and "eternal judgment." Why? Because the *results* of redemption and judgment *will* be everlasting.

So it will be with "eternal punishment." Just what is eternal about the fire and the torment? Is it not the consequences that are eternal? The end result is eternal death, the second death.

We have explicit Scriptural teaching for this point of view.

First let's look at a verse in the very brief book of Jude. The author describes the wickedness of those who lived in Sodom and Gomorrah, and then he states that:

> "[They] are set forth as an example, suffering the vengeance of eternal fire" (Jude 7).

There's that phrase again: "eternal fire." But Sodom and Gomorrah aren't still burning. That "eternal fire" went out long ago. The biblical record suggests that fire came down from heaven and rather quickly turned those cities into ashes.

Peter expresses it in this way:

> "And turning the cities of Sodom and Gomorrah into ashes, condemned them to destruction making them an example to those who afterward would live ungodly" (2 Peter 2:6).

Sodom and Gomorrah were burned up with a fire whose effects were eternal. The fire was an all-consuming fire which turned these wicked cities to ashes.

Paul said this concerning those who'd become enemies of the cross of Christ: "Their destiny is destruction" (Philippians 3:19, NIV).

Greek scholars tell us that the Greek word, translated as "destruction," is the strongest word that could be used, meaning utter loss of existence.

Jesus Himself warned: "For wide is the gate and broad is the road that leads to destruction" (Matthew 7:13, NIV).

Throughout the Bible one dominant picture of the destiny of the wicked prevails. And that is death. Prophets and apostles unite in making the picture forceful. The wicked, they all affirm, will die, perish, be burnt up, utterly consumed, become ashes, become as if they had never existed. These are the words used to describe their fate:

The wicked will die - Romans 6:23

The wicked will perish - Luke 13:3

The wicked will be burned up - Malachi 4:1

The wicked will be utterly consumed - Psalm 37:20

The wicked will be turned to ashes - Malachi 4:3

The wicked will be as though they had not been -
Obadiah 16

Satan himself will be utterly consumed and totally
destroyed - Isaiah 47:14

Friends, Scripture is clear. The wages of sin is death, not eternal life in hell. It's no good assuming that the body is destroyed in hell but that the soul goes on suffering. Jesus would disagree and warned us about the Evil One:

"The One who can destroy both soul and body in hell" (Matthew 10:28, NIV).

That's seems plain enough!

If we look at the clear teaching of Scripture we can see that death and destruction is the fate of the wicked in hell. And we can see that some metaphors, used to describe hell, really mean the opposite of what many Christians think.

Here Jesus describes hell as:

> ". . . the fire that shall never be quenched— where 'their worm does not die and the fire is not quenched'" (Mark 9:43, 44).

What does this mean? Many believers think this pictures an eternally burning hell. But Jesus is here quoting a passage in Isaiah.

The prophet speaks of the fate of the wicked and uses those phrases:

> "Their worm does not die" and "their fire is not quenched" (Isaiah 66:24).

But do you know what Isaiah is referring to there? Here is what precedes those phrases:

> "The corpses of the men who have transgressed against Me" (Isaiah 66:24).

Isaiah is talking about dead people. What does it mean, "their worm does not die?" This is a picture of worms, of maggots consuming a dead body. The picture is of a corpse being totally consumed, totally destroyed.

And what about "their fire is not quenched." Let's think about it. If the fire *were* quenched then there would be a possibility of someone living. The person might be only partially burned. But no, here the fire is not quenched, it burns completely, it destroys completely. The people are burned up. This is a picture of corpses being destroyed.

Let's look at a passage in Jeremiah that speaks of unquenchable fire. The prophet is warning about what will happen to those who persist in rebelling against God:

> "I will kindle a fire in its gates, and it shall devour the palaces of Jerusalem, and it shall not be quenched" (Jeremiah 17:27).

Eventually this prophecy was fulfilled. Jerusalem was destroyed by the Roman general Titus in AD 70. The palaces of Jerusalem were burned, burned to the ground. Those were *unquenchable* fires.

Is Jerusalem still burning today? No, of course not. What the passage means is that the fires would totally destroy, they would not be put out before they'd burned everything up.

That's the consistent picture we get from the teachings of Jesus and the Bible writers. Death, utter destruction, is the ultimate fate of the wicked.

But some believe that Satan and sinners will be tormented "forever and ever:"

> "And the devil, who deceived them, was cast into the lake of fire and brimstone where the beast and the false prophet are. And they will be tormented day and night forever and ever" (Revelation 20:10).

"Forever" in the Bible can be translated to mean "until the end of the age." The wicked are consumed, burned up, turned to ashes. The old age of sin and death ends. God ushers in a new age. God creates a new heaven and a new earth with no more crying, death, sickness or pain.

"Forever" in the Bible is often a limited time, such as long as one lives. Speaking of a slave:

> ". . . and he shall serve him forever"
> (Exodus 21:6).

What does Scripture mean? Simply, as long as he lives.

Jonah describes his experience in the belly of the whale in these words:

> "The earth with the bars closed behind me forever" (Jonah 2:6).

Again, forever is a limited time—as long as Jonah could exist in that environment.

Hannah brought her son to the temple to dedicate him to the Lord, and she said: "I will take him that he may appear before the Lord and remain there forever" (1 Samuel 1:22).

Then Hannah adds:

> "As long as he lives, he shall be lent to the Lord" (1 Samuel 1:28).

I believe these vivid images about an eternal fire and the smoke of endless torment are metaphors that emphasize the almost unimaginable tragedy of the lost.

Now, let's look more closely at another phrase used in connection with the fate of the wicked. Jesus states, in a parable, that in that final "fiery furnace" there will be "weeping and gnashing of teeth" (Matthew 13:50, NIV).

Let's look at other places where this same expression occurs. In a parable in Matthew 22, the kingdom of heaven is pictured as a great wedding banquet. The guests assemble and celebrate the marriage of the king's son. But one man has come to the feast without a wedding garment, an act of great disrespect. This presumptuous guest is thrown out.

Matthew records Christ's words:

> "Cast him into outer darkness; there will be weeping and gnashing of teeth" (Matthew 22:13).

Why such pain? Because the man realizes he's on the outside! He realizes what he's missing—cut off from this marvelous banquet.

We get the same picture in the parable of the talents. The master returns and finds that two servants have wisely used the talents he entrusted to them. So the master joyfully invites these men to:

> "Come and share your master's happiness" (Matthew 25:21)!

But one servant, lazy and mistrustful, has done nothing with his talent. This man, verse 30 tells us, is thrown outside:

> "Cast the unprofitable servant into the outer darkness, There will be weeping and gnashing of teeth" (Matthew 25:30).

Why such agony? Because the man is cut off from the abundant life the master has promised the other two.

Scripture always relates this "weeping and gnashing of teeth" to the pain of missing-out; of being left outside in the dark.

Missing out on the wonder of eternal life. That's the great tragedy. That's the agony of hell.

Does God need to arbitrarily torture the wicked in order to punish them adequately? No! The pain comes from realizing what they've missed, what they've thrown away. How pathetically limited their lives will then look! Compared to eternal life, they haven't lived at all! No wonder there is weeping and gnashing of teeth!

Friends, please don't miss out. Eternal life with God

is waiting. Life in its original abundance is waiting. Joys that we haven't even imagined wait for us.

I believe that a hell which destroys the wicked (not one which keeps them alive forever) is the best way to put together *all* of the Biblical evidence. And furthermore, it's the one that reinforces the picture of the loving God which Scripture celebrates.

Those raging oil fires in the desert of Kuwait taught us something valuable. To many people that little spot on the earth may not have seemed very significant. But when the inferno started and the smoke began billowing up, everyone took notice. It affected the environment for thousands of miles around it.

And we all knew that this ecological disaster had to be stopped. Somehow the fires had to be put out—as quickly as possible.

I don't believe that those who find a home with God on this New Earth will be any less sensitive. No one will be able to rest if there is ceaseless torment going on in some corner of God's universe.

You know, that's part of the heroism of Christ on the cross. He suffered the second death in our place; He experienced the agony of the second death. Christ had to single-handedly cap the spewing well of black, sulfurous sin that was destroying humanity. He experienced sin's wages in His own body.

Jesus Christ was tormented on Calvery's cross so that we could live forever with Him. That's the best news of all. Those who place their faith in Christ won't be touched by that final, blazing inferno. God does have a plan for cleansing our universe of sin, completely, irrevocably, eternally. He will wipe away every tear and end all suffering.

I'm sure you want to be among those who enjoy the New Earth with God and not consumed in the old world with Satan.

Think of it, to be separated from God and from loved ones forever and ever and ever. To miss out on the eternal joys of the redeemed. To disappear, with no hope of ever coming back again. That is a mind-boggling tragedy. And that, I believe, is what the fiery scenes in Revelation are making vivid for us.

But it need not be. No, not for anyone. Each of us is invited *inside,* that wedding banquet. All we must do is place our faith in Christ as Savior and entrust our lives into His hands. Jesus has promised to keep us on the inside.

Make your choice sure just now. ❏

18
REVELATION'S WORLD OF TOMORROW

L ately, there seems to be a lot of confusion about the subject of heaven! I've interviewed several people as I have traveled on planes and asked them, "What do you think heaven is like?"

Here are examples of some people's thoughts on heaven:

> A teenager: Heaven—like, that's pie in the sky, out there somewhere, like unreal—I can't believe it.

> A middle-aged woman grocery shopping: Heaven is a state of mind. It's inner peace. It's a state of calm.

> A successful business man: Heaven is my house, you should see it. It's worth three-million. My chariot is my Lexus. The angels are my kids. (Ha-ha!)

> A college student: Heaven is—are you so out of touch you still believe in those fairy tales?

> An elderly couple: We hope heaven is a real place. The older we get the more we long for it. We just hope that what we were taught in our childhood is true.

So many people, so many different answers. So many people confused regarding heaven.

They are not the only ones who are confused. Several

prominent religious leaders recently expressed their ideas to the press. In the August 19, 1999 edition of *SUN*, Pope John Paul the Second created quite a bombshell by saying that heaven is not a physical place, that paradise is not what you think, and "God is not an old man with a white beard, but a supreme being with male and female qualities and that there are no pearly gates."

Dr. Deepak Chopra, a world famous teacher that New Agers listen to says, "Heaven is as real as spirit, and spirit is the only reality . . . because this spirit is within us all along, it is possible to create a 'heaven on earth' simply by turning within and becoming aware of our innermost selves."

Why is there so much confusion about heaven? Why these hazy, ambiguous opinions?

I have been told that in the Treasury Building in Washington, DC, there are 1800 different doors. Each door has its own lock, 1800 keys open these locks. But, the superintendent of the building has one key that will unlock all 1800 doors. A master key!

God has a master key that can unlock the secrets of heaven. The Bible is the master key. Fortunately, we don't have to depend on man's theories and opinions, we have the Bible, our only safe source of information on heaven.

While John the Revelator was exiled on the little island of Patmos off the coast of Turkey, God showed him His city in vision:

> "And I saw a new heaven and a new earth; for the first heaven and the first earth were passed away and there was no more sea. And I, John, saw the holy city, New Jerusalem, coming down out of heaven from God prepared as a bride adorned for her husband" (Revelation 21:1, 2).

Few illustrations depict happiness and beauty as that of a bride preparing for her wedding day! This city is not just something that John saw and knew about, it was something known by all of God's people throughout the ages.

God tells us that all of His holy prophets had spoken about God's plan of restitution.

> "He may send Jesus Christ, who was preached to you before, whom heaven must receive until the times of restoration of all things, which God has spoken by the mouth of all His holy prophets since the world began" (Acts 3:20, 21).

What is God going to restore? He is going to restore what Adam and Eve lost! Paradise on Planet Earth, this earth made new! This old world contaminated by pollutants, waning fresh water and pure air, violence and suffering wouldn't be much of a gift! God is going to give us a new earth! A perfect world with redeemed people! Just like the earth was when Adam and Eve were created. What joy that must have been. They had perfect health and youth. Sounds too good to be true!

Sad to say, Eve listened to the temptations of the serpent and disobeyed God. She in turn gave the forbidden fruit to Adam and he also ate. Oh, what a sad day that was when they turned over the dominion of this earth to the enemy of God by being deceived by him. They lost everything. God was forced to drive them out of their home in Eden. God put a cherubim to guard the gate and keep Adam and Eve from eating of the Tree of Life.

As people multiplied on the earth, so did sin multiply until the majority of people on the earth did not know or worship the Creator. In fact, by the time of the building of the Tower of Babel, almost all the people on earth had forgotten their God and His promises. But one family in Ur of the Chaldees still worshipped the true God. That was Abraham and his relatives. God promised Abraham that his seed or descendants would inherit the earth and would see the restitution of all that was lost by Adam and Eve.

Abraham accepted by faith, that God's promises, given to him so many years ago, would be fulfilled. Abraham dwelt on the earth as a stranger, or pilgrim.

Paul wrote:

> "For he [Abraham] looked forward to the city that has foundations, whose architect and builder is God" (Hebrews 11:10, NRSV).

This same city, which the ancient patriarchs longed for, still waiting for the moment when faith becomes sight.

The story is told of Marco Polo, the Italian explorer, who returned home from China after 21 years in the Orient. His friends thought he had gone mad. He had such incredible tales to tell.

He said he had traveled to a city full of silver and gold. That he had seen black stones that burned (they hadn't heard of coal). He'd seen cloth that refused to catch fire even when thrown into the flames, (no one had ever heard of asbestos). He talked of huge serpents 10 paces long with jaws wide enough to swallow a man (no one had ever seen a crocodile). He told of nuts the size of a man's head (they had never seen coconuts).

The people just laughed at such stories. Years later, when Marco was dying, a devout man at his bedside urged Marco to recant all the tall tales he'd told. Marco refused: "It's all true—every bit of it. In fact, the half has not been told."

Words were not adequate to express the beauties the writers of the Bible have told us about the New Earth and the Holy City. As Marco Polo said, "The half has not been told." Paul wrote:

> "But it is written; eye has not seen, nor ear heard, nor have entered into the heart of man the things which God has prepared for those who love Him" (1 Corinthians 2:9).

But wait, most people don't keep reading the next verse:

> "But God has revealed them to us through His Spirit" (Verse 10).

Through God's Holy Spirit that His prophets could share with us some of the beauties of the New Earth and the Holy City, the New Jerusalem.

The book of Revelation gives us a description of the Holy City that is breathtaking! John was actually given a vision of the Holy City coming down from heaven to planet earth. John wrote:

> "Then I, John, saw the holy city, New Jerusalem, coming down from God out of heaven, prepared as a bride adorned for her husband" (Revelation 21:2).

John had difficulty describing the unimaginable beauty he saw like a "bride adorned for her husband."

The city was to be the dazzling home of the redeemed, and it will settle on Planet Earth.

John keeps writing:

> "Now the wall of the city had twelve foundations, and on them were the names of the twelve apostles of the Lamb . . . The foundations of the wall of the city were adorned with all kinds of precious stones" (Revelation 21:14, 19).

John also specified the size of the New Jerusalem:

> "The city is laid out like a square; its length as
> great as its breadth. And he measured the city
> with the reed: twelve thousand furlongs"
> (Revelation 21:16).

This square city is 1500 miles in circumference, 375 miles on each side. One mathematician estimated that the New Jerusalem could house two billion people. In other words, there will be plenty of room for every person who wants to be a citizen. What Jesus promised will certainly come true. In his Father's house there are indeed *many* mansions. And he has prepared a place for you!

The streets of the city are built out of pure gold:

> "The twelve gates were twelve pearls . . . And
> the street of the city was pure gold, like trans-
> parent glass" (Revelation 21:21).

If a city like that existed anywhere on earth today, believe me, everyone would be packing up, trying to get reservations on the next plane, regardless of the cost.

But here's the good news. Soon this city will come here as the capital of this Earth made new. As this brilliant city descends toward earth, fire flashes down to destroy the wicked and purify the planet. The surface of the earth becomes a lake of fire. All the reminders of a sin-scarred world are swept away. Back alleys and penthouses where brutality and vice festered are destroyed.

But after this holocaust, Revelation tells us, "a new heaven and a new earth" appear. The New Jerusalem settles down on a brand new planet. And this new world bursts with life just as the Garden of Eden once did. Its River of Life flows crystal clear. Its Tree of Life bears an abundance of fruit.

Yes friend, the redeemed will find themselves on solid earth. But it will be a new earth—that's what we have to look forward to. That is why the New Testament calls it the "blessed hope." It's something solid we can hang on to. And what's more, when we grasp that hope securely, it grabs hold of our lives too. Earth II will be a Garden of Eden restored. The prophet Isaiah gives us a glimpse:

> "The wilderness and the wasteland shall be glad for them, And the desert shall rejoice and blossom as the rose" (Isaiah 35:1).

Comparing our present planet to Earth II is like comparing a desert to a garden, comparing parched dirt to a blossoming rose. What flower could better describe the beauty and perfection of this new home than the rose?

This promised home is a haven where pain won't exist. No cancer, no heart attacks, no arthritis, no fevers, no illness—period, forever! Here's another glimpse from Isaiah:

> "And the inhabitant will not say, 'I am sick'. . . Then the eyes of the blind shall be opened. And the ears of the deaf shall be unstopped. Then the lame shall leap like a deer, And the tongue of the dumb will sing. For waters shall burst in the wilderness, And streams in the desert" (Isaiah 33:24; 35:5,6).

The book of Revelation echoes this same wonderful picture. It gives us this great assurance about life in the New Jerusalem:

> "And God will wipe away every tear from their eyes; there shall be no more death, nor sorrow, nor crying; and there shall be no more pain, for the former things have passed away" (Revelation 21:4).

God wipes away every tear. No more sorrow, no more death.

In the New Jerusalem, our human search, our relentless search, for that fountain of youth will, at last, find its fulfillment. We'll discover it at last in that holy city.

Note John's description:

> "He showed me a pure river of water of life, clear as crystal, proceeding from the throne of God and of the Lamb. In the middle of the street, and on either side of the river, was the tree of life, which bore twelve fruits, each tree yielding its fruit every month. The leaves of the tree were for the healing of the nations" (Revelation 22:1, 2).

The River of Life is the fountain of youth. We'll enjoy perfect bodies. We'll have boundless energy to explore the wonders about us. We'll always be refreshed by the River of Life and the Tree of Life. We'll always be refreshed because we'll always be with God.

The Bible is full of promises about the home that awaits us in this earth made new, this Earth II.

Isaiah expressed it well:

> "Violence shall no longer be heard in your land, Neither wasting nor destruction within your borders" (Isaiah 60:18).

No violence. No fear. Just peace, harmony and love. And this new spirit will even affect the animal kingdom.

Isaiah continues:

> "The wolf also shall dwell with the lamb, the leopard shall lie down with the young goat, the calf and the young lion and the fatling

together; And a little child shall lead them. The cow and the bear shall graze; Their young ones shall lie down together; And the lion shall eat straw like the ox . . . They shall not hurt nor destroy in all My holy mountain, For the earth shall be full of the knowledge of the LORD As the waters cover the sea" (Isaiah 11:6, 7, 9).

Nature will no longer be red in fang and claw. No more kill or be killed.

No need for burglar alarms. No need for locks and bolts on our doors and windows. No need for safety-deposit boxes.

No more fear, period. Death and sorrow have passed away. No more exhaustion or burnout or depression. We will be renewed. We will live exuberantly.

Our hands, designed by God to work out the visions of our minds, will build and create freely. We'll be able to produce anything we can conceive! And our energy will be renewed, from week to week. We'll have wonderful worship and communion with our Creator.

Further, Isaiah tells us:

"From one Sabbath to another, All flesh shall come to worship before Me, says the LORD" (Isaiah 66:23).

The Sabbath celebration even now brings us new life and vision on this marred old Earth. It will energize us in an even more wonderful way amid the splendors of heaven. Our sense of community, our experience of praise—all that will exceed anything we've witnessed here below.

But God has promised that one day soon, this earth will be the center, the capital, of His universe!

John wrote:

> "And I heard a loud voice from heaven saying,
> 'Behold, the tabernacle of God is with men, and
> He will dwell with them, and they shall be His
> people. God Himself will be with them and be
> their God'. . .They shall see His face"
> Revelation 21:3 and 22:4).

We can have this great hope—even here, even now in a world that has so much suffering and sorrow. Even in the darkest places on our planet, that great hope can light our way.

His name was Juliek. The Nobel prize winning author Elie Wiesel tells about him. Elie met the boy during a terrible night on the way to a Nazi death camp. He and hundreds of other Jews were forced into a barracks for three days in the town of Gleiwitz. They were jammed into a room so tightly that many actually smothered to death. The sheer mass of human bodies simply cut off sources of air.

Among these twisted bodies, Elie noticed one young emaciated Warsaw Jew named Juliek. He clutched tightly to his chest—a violin. Somehow, Juliek had managed to hang on to the instrument, mile after mile through snowstorms, during the forced death march to Gleiwitz.

Now he struggled to free his limbs. Crammed among hundreds of the dead and dying, he slowly drew his bow across the strings. And Juliek began to play a piece from a Beethoven concerto. A beautiful, lilting melody arose, pure and eerie in that horrible room.

In the darkness, Elie heard only those sounds of the violin. And he felt as if Juliek's soul were in the bow, and his whole life gliding on the strings. Elie would always remember the youth's pale, sad face as he said a tender, gracious farewell to his audience of dying men.

That night Elie fell asleep to Beethoven's concerto.

In the morning he saw Juliek slumped over nearby, dead. Beside him lay his violin, broken and trampled.

But the song remained. Juliek's final melody still rose above the horrors of that death march. Not even Nazi cruelty could suffocate its gentle winsomeness. Juliek's song echoed the beauty of another world. It made an eloquent statement: there's something beyond all this. There's something beyond this suffering and inhumanity. Beauty and grace are what count in the end. Those qualities last forever.

Juliek's final song was his way of reaching toward heaven.

How about you? Are you standing on heaven's border? Have you found a song you can play—even in the darkest night?

Friends, eternity stretches ahead of us. Here on this earth we have maybe 70 or 80 years of life. But think of life in heaven, think of 70 thousand years, 70 million years, 70 billion years on Earth II—and we'll have only just begun!

How can we make certain we will be citizens of the Earth made new? How can we know that our name is on one of those mansions in the New Jerusalem?

The answer is simple. God promised Abraham centuries ago that his seed would inherit the earth. And we know that Abraham's seed are those who are in Christ, those who inherit the promises by faith, those who accept Christ as their Savior.

If you belong to Christ, you belong in the promised land; you belong in heaven. Count on that. The road may seem rough. But with Christ as your guide, your arrival is secure. Count on it. He has a place for you in those many mansions He has prepared for us. ❏

19

REVELATION'S NEW LIFE FOR A NEW MILLENNIUM

The banners spread across Eastern Europe like butterflies struggling in flight. Voices joined together, growing stronger and more confident with each step. Voices of Polish workers, Hungarian students, Czechoslovakian dissidents, East Germans youths, Romanian shopkeepers. A varied chorus of languages rose up—all energized by one magical, powerful word: freedom. In the last few months of the 1980s, the world watched spellbound as decades of totalitarian rule washed away before an incredible human wave of democracy.

Future historians will look back on 1989 as one of the pivotal points of history—ushering in a new era for Eastern Europe. People all over the world seemed to be celebrating the triumph of democracy in the most unexpected places. We are living in exciting times.

What most observers fail to really see, however, is the spiritual dimension of these revolutions against tyranny. Much more is happening than just a change of political systems.

In most of the countries struggling under various forms of dictatorship, reformers found a source of strength and inspiration in the church. They gathered in cathedrals and chapels to fan the flame of freedom. Worship services united believers in their stand against tyranny.

Those of us who've lived all our lives in relative security and freedom may find it hard to grasp just how priceless such things are. And we may have forgotten just how deeply God Himself is committed to freedom.

The prophet Isaiah says this about God's Servant, one "anointed to preach good news:"

> "He has sent me to bind up the brokenhearted, to proclaim freedom for the captives and release from darkness for the prisoners" (Isaiah 61:1).

God is in the business of freeing people from oppression—all kinds of oppression. The Almighty is described as One who lifts the yoke from our necks, as a Victorious Warrior rescues the enslaved from the tyrant.

And this God of freedom stands in opposition to the empire of Satan in all its forms. Satan seeks to enslave by whatever means: vice, deprivation, ignorance, political oppression. God's way and Satan's way are at war.

This is the great conflict that the book of Revelation reveals through vivid symbols. It's the Lamb of God vs. the Red Dragon. It's the pure woman crowned with stars vs. the harlot of Babylon. It's the ten-horned beast vs. God's faithful people.

And one of the things that Revelation emphasizes is that this is a battle of freedom vs. coercion, of love vs. force.

The Lamb of God invites us to a wedding feast. One of the greatest invitations of all time is found in the Bible's last book: "Blessed are those who are called to the marriage supper of the Lamb" (Revelation 19:9).

The marriage supper of the Lamb is a symbolic description of Christ's union with His people in the great victory celebration as they ascend to heaven at His Second Coming.

This is all possible because Jesus made the total, all-out commitment for us on the cross. John describes our Lord's sacrifice this way:

> "To Him who loved us and washed us from our sins in His own blood, and has made us kings and priests to His God and Father, to Him be glory and dominion forever and ever. Amen" (Revelation 1:5,6).

Jesus made the supreme commitment for us and He invites us to make the supreme commitment to Him.

One of the places where we learn about a total commitment which leads us to freedom is in the experience of Romanian Christians during the Communist years.

Nicolae Ceausescu held that country in an iron grip for over three decades. Toward the end of his rule he had become, by all accounts, one of the worst dictators in modern history. Ceausescu exported food and fuel to pay off his government's debt, but kept his citizens malnourished and shivering in the cold.

Ceausescu's dreaded Securitate forces, 180,000 strong, better equipped than the army, and fanatically loyal to the dictator, kept everyone in line.

Few leaders have been more widely and deeply hated by their people. But what could the Romanians do? They lived in a state of constant terror. Often it seemed that half the country was spying on the other half.

And yet this dictator fell faster than any of his contemporaries. He passed from secure, confident tyrant to a hunted fugitive in a matter of hours. How did it happen?

The spark of revolution came from a most unexpected

source: an obscure pastor of the Reformed Church in the city of Timisoara. Laszlo Tokes simply couldn't remain quiet about the terrible abuses of Ceausescu's regime. He spoke against the government's plan of bulldozing thousands of villages and forcing farmers into apartment complexes.

As a result, the pastor was harassed and beaten. A court order was issued for the minister's eviction from his church. At this point his fellow believers and supporters decided to take a public stand. They came to the church and formed a human chain around it. When police came to take Tokes away they refused to move.

That's when Ceausescu's dreaded Securitate forces came into play. They ordered the army units that were gathered around the church to fire into the crowd. The troops refused; several of their officers were shot. Then the massacre began. The Securitate men fired a barrage of warning shots, and then, incredibly enough, mowed down a row of children who were standing in front of the crowd. Next they shot down unarmed adults who were maintaining their vigil.

Word of the massacre in Timisoara spread through the country. The courageous stand of those people around their church inspired others to take a stand. Demonstrations broke out; factory workers went on strike.

At this point, Ceausescu decided to stage a propaganda rally in Bucharest outside his presidential palace. But that rally suddenly turned into a huge protest. For the first time, Romanians publicly defied this tyrant, face-to-face. Their voices of protest drowned his voice out; some shouted a demand that he tell the truth about Timisoara.

And that was the end. That's when Ceausescu fled the scene and lost his hold on the country.

Almost everyone in Romania longed for freedom; almost everyone hated their dictator. But they remained paralyzed and helpless *until* they were willing to make a public stand, a public commitment. Everyone cherished freedom secretly in their heart. But that did not become a reality until a group of believers linked their arms and stood in a circle around a church in Timisoara.

Friends, each one of us has to deal with tyranny in our own lives. Satan is seeking to enslave each of us in some way; he wants to entrap us in his kingdom of oppression. Revelation shows us Satan as a dragon who attacks God's people. John speaks of the church as a pure woman, and he writes:

> "And the dragon was enraged with the woman, and he went to make war with the rest of her offspring, who keep the commandments of God and have the testimony of Jesus" (Revelation 12:17).

Peter describes our enemy in a similar way:

> "Your enemy the devil prowls around like a roaring lion looking for someone to devour. Resist him, standing firm in the faith. . ." 1 Peter 5:8, 9, NIV).

This is the earth's ultimate tyrant, always on the lookout for victims. Now, you may say you'll never give your allegiance to this roaring lion, Satan. You may cherish spiritual freedom in your heart. You may hate and despise evil. *But*, you will still remain trapped in this tyrant's empire *unless* you resist by taking a firm stand.

Why? Because we're not just neutral observers in this war between the kingdom of God and the kingdom of Satan, the realm of the dragon and the beast. We don't stand apart from it all somehow. No, we're very much caught up in the tragedy of Satan's kingdom. Like the citizens of Romania we find ourselves under the influence of a tyrant.

So how do we escape? How do we find freedom? It's not enough just to wish this tyranny away. We have to take a stand, declare another allegiance. And of course that allegiance must be to the One who came to set us free, Jesus Christ.

The book of Revelation describes a group of people who have declared just such an allegiance; they are a group which has gone through the last upheavals of history and made it to the very throne room of God. You may recall this text describing the secret of their strength:

> "These are the ones who came out of the great tribulation, and washed their robes and made them white in the blood of the Lamb. Therefore they are before the throne of God, and serve Him day and night in His temple" (Revelation 7:14, 15).

These people washed their robes and made them white in the blood of the Lamb. But did you know that there is a particular Christian practice that symbolizes this washing, this making things white in the blood of the Lamb? There is actually a way in which we can affirm that publicly in our own lives? I'm talking about the affirmation, the public statement of baptism.

Baptism is mentioned more than 80 times in the New Testament. Jesus gave final instructions to His disciples:

> "Go therefore and make disciples of all nations, baptizing them in the name of the Father and of the Son and of the Holy Spirit, teaching them to observe all things I have commanded you, and

lo, I am with you always, even to the end of the age" (Matthew 28:19, 20).

Throughout the New Testament, baptism is a symbol of a public commitment—a symbol of allegiance or commitment to Jesus Christ.

Bible baptism declares whose side we are on. To be "washed in the Blood of the Lamb" is to make a public statement of loyalty in baptism.

No doubt about it. The book of Revelation shows us that Jesus is the one who stands against the evil empire of Satan; He is able to deliver us from the grip of the tyrant. And He asks us to give our absolute allegiance to Him as our Savior.

But here's the problem. Many people today give a sort of vague assent to Jesus as Savior and keep their allegiance a rather private affair. They believe in Him, they say, but that belief, for some reason, never becomes a public statement.

The Bible doesn't tell us to just nod toward Christ and away from Satan. We need something more definite than that in our lives. Private allegiances tend to wither away. Unexpressed beliefs tend to bend with the circumstances.

So how do we take a stand? The early Christians show us how very clearly. After one of Peter's first sermons, his listeners were deeply convicted about the claims of Christ. They asked, "What shall we do?" Peter answered:

> "Repent and let every one of you be baptized
> in the name of Jesus Christ" (Acts 2:38).

These people were ready to call Jesus their Lord and Savior. How were they to take a stand? By making a public statement, by being baptized.

Let's study the method of baptism. Let's look at how Jesus was baptized. He is a safe example to follow:

> "Jesus came from Nazareth of Galilee, and was baptized by John in the Jordan. And immediately, coming up from the water, He saw the heavens parting and the Spirit descending upon Him like a dove" (Mark 1:9,10).

Jesus was fully immersed by John in the Jordan River. John states:

> "Now John was baptizing in Aenon near Salim because there was much water there. And they came and were baptized" (John 3:23).

True Biblical baptism requires "much water." Sprinkling does not require much water. Pouring does not require much water. Only immersion requires much water. Paul wrote:

> "One Lord, one faith, one baptism" (Ephesians 4:5).

According to Scripture, there is only one genuine faith—saving faith in Christ. There is only one Lord—Jesus our Savior and Lord and there is only one genuine method of Bible baptism—baptism by immersion.

In one of the earliest baptismal paintings we have depicting our Lord's baptism was discovered in Africa and now residing at the World Council of Churches in Geneva, Switzerland. Jesus is being immersed. In numerous ancient churches there are large baptisteries for immersion.

Full immersion is the only method of baptism described in the Bible. Note how the Apostle Philip baptized an Ethiopian eunuch:

> "And both Philip and the eunuch went down
> into the water, and he baptized him" (Acts
> 8:38).

Both Philip and the Ethiopian entered the water.
Philip immersed the new believer.

Why is this the New Testament method of baptism?
Because of what it symbolizes.

In the New Testament picture of baptism, the new
believer was lowered into water in the name of the Father,
Son and Holy Spirit, and raised out of the water as a committed individual who had accepted the forgiveness and
cleansing of Christ. Baptism is a way of identifying ourselves with Christ. We join ourselves to Him publicly, in
the same way that a man and woman join themselves in
marriage through a wedding ceremony. In baptism we
declare that we are dead to Satan, this roaring lion, and
committed to Jesus, the One who can set us free.

Jesus' sacrificial death and His resurrection is our
great hope. And God gave us a way to identify with it, to
accept it. Paul put it this way:

> "Don't you know that all of us who were bap-
> tized into Christ Jesus were baptized into his
> death? We were therefore buried with him
> through baptism into death in order that, just
> as Christ was raised from the dead through the
> glory of the Father, we too may live a new life"
> (Romans 6:3, 4, NIV).

Baptism is a memorial of Christ's death and resurrection. Being immersed in the water symbolizes our
burial with Christ. Being lifted up out of the water pictures our resurrection with Him.

Baptism represents three things—

1. Dying to the old sinful way of life. That is, turning sincerely away from it. We identify with Christ's death on the cross.
2. Burying our sins in the watery grave—just as Christ was buried in the tomb. We acknowledge that Christ's sacrifice covers our sins.
3. Rising again out of the water to walk a new life—as Christ rose again in triumphant resurrection.

That's why baptism can be like a great banner of freedom waving over our heads. It is God's chosen method of taking a stand against the kingdom of evil.

But let's make one thing clear. Baptism does not save us. It is not a magical ceremony that gives us eternal life. Faith in Jesus Christ is what saves us; we receive eternal life by believing in Him and accepting Him as Savior, period.

Baptism doesn't mean you're perfect; it means you're committed. It means your face is toward the kingdom of God and you're walking forward with Christ.

Baptism is simply a way of declaring that—publicly. But, as a public statement, it can give us something invaluable: a new sense of direction, a new freedom, and a new spiritual power.

When we make a public stand in baptism, the abstract idea of following Christ becomes more of a living force and our commitment becomes more real. God doesn't want us to just keep struggling alone; He wants us to be part of a great movement.

Here's what happens when we are baptized:
1. Every sin is forgiven and its guilt gone. The Scripture says, "Repent and let everyone of you be baptized. . . for the remission of sins" (Acts 2:38).
2. We receive new spiritual power to overcome Satan's temptation. Acts 2:38 continues: " . . . and

you shall receive the gift of the Holy Spirit." When Jesus was baptized, "He saw the Spirit of God descending like a dove and alighting upon Him" (Matthew 3:16). The same Holy Spirit fills the hearts of committed believers at baptism to empower them to face Satan's temptations.

3. We are adopted into the family of God. We become part of Christ's Body and His church.

"Then those who gladly received his word were baptized; and that day about three thousand souls were added to them. And they continued steadfastly in the apostles' doctrine and fellowship, in the breaking of bread, and in prayers. . . . praising God and having favor with all the people. And the Lord added to the church daily those who were being saved" (Acts 2:41, 42, 47).

"For as the body is one and has many members, but all the members of that one body, being many, are one body, so also is Christ. For by one Spirit we were all baptized into one body— whether Jews or Greeks, whether slaves or free—and have all been made to drink into one Spirit. For in fact the body is not one member but many" (1 Corinthians 12:12, 13, 20).

In baptism we express our union with Christ, but we also express solidarity with other believers. We primarily commit ourselves to Christ, but we also commit ourselves to His body, to the church. We become part of God's great movement for freedom on this earth.

Personal, private values are fine; private goals are good to have. But we are faced with overwhelming evil in the world. It's not just political oppression that threatens us. We are all but inundated in a sea of drugs and alcohol today. Look around you. Children are being scarred for life by the trauma in their homes. Materialism is choking out our spiritual ideals.

We need to take a stand together. We need to raise up a great demonstration against evil in this world. We can't win the war privately. The church may appear to be badly flawed; religious leaders may let us down; the group of believers in your neighborhood may seem pretty small and insignificant. But joined together in Christ we *can* become a movement. Publicly committed to Christ, and to each other, we *can* make a difference.

Some people say they just want to be baptized into Jesus but not into the church. I would have to ask, do they want to cut off the Head from the body? The church is imperfect to be sure. But it's still the body of Christ; it's the way He manifests himself on earth.

Please, don't fool yourself, you need the strength of other believers, you need fellowship, you need to identify with a group which is identified with Christ.

Baptism serves as a unifying experience for believers. It binds together those who have been through spiritual struggles. Through baptism we can all share in the victory Jesus Christ.

I'll never forget the baptism of a young man named Peter, who lived in Poland. He was a Polish Neo-Nazi, a pretty tough kid. He also became involved in worshipping Satan. Peter wanted nothing to do with Christianity.

But then he got cancer. They had to operate on his brain. They operated three times. But they couldn't get all the cancer. Peter began wasting away. His skin turned yellow.

Well, Peter's Christian mother would take audio tapes home from my lectures. And Peter listened to them. After a while he said, "I want to give my heart to Jesus." He took all his Nazi materials and his Satanic materials and threw them away.

I came to see Peter and studied the Bible with him. One day his mother called and said, "You've got to come quickly. The doctor is here. Peter's dying. He'll only live about two hours."

I went to the house and found Peter in terrible shape. He was vomiting. He hadn't been able to keep food down for about three weeks. The house was dirty and smelly.

I remember fetching a basin and holding Peter in my arms as he kept retching his frail life away. All I could do was hold him.

Peter looked up into my eyes and said, "Pastor you've got to baptize me before I die."

Peter knew those passages in the Bible which speak of the supreme importance of Bible baptism. He remembered the words of Jesus:

> "He who believes and is baptized will be saved" (Mark 16:16).

Peter was extremely concerned that without Bible baptism he would not be saved.

I said, "Peter I can't baptize you. I can't take you to church; you're too weak."

Peter said it again, "Pastor, I'm going to die, you have to baptize me."

I tried to explain. "Peter, Jesus accepts you completely, right now—even if you can't be baptized. You're like the thief on the cross."

But Peter whispered to me, "But it's my dying wish. Won't you give a dying man his last wish?"

What could I say to that? I told Peter's mother, "Fill the bathtub as high as you can, to the top."

She did. I helped Peter strip down to his waist. Then I took that young man in my arms, just skin and bones, and I carried him to the bathroom.

I knelt on the floor and I began to pray for Peter, and I'll tell you something. There are times in your life when you're almost afraid to look up, times when a place feels so holy that you think you'll see God, right there.

Peter's mother knelt with me. Peter's wife knelt with me, with their baby in her arms. And I still had Peter in my arms with his hands around my neck. As gently as I could, I lowered him into the warm water and I had the privilege of baptizing that man in the name of the Father, Son and Holy Spirit.

That was a holy place for me. God was present. I lifted Peter out of the tub and we dried him off with towels. And for the first time in three weeks he asked for tea.

Peter didn't die that day. He didn't die the next day, or the next. For one month his mother had the most wonderful time in her life with her son, sharing together.

And then, just before Peter closed his eyes for the last time, I leaned over and asked him, "Do you have any message?"

He told me, "I do, Pastor. As you go to every place, tell them my story, and tell them, pastor, not to wait too long. Tell them to move ahead, accept Christ and be baptized because he's calling them."

Jesus Christ is calling you, friend. It's time to come home. Paul appeals to us: "Behold, *now* is the accepted time; *now* is the day of salvation" (2 Corinthians 6:2).

Think of the urgency of Ananias to Paul:

> "What are you waiting for? Get up, be baptized and wash your sins away, calling on His name" (Acts 22:16, NIV).

If you've never been baptized by immersion, it's time to step into that water; it's time to identify completely with the life, death and resurrection of Jesus Christ.

If you've turned your back on God; if you've wandered far away from Jesus, perhaps you want to be rebaptized. Perhaps you need to make that statement to God now, to make a new beginning.

Christ longs to say to you exactly what the Father said to him: "This is my beloved Son in whom I am well pleased." He longs to give you that commendation.

I invite you to listen to that voice, to listen to the Spirit's pleading. If you feel that conviction, please do not delay. I invite you to make a decision. Come home now. ❏

20
THE REVELATION LIFESTYLE
DISCOVERING A LIFE OF ABUNDANT
HEALTH AT END-TIME

D r. Neil Nedley tells a fascinating story in his new book, *Proof Positive*, on how to combat disease and achieve optimal health. Dr. Nedley was giving a treadmill test to a patient whom he suspected had heart disease. Harold, the patient, looked up and said, "Doctor, I really don't think it matters how I check out on the test today. We each have a time we are going to die; that time is set and there is nothing we can do about it."

Here was Harold's thought: "God determines if you live or die. When God calls your number, it's up. There is nothing you can do about it." This statement fails to take into account how our own personal lifestyle choices affect our health. It is totally out of touch with the overwhelming amount of scientific evidence which clearly demonstrates that our daily choices affect our likelihood of living a long and healthy life.

I am convinced that the devil is anxious to destroy our health and God wants to build it up. In the book of Revelation, in this titanic struggle between good and evil, Satan is the destroyer and Jesus is the Restorer. One of Satan's tools of destruction is deception. He deceives to destroy. He deceives millions of Christians into thinking it does not make any difference how they treat their bodies as long as their "hearts" are right with God.

John exposes Satan for who he is:

> "So the great dragon was cast out, that serpent
> of old, called the Devil and Satan who deceives
> the whole world" (Revelation 12:9).

He deceives people into defiling their bodies thinking it makes little difference. They accept the temporary pleasure of some physical indulgence—drugs, alcohol, tobacco, harmful articles of diet, sexual immorality—and in the process destroy both their bodies and their souls.

Read John's words:

> "And they shall bring the glory and honor of
> the nations into it. But there shall by no means
> enter into it anything that defiles, or causes an
> abomination or a lie, but only those who are
> written in the Lamb's Book of Life"
> (Revelation 21:26, 27).

Here is an incredible contrast picture: Those who give God glory in their entire lifestyle enter God's eternal city, New Jerusalem. Those who accept Satan's lies and defile their bodies are outside the city.

God gives us specific instruction in Revelation which relates to our total lifestyle:

> "Fear God and give glory to Him, for the hour
> of His judgment has come; and worship Him
> who made heaven and earth, the sea and
> springs of water" (Revelation 14:7).

Giving glory to God includes total commitment, an absolute surrender of our physical, mental and spiritual choices. Our bodies are no less God's than our hearts and minds. Giving glory to God involves a commitment of our entire being.

Just how do we give glory to God? Does this have anything to do with our lifestyle? Paul asks:

> "Do you not know that your body is the temple of the Holy Spirit who is in you, whom you have from God, and you are not your own? For you were bought at a price; therefore glorify God in your body and in your spirit, which are God's" (1 Corinthians 6:19, 20).

We are to glorify or honor God in our bodies. We are to treat our bodies as temples of the Holy Spirit. Our bodies are not our own. We belong to Christ. He created us. Life is a gift which comes from Him. He redeemed us. Paul continued:

> "So whether you eat or drink, or whatever you do, do all to the glory of God" (1 Corinthians 10:31).

Look at earnest appeal:

> "I beseech you therefore, brethren, by the mercies of God, that you present your bodies a living sacrifice, holy, acceptable to God, which is your reasonable service" (Romans 12:1).

Here is how The New International Version of the Bible translates Romans 12:1, "Offer your bodies a living sacrifice, holy and pleasing to God. This is your spiritual act of worship." Offering our bodies to God is a spiritual act of worship. It's part of the believer's commitment at anytime in world history but especially in the final controversy between good and evil.

Revelation's final appeal is to worship the Creator and not worship the Beast. One of the ways in which we worship the Creator is to cooperate with Jesus, the great Creator and Restorer of our health, to keep our bodies in good health. One of the ways we side with Satan is to accept his deception that what we do with our bodies doesn't matter and destroy our health.

Now let's be very practical. Most leading authorities and researchers in the field of Preventive Medicine believe that it is our lifestyle practices which are killing us. Our choices contribute to premature disease and death.

Let's look at some of the many practices which are destroying the lives of millions of Americans and what we can do about them. You can add years to your life— happy, productive, fulfilling, joy-filled years.

Dying For a Smoke?

The sixth commandment says, in Exodus 20:13 KJV, "Thou shalt not kill." Some think that refers to taking a gun and shooting some one, but it means not only that you shouldn't kill other people—it means you shouldn't kill *yourself,* Dr. Linus Pauling, one of the few scientists ever to win two Nobel Prizes, said that every cigarette you smoke takes 14½ minutes off your life. In other words, smoking is *committing slow suicide.*

Are you aware of research done at the Sloan-Kettering Institute of Cancer? They developed a smoking machine that extracts tobacco tar from cigarette smoke. When they painted that tar on the backs of mice, the mice developed cancer indistinguishable from human cancer. Today we know there are 29 cancer-producing chemicals in the smoke of every cigarette!

Aside from *cancer,* there's *emphysema.* At least 80 percent of all emphysema cases are caused by cigarette smoking. A victim of emphysema usually carries around an oxygen tank to get air.

Then, of course, cigarette smoking is related to *heart disease.* The very first puff of smoke reaching a person's lungs causes his blood vessels to *contract,* constricting the flow of blood, forcing the heart to work harder. You have a 25 percent greater chance of getting a heart attack if you're a smoker than if you're a non-smoker. So cancer, emphysema and heart disease are all related to cigarette smoking.

Someone says, "Pastor, I'd really *like* to quit smoking, but I *can't."* Question: is the power of tobacco greater than the power of Jesus Christ? No, Jesus is stronger than a cigarette. I, personally, have seen Jesus deliver thousands of people from the tobacco habit. I think of Ed. He was a two-pack-a-day smoker. Ed was the kind of person who could do everything—except quit smoking. He just couldn't quit. He smoked a pack and a half to two-packs a day for 15 to 20 years.

CHRIST CAN DELIVER YOU

So I talked to Ed about the Bible. I said, "You know, in Bible times when Christ touched blind eyes, they were healed. When Christ touched the paralyzed man's withered arm, it was healed. Those people had afflictions, and you have an affliction of tobacco. You can't quit yourself, but Christ can deliver you. Would you like to kneel down with me, so we can pray about it?"

I had him bring his cigarettes, and he put them on the floor. Then we began to pray. Here's how he began to pray—it was the weakest prayer I've ever heard—"Oh, dear Jesus, I can't quit. You know I can't quit. I'm so weak, Lord. Tobacco has a grip on me. I can never give it up."

I couldn't take it anymore. I shook him as he prayed.

I said, "Stop praying like that!" He looked up at me and said, "Pastor, what did you say?" I said, "Don't pray anymore. You're going to be worse after you pray than you were before." Now, he'd never heard a preacher talk to him like that, but nevertheless I did. "Look, you're convincing yourself in your prayer that you can't quit smoking." but Jesus says in Matthew 7:7, 8:

> "Ask, and it will be given you; seek, and ye will find; knock, and it will be opened unto you. For every one who asks receives; and he who seeks finds; and to him who knocks it will be opened."

I told Ed, "Get down on your knees and tell God, 'I know I'm weak, but You're strong, God. You've got almighty power. You touched blind eyes—and they were opened. You touched deaf ears—and they were unstopped. Lord, Your power is greater than tobacco.'"

"Ed, your problem is that you think tobacco is greater than Jesus, but you need to tell Jesus you believe that *His* power is greater. Please pray your prayer over again right now."

He bowed his head and prayed, "Dear Jesus, I'm so weak, but You're strong. You're almighty. You can deliver me, Lord. I may have a craving, but You're greater than that craving. I may want to run out and get some tobacco, but You're greater than that, Lord. Please deliver me."

That man was delivered by the grace of God! And you too can be delivered. You don't need to be bossed around by a little cigarette. You can be delivered by the grace of God. Your lungs don't need to be polluted. Jesus can deliver you. I'm not saying it's going to be easy. You've been putting nicotine in your body for 10, 15, 20 years, and your body's going to cry out. It'll say, "What are you doing to me now?" You've been putting that stuff in for years, to keep feeding that habit. But you don't *have* to do that. You see, Jesus' power is greater.

One scientific textbook says, "Nicotine causes the arteries to shrink. This combination of *fat buildup* and *shrinkage* of the arteries hinders the blood vessels from supplying enough blood to the heart, brain, extremities, and other organs. As the condition becomes worse, tissue damage results. At this point, it takes only a small blood clot caught in the constricted blood vessel to cause a heart attack or a stroke." That's what happens, friends. A lot of people look fine while they're smoking. but their arteries are getting smaller and the fat's building up. Then one day something happens. They feel pain in their chest. And it gets worse—like an elephant is stepping on their heart! The pain radiates through their chest, and they fall over— often to die. That's the cumulative effect of smoking.

QUITTERS ALWAYS WIN

But, by the grace of God, you *can* quit. The good news is that when you stop smoking, your vessels begin to clear up. Your lungs improve, the irritation stops, the inflammation stops, the congestion stops, the dripping mucous stops, the shortness of breath stops. The beneficial health effects are almost immediate. *I thank God* that Christ can give us abundant health, can give us power to *overcome*—and live!

Furthermore, much evidence exists today, too, about second-hand smoke, about what smoking does to people living in the home of a smoker. What does smoking do to women who are pregnant? The Chicago *Tribune* ran an article that said: "Women who smoke during pregnancy are damaging their baby's blood vessels." Smoking affects not only you. If you're pregnant, it affects your baby. If you have little children, two, three, five years old in the home, it affects them. They have more colds, and through your second-hand smoke, they can develop cancer. There's no question about it. You pollute the atmosphere surrounding your kids. Women who smoke have premature babies much more frequently. Those tiny babies have to be put in incubators, and have a difficult start in life. Smoking is harmful to everyone around you, so you have every reason to quit.

The power of God will enable you to quit. By the grace of God, you can be free. You can present your body "a *living* sacrifice." Paul wrote:

> "Don't you know that when you offer your-
> selves to someone to obey him as slaves, you
> are slaves to the one whom you obey"
> (Romans 6:16, NIV)?

You're a slave to tobacco or to Jesus. It's a wonderful thing—even though it's difficult sometimes when we have that craving—to say, "I'm not a slave to tobacco anymore. I want to be a servant to Jesus Christ, I want to be a child of the King." And He comes into our lives and grants us His power over those habits!

Fighting the Battle of the Bottle?

Alcohol destroys cells immediately—brain cells, incidentally, which never regenerate! So they're gone forever. Dr. Melvin Knisely has developed an electron microscope that he used on college students. He can look through that microscope into the blood vessels in their eyes and see the coagulation of the blood carrying oxygen to the brain. He can tell if a person has taken two drinks, six drinks, or eight drinks by looking into their eyes with the new electron microscope. He warns that drinking alcohol cuts off oxygen supplies to the brain. Question: Where does the Holy Spirit communicate with you? Does He communicate through your fingers? Does He communicate through your toes? Where does He communicate? Through your brain! Do you see why the devil brewed alcohol in the laboratories of hell? Because alcohol affects the brain!

The human brain is the only place where God can communicate with us through His Holy Spirit. Have you ever noticed that when people start drinking, after a few drinks they lose their inhibitions? Drinking and sexual immorality often go together. Drinking often precedes a moral fall. Why? It's because the devil destroys our brain cells, and we can't hold back from doing what we *know we shouldn't* do. That's why Soloman says in Proverbs 20:1, "Wine is a mocker, intoxicating drink arouses brawling, and whoever is led astray by it is not wise."

Two out of every five people who use alcohol develop serious drinking problems—that's 40 percent! But someone still will say, "Oh, I can drink socially with no problem." Friend: If you had a dog that bit only two of five people who came to your house, and it sent them to the hospital, would you keep that dog around? Not at all! Two out of every five people who take even one drink, develop serious marital problems, other family problems, and job-related problems, as a result of drinking. You don't know if you're one of those two. That's why the Bible says "Wine is a mocker. It will deceive you." God says, "Don't take that chance—don't even begin."

The Word of God doesn't have good things to say about liquor. In fact, Soloman puts it this way:

> "Who has woe? Who has sorrow? Who has strife? Who has complaints? Who has need-

less bruises? Who has bloodshot eyes? Those who linger over wine, who go to sample bowls of mixed wine. Do not gaze at wine when it is red, when it sparkles in the cup, when it goes down smoothly! In the end it bites like a snake and poisons like a viper. Your eyes will see strange sights and your mind will imagine confusing things" (Proverbs 23:29-33, NIV).

That last sentence describes the hallucinations and *delirium tremens* which plague many drinkers of alcohol.

Someone says, "Wait a minute, Pastor. Wait a minute! Jesus created wine at a wedding feast." And I ask, did you ever study that passage? I looked at the measurements. The wine He created at that wedding feast was a large amount: John says it was enough to *fill* "six stone water jars . . . to the brim" and describes the jars as "each holding twenty to thirty gallons" (John 2:6, 7, NIV). That's between *120 and 180 gallons of wine!* It was enough for everyone at that wedding feast to get sauced— to get *really drunk* if it were *fermented* wine. Can you believe that Christ created fermented wine that intoxi-cates? Look at those quantities! If those people drank like that, then some man will go after another man's wife. Another one's going to drive an ox cart off the road on the way home. And someone else will go home and beat his children. Do you mean Jesus is responsible for those kinds of things? Don't believe it for a minute, friend.

I don't want to be sidetracked into a deep discussion of linguistics, but we must look at things from the Biblical perspective. The fact is that the Bible uses the English word "wine" to refer to two distinctly different grape bev-erages: one, *unfermented,* refreshing and lawful; the other, *fermented,* intoxicating and unlawful. The sacred

Scriptures translate the Hebrew word *yayin* in the Old Testament and the Greek word *oinos* in the New Testament into our English word "wine."

In Bible days, both *yayin* and *oinos* could mean *either* the fresh, unfermented juice of the grape OR the fermented, intoxicating drink we call "wine" today. Since the Bible is not a lexicon which defines its words, the meaning of its words must often be derived from their context. Therefore, we can't merely read the word "wine" and assume it means an alcoholic drink that makes one drunk or a delightful drink of grape juice even our children can enjoy—we must look at the context. When the Bible *condemns* "wine" and the problems of drunkenness it causes, we know it refers to the intoxicating variety. When it *praises* "wine" as a refreshing and healthful blessing to mankind, we may be sure it refers to the unfermented variety—pure grape juice!

When Jesus went to that wedding feast at Cana, He performed His first miracle. John says in John 2:9, 10 that the wine the wedding guests drank at the end, which Jesus created, was *different* from that at the beginning. People said, "This is the sweetest and the best wine we've ever tasted." Jesus miraculously created *non-alcoholic* wine which you can buy in the stores today. He didn't create fermented, intoxicating, alcoholic wine for those people to get. Not at all! My Lord created wine that was so sweet, so magnificent, so bubbly that it gave them energy. It didn't destroy their brains. Jesus will never create something that's going to cause people to lose control their minds—not for one second!

I get agitated about these things because the devil is destroying people's spiritual life! Someone has to stand up and say, "My brother, my sister, Jesus is coming soon! Let's get our bodies ready and keep our minds clear in preperation for the second coming of Christ." Someone has to face the liquor industry and say, "You're deceiving our teenagers. You're raping the minds of American young people."

Don't talk to me about 'responsible drinking.' There's no such thing! You become *irresponsible* when you drink because it deceives you." Shakespeare said of alcohol: "O God! that men should put an *enemy* in their mouths to steal away their brains."

Jesus wants adults to set the tone for young people. If you are drinking socially, how can you tell your teenage son or daughter not to drink? And even if you can "handle it," how do you know they'll be able to "handle it?" Many young people have started drinking at home by taking beers out of the refrigerator when parents are gone— or drinking and sipping wine when parents are away. That's right, they do. You can never lead your children to get ready for Jesus' coming unless you, yourselves, put your bodies on the altar. But the only way is to abstain totally. Say, "I'm going to clean myself up for You, dear Jesus." People think they can "handle it," but they can't—not when they sip wine and other alcoholic beverages that destroy health and destroy lives by drunk drivers and other irresponsible acts.

When we put our bodies on the altar by refraining from alcohol, tobacco, and drugs, they're clean before God. It sounds like a corny cliche, but the only way to be safe from them is to say "No," to these drugs—there's no other way. Our bodies are the temple of God. I'm not my own, for Christ bought me on the cross, and now I'm His.

NONE OF THESE DISEASES

In the Old Testament, God made a wonderful promise to ancient Israel. Moses said:

"If you diligently heed the voice of the Lord your God and do what is right in His sight, give ear to His commandments and keep all His statutes, I will put *none of these diseases* on you which I have brought on the Egyptians. For *I am the Lord who heals you.*" (Exodus 15:26, Emphasis supplied).

When God led Israel out of Egyptian bondage, the Psalmist wrote: "There was *none feeble* among His tribes." (Psalm 105:37, Emphasis supplied). The Israelites followed God's health principles, but the Egyptians did not.

Today we know the Egyptians' health practices because we've been studying the mummies. Through hieroglyphics, we know the lifestyle of the Egyptians. The Egyptians drank a lot of alcohol and were generally overweight because they ate a diet high in fat. They ate roast pork a great deal, which has the highest fat content of all meats. The Egyptians also had a lot of sugary foods in their diet.

Loma Linda University, in Loma Linda, California, conducted some magnificent studies on health and disease in the ancient world. Other researchers, looking at some of those studies, performed autopsies on literally thousands of Egyptian mummies. From these autopsies we have learned much about Egyptian culture and health habits. They actually did an autopsy on Egyptian Pharaoh Ramses II. The autopsy showed almost completely clogged arteries. He probably died of a massive heart attack.

They also x-ray the mummies. Dr. Rufeis, a French physician and Egyptologist, x-rayed mummies extensively. He found they had cancer, heart disease, arthritis, and rheumatism. Ramses II—what a specimen he was, with his heart disease and arthritis. The ancient Egyptians had the same diseases we have today. They had sexually transmitted diseases—syphilis and gonorrhea—because of their immoral lifestyles. They turned their backs on what the Bible said and violated God's health principles. As the result of those violations, they had everything from atherosclerosis to tooth decay, from obesity to heart disease, from cancer to arthritis.

Frequently, people ask me, "Mark, what about diet in the Bible? Does the Bible offer any help in choosing the best diet?" It certainly does. And what are the health principles God gives when it comes to diet?

Principle #1: When God created the human race, He gave them a magnificent diet of vegetables, grains, nuts, and fruits—a vegetarian diet.

> "God said, See, I have given you every herb that yields seed, which is on the face of all the earth, and every tree whose fruit yields seed: to you it shall be for food" (Genesis 1:29).

The original text was fruits, nuts, grains, and vegetables. No animals killed to provide a meat diet. It was God's desire they live long lives on the diet, which incidentally provides very adequate *protein*. Strong animals like the horse and cow get all the protein they need from the oats and corn and other grains they eat. They get their protein firsthand, from the earth, and grow big and strong. The man who kills them and eats their flesh is getting his protein secondhand, with accompanying health problems.

When Adam and Eve left the Garden of Eden, their diet also included root vegetables, a great diet of fruits, nuts, grains, and various kinds of vegetables. It wasn't until after the time of the Flood in Noah's day that God gave people permission to eat flesh food for what seems to be obvious reasons. But flesh food was not the original diet God gave Adam and Eve. If you want to eat His original diet, you must go back to Adam and Eve's diet.

Seven generations from Adam, there was a man named Methuselah. His name Methuselah means: "When he dies, the flood waters will come." (Incidentally, God did lay him to rest the very year the Flood came.) But he lived to be 969 years old. The average life span before the Flood was 900 years. Seven generations before Methuselah, Adam lived for 930 years. Noah lived 950 years. Genesis 5:5; 5:27; 9:29. Some people ask me, "Did they really live that long?" They certainly did. Nine hundred and sixty-nine years were nothing. God had designed for them to live—and wanted them to live—forever and ever and ever! When God makes something, He doesn't make junk. He makes something to live and to last for a long time. God wanted them to live *forever*.

FLESH FOOD SHORTENED LIFE SPAN

But after the Flood—since the catastrophic deluge ripped up trees and plants and temporarily destroyed all vegetation—God gave Noah and his family permission to eat meat. Immediately their life spans were shortened by hundreds of years. Look, seven generations from Adam is Methuselah, and those patriarchs lived long, long lives. But seven generations from Noah's son Shem, you come to the patriarch Nahor. Genesis 11:24, 25 says he lived only 119 years. So mankind's life span went down very, very rapidly once they began eating a diet other than what God gave originally.

Some may wonder, "Is it a sin to eat meat?" The answer is no, it's not. God gave permission to eat meat if people choose to do that. But you must realize that if you eat meat, you'll have more animal fat in your diet—and in your arteries. So it's important not to abuse that privilege, for you need to cut down on that high fat in your diet. If you want the best diet, of course, you'll choose a vegetarian one. That's what God really intended us to eat.

When you study the days of the Flood, you find something very interesting. God told Noah *how many* of each species of animal to bring into the ark:

> "You shall take with you seven each of every clean animal, a male and his female; two each of animals that are unclean, a male and his female" (Genesis 7:2).

So God said there are two kinds of beasts, clean and unclean.Why should Noah take the clean animals into the ark by sevens? Because he and his family were going to eat the clean ones and also use some of them for sacrifice. They were to take seven pairs—the original Hebrew tells Noah to take "seven, a male with his female"—so the animals could multiply. Why should Noah take the *unclean* animals in by only two? Because they're scavengers—not to be either eaten or sacrificed. The scavengers were created to eat the garbage of the earth. They were God's garbage-disposal system long before our modern garbage disposal was invented. As unclean creatures, they're unfit for human consumption.

Stop and think: Noah took the unclean animals—scavengers like the pig and the vulture—into the Ark only by two, a male and female pair, simply to preserve and perpetuate the species. If Noah and his family *had* eaten either one of the pair of those animals God says are unclean, we wouldn't have any of those animals around today!

The two categories of animals are *clean* and *unclean.* Note that God made this designation *before the Jewish race existed!* Some people say that clean and unclean came in only as a Jewish pracitce. Not true! Noah was not Jewish. The first Jew was Abraham, born about four centuries after the Flood. Only eight humans were saved in the Ark: Noah, his three sons, and their wives were the sole survivors of the human race at that time. When God applied this distinction for these survivors, it's obvious He applied it to all humanity, not just Jews, who didn't exist as a race or nation until much later.

Furthermore, when God *did* tell Noah the proper number of beasts to save aboard the Ark, Noah didn't ask for the clean-unclean distinction to be explained, so it must have been in effect even earlier.

Some say, "The clean-unclean distinction was only for *Old* Testament times." Simply not true, on the basis of both theology and common sense. Isaiah wrote that God's distinction between clean and unclean foods will *still be in effect* at the time of Jesus' second coming: "Behold, the Lord will come with fire, . . . and the slain of the Lord shall be many. Those who sanctify themselves, . . . *eating swines' flesh, and the abomination, and the mouse,* shall be consumed together, says the Lord" (Isaiah 66:15-17, Emphasis supplied).

And common sense tells us that God's prohibition against unclean beasts is not based on a ceremonial or religious ritual, like circumcision, that became obsolete at the Cross. *It's a health principle*—good for all time—because it's based on what God, the Creator, knows about those scavenging beasts, their anatomy and their eating habits. He knows what He designed all creatures for—He made the horse to be an excellent beast of burden, and He made the pig and the vulture and the catfish to be scavengers to keep their environment clean, just as we make garbage disposals and sewers.

The ideal diet is, of course, vegetarian, as God originally prescribed. In the emergency after the Flood, God did say man could eat meat in limited amounts. But God never said we could eat the unclean animals! Nor should we want to! Someone observed that "He was a valiant man who first ate an oyster!" We'll be so much healthier if we follow God's principles of health and diet just as He gave them in the Bible.

Science Validates God's Prescription

But you may ask, "What are some of those principles, and which animals are clean and unclean?" That's a very good question.

The first thing we need to notice when eating any kind of meat is the specific instruction God gave us:

> "It shall be a perpetual statue [not just in Old Testament times but always], throughout your generations, in all your dwelling places that you *eat neither fat nor blood*" (Leviticus 3:17, RSV).

Is science just catching up with the Bible? What did God say thousands of years ago? *Don't eat the fat.* What do we hear everywhere today? Eat a low-fat diet. You read about the importance of a low-fat diet in all kinds of books and weekly magazines. But God said it long ago. The scientists are just catching up with God. Why not eat fat? Among other problems, because of the cholesterol. Why not eat blood? Because disease is transmitted through the blood. They're just now seeing cancer as a virus transmitted through blood. Indeed, studies are being done in these areas. If you do eat meat, certainly cut out those *high-fat* meats and certainly don't eat *rare steaks* filled with blood.

The Bible gives very clear, very specific instructions to help us know which animals are clean or unclean. Two entire chapters—Leviticus 11 and Deuteronomy 14—are devoted to this instruction. If you do eat meat, whatever you do, don't eat animals God tells us are unclean. Now, which are the clean animals?

Moses wrote:

> "You may eat every animal with cloven hooves, having the hoof split into two parts, and that chews the cud" (Deuteronomy 14:6).

What does chewing the cud mean? It means that the animal chews its food, swallows it, spits it up, and chews it again. Some examples of clean animals are the ox or cow, the sheep, the goat, the deer, the gazelle, the antelope, the mountain goat and mountain sheep. All those animals fit God's description as clean animals.

What animals are *unclean?* What animals should we not eat, according to the Bible? What about the camel?

Moses continured:

> "Ye shall not eat of . . . the camel, and the hare, and the coney: for they chew the cud, but divide not the hoof; therefore they are unclean unto you" (Deuteronomy 14:7).

So the camel is unclean. Now, I want you to go home and take all the camel meat out of your refrigerator and throw it away! No more camel sandwiches for lunch! The Bible says the camel is unclean to you. Are you willing to give up eating camel because you love Jesus? You may smile because you don't eat camels. Maybe there's only one or two camels in the zoo.

So we don't have to worry about eating things that are unclean, because you wouldn't eat anything that's unclean. We'd better keep reading the Bible. Right? We've learned about the camel, the hare—that's a rabbit—and the coney. What's a coney? A coney is like a rock badger, an animal like a large rat that lives near the ocean. So no more coney in the mornings!

Going on, Moses said further in Deuteronomy 14:8: "Also the swine is unclean for you"—what's swine? Pig! Pork! Why does God mention it?—"because it has cloven hooves, yet does not chew the cud, you shall not eat their flesh, or touch their dead carcass." We can skip that because no one eats pork, right? God says not to eat it. Someone asks, why? Well, let me give you a few scientific reasons—but even if I didn't know the scientific reasons, I'd follow God, wouldn't you? The Bible says: Pork, don't eat it, get rid of it, throw it away. It's good fertilizer.

Here's a verse you should remember: The Psalmist says, "No good thing does the Lord withhold from those who walk uprightly" (Psalm 84:11, NRSV). If pork were good, God wouldn't hold it back from us. But since it's not good, He says: "Don't eat it." Cows, yes, you may eat. But pigs, God says, "No, don't eat the pig." Why? *Reason #1*—It has the *highest fat content* of all meat. Ounce for ounce, no meat is higher in fat than pork. It clogs the arteries and gets you ready for a heart attack.

Reason #2—Dr. McNaught examined pork specimens in the San Francisco meat markets and found that one out of four had *living trichina larvae* in it. Trichina are parasite worms. Trichinosis is breaking out again. If you put pig meat under a microscope, you'll see the trichina larvae, which may have millions of little eggs. Those eggs hatch in your stomach and then invade your muscle tissue, causing serious symptoms like arthritis or rheumatism.

Someone said to me once, "Oh, but we cook it so hot

that we kill them all." Does it give us more comfort to know we're eating dead worms rather than live ones? In fact, many cases of trichinosis that break out afflict people who thought they cooked their meat sufficiently. I'd rather follow God, friends. And I know you would too, wouldn't you? We can learn to control our appetites. We can eat to live rather than live to eat. We don't have to be among those God speaks of in Philippians 3:19, "Whose end is destruction, *whose God is their belly."* The Lord will gladly help us sanctify our tastes if we ask Him. Instead of junk food, we can learn to enjoy the premium fuel our bodies deserve.

YOU ARE WHAT YOU EAT

Look at everything God gave us to eat! We can follow a diet with real meal appeal! We can feast on the flavor of all those wonderful fruits and vegetables and nuts. And if you still prefer meat, there's beef, or lamb. But isn't it wiser to follow our Creator's way and not weaken or destroy these God-given bodies of ours? I don't want those parasitic trichina worms inhabiting my body in any way nor do I want high-fat foods clogging my arteries. I want my body as healthy so my mind can be clear.

What about fish? Moses said:

> "These you may eat of all that are in the waters: you may eat all that have fins and scales. And whatever does not have fins and scales you shall not eat; it is unclean for you" (Deuteronomy 14:9, 10).

If a fish has fins and scales, you may eat it—no problem. But if it's in the water and doesn't have fins and scales, eating it is simply digesting garbage. When you eat garbage, your digestion transports it into your flesh and makes you a candidate for disease and premature death.

During World War II, after the tragedy of Pearl Harbor, the American government hired Bruce Halstead, a marine biologist. Many American fliers—Marine and Naval aviators—who were shot down in the Pacific ate seafood to survive but were getting sick. So the American government said, "Okay, Dr. Halstead, we'll give you a year. We'll pay you a good salary, give you a boat and a crew, and we want you to tell them which fish they can eat, and which fish they shouldn't eat. Okay?" So Bruce Halstead went out and made a manual—a large study manual to tell the Navy fliers what they could and couldn't eat.

The interesting thing he said was this: "If you lose this manual, remember one thing: if it has fins and scales, you can eat it. If it doesn't have fins and scales—such as crab, lobster, shrimp, oyster, clams—don't eat it, because they have a high level of toxicity." This man of science, this twentieth-century marine biologist, echoed the words of God in Deuteronomy 14:10, "Whatever does not have fins and scales ye may not eat; it is unclean unto you." We seek out and respect *expert advice*—from doctors, nutritionists, and other medical specialists. But God is the divine Expert who made us. As the Creator, He knows whereof He speaks!

POISON ON THE PLATE

You know, I was brought up on the Atlantic Ocean, not the Pacific, and I used to go crabbing. I didn't know about clean and unclean food. I'd go down to the fish stands, and after the fishermen came in, I had a friend who'd cut off the heads and the tails of the fish and gut them. I'd go to this fish house to get the stinking smelly heads, these stinky, smelly guts. Then I'd take a string and tie it on a fish head—an old, rotten, decaying, smelling, worm-filled, maggot-filled, fish head. I'd drop it down off a bridge, and along would come some crab looking for his dinner. He's see that worm-filled, maggot-filled fish head. Then old Mr. Crab began to eat it. I'd begin to pull up, so gently on my string, and the crab would still hang on. Then we'd pop him in the net.

Do you know anything about crabs or lobsters? When you catch a crab or lobster, do you kill it right away and leave it lying there in the boat? No, you don't kill it right away. You have to keep it alive, because if you kill it, the poison goes right through it. The only way to cook a lobster is to put it live into boiling water, right? Don't kill it ahead of time, because the poison would quickly permeate it. What does that tell you about the poisons in those scavenger shellfish?

Prevention magazine had an article some time ago entitled "Shellfish Are Dirty and Dangerous" which blows the whistle on shellfish which carry so much disease and poison. It stated that "No other animal food offered on the menu of your favorite eating place would be served to you along with it's *feces*. Yet this is the case with seafood. It is offered whole, complete with its intestinal tract"!

I used to go out and get quahogs. They're like clams, but they have a harder shell. You have to go in the muddy parts, sometimes where the sewers come out. Quahogs go close to the sewers, you know, because they want to get all that nourishment! I'd go along with my bare feet, feeling for quahogs or clams. Then I'd reach down, take it, and throw it to my grandfather on shore. He's take a knife and pry it open, put salt on it, and hand it back to me—and I'd slurp it into my mouth. I probably shouldn't tell you what I used to do! But I always have had problems with my stomach! Do you understand why?

But when I came to Jesus, I gave up the clams and the quahogs and the lobsters and the pork. I've been energetic ever since! Praise the Lord, we can give up all that stuff. If Jesus asks me to give it up because He knows it's not good for me, I'll do it. I don't want to drift toward disease and premature death.

But some say to me, "Mark, wait a minute, in the New Testament all that changed. When Jesus came, He said we could eat anything." You know what I reply? "If something was bad to eat and unhealthy before the cross, it's going to be bad to eat and unhealthful after the cross."

PETER'S CORRECTIVE VISION

Then someone else asks, "What about Peter's vision when he saw all those unclean animals and God said, 'get up and eat.' And Peter said, 'No, I can't eat that.' And God said three times, 'Eat it.' What did that mean?"

Let's look at that passage in Acts 10:1-35, which talks about two visions given by God. The first was given to Cornelius, a Roman centurion who, although of heathen birth, worshipped God the best he knew how. While Cornelius was praying, "he saw a vision . . . an angel" who told him to contact Peter for instruction. So he sent messengers to do just that.

Then the Bible says while Peter was praying "he fell into a trance" and saw in vision a large sheet that came down with many unclean animals in it. There were rats and alligators and crocodiles and crabs and lobsters and pigs and snakes, and three times God said, "Kill, and eat." But Peter said, "Not so, Lord; for I have never eaten anything that is common or unclean." Then the sheet went back up. Peter's reply proves that during his entire three-and-a-half years with Jesus, he never heard about any changes in the status of unclean foods. Jesus had not changed the prohibition against eating the forbidden animals—if He had, Peter would have known about it and wouldn't have responded as he did. The Bible says Peter was so confused, he didn't know what the vision meant.

Just then there was a knock on his door, and the men Cornelius sent were standing there. They said, "Peter, our master Cornelius lives in a neighboring town. He's a Roman centurion and a Gentile. Please go visit him." Peter, being prejudiced against Gentiles, had always called them unclean and never wanted to go near them. Peter thought of Gentiles as rats and snakes! But now Peter understood the vision God sent him. It had nothing to do with eating unclean animals! When Peter explained his vision, he said, "God showed me that *I should not call any MAN common or unclean."* And he went and taught Cornelius about Christ.

God didn't really want Peter to eat the rats, snakes, crocodiles, or rodents in that sheet. God used them only as an illustration to show Peter he had prejudice against people of another race—not that it was right to eat unclean animals.

The lesson Peter got from the vision was this:

> "I now realize how true it is that *God does not show favoritism but accepts men from every nation* who fear Him and do what is right" (Acts 10:34, 35, NIV, emphasis supplied).

Peter realized God gave him the vision to correct his attitude toward people, not toward food. I'd rather let Peter interpret the vision than another human being, wouldn't you? It only makes sense that if things were unhealthful before the cross, they'll be unhealthful after the cross.

God will give us insight to see that we have a moral and religious duty to preserve our health, which comes to us as a sacred trust. We need to see that a failure to care for this priceless machinery called our body is an insult to the Creator. Jesus wants us well!

Now friend, you may feel too weak to change some habits. You may say that you love pork, are addicted to tobacco, and can't get along without alcohol because it calms your nerves. But Jesus says, "My child, come to Me. Give your body as a living sacrifice to Me. I'll give you health, joy, meaning, and purpose in your life. I love you so much! When I hung on the cross, I bought you. You're Mine—you're My son, My daughter."

You may have tried on your own power, to stop smoking. You may have tried to give up alcohol. You may have tried on your own to give up bad habits and be healthier. But in John 15:5 Jesus says, "Without Me, ye can do nothing." Paul triumphantly proclaims in Philippians 4:13, "I can do all things through Christ who strengthens me." He doesn't say, "I can do all things through Christ—except quit smoking. I can do all things through Christ—except give up this destructive relationship. I can do all things through Christ—except give up drugs, and alcohol, and unclean foods."

Without Christ, we can do nothing. Jesus says to you right now, "Come to Me. Put your tobacco on the altar, put your alcohol on the altar. If you're in some destructive relationship, put your life on the altar. If you're abusing your body with drugs, put that body on the altar." Lovingly, Jesus reminds you, "I've worked many miracles. I delivered demoniacs and they went free—their chains were broken. I delivered people who were blind and crippled, and they went free with great joy. When you surrender all, I'll work miracles in your life. When you put your life on the altar, when you come forward and give Me your heart, My welcoming arms will be out for you!"

Those arms are very strong. You can trust them. Let Him give you the desire and the power to be free from whatever is destroying your physical and moral health. ❏

21
REVELATION'S FOUR HORSEMEN REVEAL—WHY SO MANY DENOMINATIONS?

I magine that you're visiting a town you've never been to before. And imagine that you're a brand-new Christian; you've just made the exciting discovery that Jesus Christ is your personal Savior, and that His followers all around the world are your brothers and sisters.

The weekend is coming up and you want to fellowship with others of the Christian faith. Well, that shouldn't be too hard, you think, I'll look in the phone book.

So you turn in the yellow pages past Automobile parts, past Banks and Bicycle Shops—to Churches. There we are. But, what you find as a new believer, is rather overwhelming: page after page of denominations. Baptists and Presbyterians, you may have heard of them before. But Foursquare Gospel, Unitarian Universalist—what are those? It's pretty hard to find a church that's just—well, Christian.

Protestants are now divided into over 200 major denominations. And most of these church organizations are further sub-divided into many groups. There are, for example, twenty different kinds of Baptists alone, at last count.

An Anglican bishop once said, "Divided Christendom is a source of weakness in the West: in non-Christian lands it is a . . . stumbling block." This man was referring to the confusion faced by new Christian believers in Hindu or Buddhist or Muslim lands who, when they decide to follow Christ, must choose between scores of denominations all competing for their allegiance.

In the 1940s, when Jews were flocking to Palestine with the hope of someday building a new nation of Israel, Christian churches sent missionaries to that land. It seemed a great opportunity to challenge the Jewish people with the claims of Christ as their Messiah.

Around that time there were 172 Christian missionaries in Palestine, representing almost as many churches and mission societies. Some of these people worked together well. Unfortunately, some others engaged in heated battles to win new converts to their group.

Sooner or later every believer faces a disturbing question: Why so many denominations? Why so much squabbling? If Christ is supposed to bring human beings together, why have His followers split into so many factions? Why do so many different groups claim to be the One True Church?

I believe that the God who has revealed His secrets to His servants the prophets, has given us some good answers. Those answers are embedded in the book of Revelation, specifically in a vision of Christian history in chapter six. Chapter six shows us Christian history as a scroll being unfolded by God. As the scroll unfolds, four horses gallop across the sky. These four horses represent four successive ages in the history of the church.

The Lamb, or Christ, is pictured opening a series of seals; He is, in effect, unrolling the scrolls of history, giving John the Revelator views of the future. This is what John reported:

> "And I looked, and behold, a white horse. And
> He who sat on it had a bow; and a crown was

given to him, and he went out conquering and to conquer" (Revelation 6:2).

Now, white is a symbol of purity. And the one riding that horse, wearing a crown is Jesus. He goes out "conquering and to conquer." When did that happen? In the earliest days of the Christian church. The church of apostolic purity swept over the world, conquering with the gospel.

The New Testament church was like a Roman general riding on a white steed. Everyone in that era would have understood the symbol. The Early Church, with Jesus as its general, marched into the citadels of Satan and conquered.

The New Testament church was, as Paul said in Colossians 1:23, grounded and settled in the faith. They were faithful to the gospel, faithful to Bible doctrine. They endured fierce persecution, but their faith spread through the world. These people were totally committed, totally consecrated. They were like the apostles who, when ordered not to preach in Jesus name, replied, "We ought to obey God rather than men" (Acts 5:29).

One big reason almost all Christians feel a call to go back to the purity of the early church is because of people like Phileas. Phileas was executed for his faith in 306 AD at Alexandria. But before this Christian died, he left a beautiful testimony for his faith, recorded by eyewitnesses.

Phileas was young, wealthy, and came from the upper class. He'd served honorably in public affairs, and had a wife and children. Becoming a Christian involved, for Phileas, the risk of everything. But he gladly took that risk.

After his arrest, the Roman prefect of Egypt tried to persuade him to give up his faith: "Free your mind of this madness which has seized it."

Phileas calmly replied, "I have never been mad and am quite sane now."

"Very well then," the prefect replied, "sacrifice to the gods."

Phileas answered that he could sacrifice only to one God.

"What kind of sacrifices does your God like?" he was asked.

"Purity of heart, sincere faith, and truth."

During the whole ordeal of the interrogation, as this man stood before the judge with his weeping family in the courtroom, he testified eloquently for his faith.

When pressed again to give in, Phileas said, "The Savior of all our souls is Jesus Christ whom I serve in these chains . . . I have given much thought to my situation and I am determined to suffer for Christ."

Shortly afterward Phileas was beheaded. He was not alone. There were many others in the early church who gave up their lives gladly. The church historian Eusebius was an eyewitness of the suffering of believers in Egypt. He wrote: "We saw the most marvelous inspiration, a force which was truly divine, and the readiness of those who had faith in the Christ of God. Immediately when a sentence had been pronounced on one group, another party came before the tribunal . . . acknowledging themselves as Christians and remaining unmoved before dangers and torments of all kinds. Indeed, they reasoned bravely and clearly concerning the service of God . . . lighthearted and happy, they received with joy the final sentence of death. They sang hymns and offered thanksgiving to the God of all until their last breath."

No wonder Paul could make this incredible statement regarding the effectiveness of the New Testament Church: ". . . the hope of the gospel. . .you heard, which was preached to every creature under heaven" (Colossians 1:23).

The church's white-horse period was one of apostolic purity, lasting to about AD 100. And then we come to the second age of church history. It is represented in Revelation by another horse.

Look at Revelation 6:4:

> "And another horse, fiery red, went out. And it was granted to the one who sat on it to take peace from the earth, and that people should kill one another; and there was given to him a great sword."

This red-horse period represents a time of fierce persecution. Historians date this period from about AD 100 to 313—during the days of the Roman Emperors Decius and Diocletian. The ten worst years were from AD 303 to 313.

Satan saw how the Christian faith was conquering hearts and minds everywhere. So he roused pagan emperors to try to stamp it out. Believers were burned at the stake, thrown to lions, torn apart on the rack. A great bloody sword was lifted over the church.

But, remarkably, the church kept growing, believers kept multiplying. The world looked on and saw individuals who were willing to give up everything for their faith; Christians who were willing to die for what they believed. And the world took notice. It was an argument for the Christian faith that was hard to ignore. That's what moved people then and that's what moves people now. People are looking for a church that stands for principle, believers who say, "God whatever you ask me to do, I will do it."

Pagan persecution failed to destroy the Christian church. Believers only grew stronger. And so Satan decided to change his strategy. He decided he'd try to destroy the church from within. The third period in church history is represented, ominously enough, by a black horse.

Look at Revelation 6:5:

> "When He opened the third seal, I heard the third living creature say, 'Come and see.' And I looked, and behold a black horse, and he who sat on it had a pair of scales in his hand."

If the color white implies purity of faith, black represents corruption of that faith. Also the rider carries a balance scale, depicting the church weighed in the balances and found wanting.

The next verse describes wheat and barley being sold for inflated prices. It's a picture of scarcity, of famine—a vivid picture of famine for spiritual food, a famine for the Word of God, because it was lacking in the church!

The words of Amos the prophet were certainly true of this period:

> "'Behold the days are coming,' says the Lord God, 'That I will send a famine on the land, not a famine of bread, nor a thirst for water, but of hearing the words of the Lord. They shall wander from sea to sea, and from north to east; they shall run to and fro, seeking the word of the Lord, but shall not find it'" (Amos 8:11, 12).

Satan, during this period, infiltrated the church. Pagan beliefs and practices crept into the life of the church and became accepted as part of the faith. Believers compromised with their pagan environment. Gradually God's Word was replaced with tradition. The church became very powerful in the Middle Ages, as powerful as the Roman Empire once had been. It boasted great cathedrals and wielded absolute authority over believers.

Churchmen actually changed the law of God to accommodate pagans and get more people into the church. Let me give you one key example of how this happened.

When the Roman emperor Constantine publicly accepted the Christian faith in AD 312, it spelled a new day for the church. Just a few years before, believers had been thrown to the lions in Rome, and hunted down like wild animals in North Africa. But now, Christianity was accepted; soon it would become the official religion of the Roman Empire.

And so all kinds of pagans, who'd worshipped Zeus or Caesar before, now wanted to join the Christian church for obvious reasons. Unfortunately, many church leaders decided to make the transition easier by allowing the new members to hang on to some pagan ideas, images and customs.

God's command however, was clear. The second commandment is plain:

> "You shall not make for yourself any carved image, or any likeness of anything that is in heaven above, or that is in the earth beneath, or that is in the water under the earth; you shall not bow down to them nor serve them" (Exodus 20:4, 5).

The second commandment's clear teaching not to make images was compromised to accommodate the pagans.

The heathen worship of many gods and heroes, for example, eventually evolved into the veneration of saints. The cults of Diana and Isis, two female deities, made it easier to evolve into the veneration of Mary, the mother of Jesus.

Some pagan idols were given new names and brought into churches. An image dedicated to Jupiter became a statue of Peter. A fertility figure became Mary, Mother of Jesus.

Sun worship also had a very strong hold on the people of the Roman Empire. And, it didn't wither away when pagan began calling on the name of Jesus.

So, the Emperor Constantine thought of a way to make sun-worshipers feel more at home in the Christian church. In March, AD 321, he issued this decree: "On the venerable Day of the Sun let the magistrates and people residing in cities rest, and let all work shops be closed."

This was another step toward establishing Sunday as the official day of worship for Christians. Soon the church itself would forbid all work on Sunday.

What most people don't realize today is that the seventh-day, Saturday, remained the Christian day of worship for some time after Christ's death. That was the Sabbath for early believers. There is certainly no evidence for the change of the day of worship in the New Testament.

But finally church leaders decided to accommodate sun-worship. After all, they said, Sunday was also the day of the Lord's resurrection.

Now, why is this important? Does it really matter what day of the week we go to church on? Isn't God happy when we worship Him, no matter what day it is? Of course He is.

The important thing was this: what people were saying in their hearts when they began to worship on Sunday. What did this new sign of allegiance mean to them? That's what God cares about. Were they really worshipping Jesus Christ, the Creator of heaven and earth?

As we look at the history of the church, it's obvious that quite a number of its members were still worshipping someone or something besides Jesus. In the middle of the fifth century, we find Pope Leo I rebuking worshippers at St. Peter's because they kept turning around and bowing toward the sun before entering the basilica.

This mixing of pagan customs with Christian teaching greatly weakened the church.

This rather arbitrary change in the day of worship from Saturday to Sunday also contributed to another problem: the problem of church authority. The Christian church in Rome kept increasing in power and in authority for centuries to come. It became the official interpreter of Scripture. And eventually it began to persecute those who questioned its authority.

When individuals challenged the church on these points, church leaders sometimes defended their right to decree what God's truth is in a very interesting way. They pointed to the observance of Sunday. "We did that by our own authority," they said. "There's no basis for it in Scripture."

This thinking persists in some doctrinal catechisms. Catholic writer Stephen Kennan, for example, asks the question: How do you prove that the church has power to institute festivals? This is his answer:

> "Had she not such power, she could not have done that in which all modern religionists agree with her;—she could not have substituted the observance of Sunday the first day of the week, for the observance of Saturday the seventh day, a change for which there is no Scriptural authority." *A Doctrinal Catechism,* page 174.

Do you see the danger of making up our own rules, our own signs? It can become a question of allegiance. Who are we really following? If Scripture, and Scripture alone, doesn't have the last word, then we get into trouble very fast.

God does not want "baptized paganism." He calls us away from compromises with evil. He calls us back to his Word, back to his commandments, back to faithfulness to Jesus Christ.

Now let's look at the fourth horse riding across the sky in Revelation, chapter 6:

> "And I looked, and behold, a pale horse. And the name of him who sat on it was Death, and Hades followed with him. And power was given to them over a fourth of the earth, to kill with sword, with hunger, with death, and by the beasts of the earth" (Revelation 6:8).

A corpse is riding a pale horse! Rather graphic. This pictures the church at its lowest. Compromise has become spiritual death. We know that by 538 AD, church councils took the place of the Bible. Church leaders became "vicars of Christ." This period for hundreds of years is known as the Dark Ages. The stagnation was widespread; the arts didn't flourish; scholarship and learning were repressed.

During this period the church wielded the power of the state. It actually killed with the sword and with hunger. The Inquisition was one horrible example of religion using brute force to ensure orthodoxy. Outwardly the church was splendid and majestic and influential. But inwardly, was widespread death and decay.

But, as the panorama of this prophecy shows us, God knew in advance just what would happen. He knew about

Satan's future strategies. He warned his people about the dangers ahead.

What John saw was that the church that was once white with apostolic purity and a conquering force in the world had been reduced to a ghostly horse ridden by death, fleeing Hades.

From the time of the white, pure church to the red of bloody persecution, to the black period of compromise, to the pale period of spiritual death—all this took four to five hundred years, from about AD 100 to 600. That's a long period of steady decline.

Many people must have wondered, would the light of truth ever shine again? Would God's sun ever rise again?

Jesus made this fascinating statement regarding His church:

> "I will build My church, and gates of Hades shall not prevail against it" (Matthew 16:18).

Error would not triumph forever. Human traditions would not always overshadow death. Before the coming of Jesus, Revelation's prophecies would be fulfilled—the light of truth would penetrate the darkness.

Job predicted:

> "After these things I saw another angel coming down from heaven, having great authority, and the earth was illuminated with his glory" (Revelation 18:1).

Ultimately, light would penetrate darkness. One day truth would prevail.

God's truth did indeed rise again. It was championed by some very brave men and women. The roots of the Reformation really go back to 1200-1300 AD.

People like the Waldenses lived in northern Italy and

southern France. Their faithfulness to the clear teachings of God's Word provoked fierce opposition. They often had to live in caves and meet in remote mountainous regions. These people copied the Bible by hand and passed it down from generation to generation. They secretly shared the good news around Europe. They helped fan these sparks of truth into the great spiritual fire that would one day light up the Dark Ages.

The Waldenses' only creed was the Bible. Their constant appeal was to the Scriptures as the only basis of their faith. They accepted Paul's words to Timothy:

> "All Scripture is given by inspiration of God, and is profitable for doctrine, for reproof, for correction, for instruction in righteousness" (2 Timothy 3:16).

For the Waldenses, the Bible became their chief instructor, not the church. The Bible was the basis of their faith, not church tradition.

John Wycliffe, an internationally known theology professor at England's Oxford University, decided to make the Bible his guide, and the Bible alone. He translated the Bible into English, the common language of the people.

Now, if you're in a dark room and you suddenly walk out into sunlight, what happens? You can't see at first; you're blinded.

> "But the path of the just is like the shining sun, that shines ever brighter unto the perfect day." (Proverbs 4:18).

God leads His people gradually from darkness to the full light of day.

God doesn't blind us every morning. Did you ever

think of that? He doesn't just throw a switch and turn on the sun. No, we have sunrise. Slowly the dark sky begins to lighten, slowly golden light spreads toward us from the East, slowly our world turns to living color.

God's way with light is also God's way with truth. He brings it on us gradually, step by step. He does this so we can grasp it, so we're not blinded by it.

Huss and Jerome rediscovered the gospel and began to proclaim it. They were honest, committed priests who began to realize that the teachings of the New Testament were very different from many of the teachings of the church. John Huss of Bohemia rose to become chaplain to Queen Sophia and rector of the University of Prague. He remained an earnest advocate for religious enlightenment and human freedom. Church leaders silenced them in 1415 by having them both burned alive at the stake. Huss and Jerome made obedience to God their motto.

God didn't pour out all truth on one person. He blessed people like the Waldenses with the idea of God's Word as the foundation of faith. He showed John Huss and Jerome that obedience to God has to take precedence over obedience to the church. He showed Martin Luther the wonderful truth of justification by faith.

People were coming out of the Dark Ages. Important truths had been hidden for centuries. And so New Testament faith had to be rediscovered one step at a time. The lights had to come on one at a time.

The Anabaptists rediscovered the truth of adult baptism by immersion, of individual commitment to Jesus Christ.

John Wesley rediscovered the truth of sanctification, of how the Spirit works in our lives.

Early Adventists in the 1830s and 1840s rediscovered the truth of the Second Coming of Jesus Christ.

Churches formed around the people who made these discoveries, denominations formed around the new light rediscovered. New religious traditions were developed.

That's why we have many different denominations. Each one celebrates a particular rediscovery of truth.

Here is where the problem lies. God longs to restore all of His truth to His people at the end-time. God wants us to keep following light. God wants us to keep making discoveries. God has more light to give us. And churches tend to remain static. Lutherans, of course, focus on what Martin Luther taught. Calvinists talk about what John Calvin taught. Methodists want to talk about what John Wesley taught. Episcopalians and Presbyterians and Baptists want to talk about what their church traditions teach.

It's good to preserve important truths, but it's not good to build a wall around them. It's not good to stop there, when light continues to lead us forward.

God's intent was that each generation should accept the truth of earlier generations until the entire truth of God's Word would be restored. God's plan was to have a people who would put the crown jewel on the restoration of truth at the end-time. God's plan was to gather a remnant people at the end of time, to call them from all churches and to join them together in a final movement, a movement that would restore God's truth as it was known in New Testament times.

Sometimes people ask me, "Mark, what religion are you?" I say, "Well, I'm like the Waldenses because I believe the Bible and the Bible only. Don't you? And I'm kind of like Huss and Jerome because I believe in obedience to God, not man, don't you? And I'm like Lutherans because I believe that salvation comes only through faith in Jesus Christ, don't you? And I'm like a Methodist because I believe that when Christ is in your heart, a life of holiness is possible. Don't you? And I'm like an Adventist because I certainly have a hope in the Second Coming of Jesus Christ, don't you?"

The Bible teaches that there *will* be a final restoration of God's truth:

> "Go therefore and make disciples of all the nations, baptizing them in the name of the Father and of the Son and of the Holy Spirit, teaching them to observe all things that I have commanded you; and lo, I am with you always, even to the end of the age" (Matthew 28:19, 20).

Christ calls us to teach people to observe how many things? All things. All things, to the end of time.

As we come to the end-times restoration of truth will be fully restored. God's people will gather who will not compromise with paganism or with secularism. They will not be like those who tried to combine sun worship with Jesus worship. They will cling to all the symbols of loyalty to Christ, worshipping Him alone, in His way, on His Sabbath day.

John describes the last-day church:

> "Here is the patience of the saints; here are those who keep the commandments of God and the faith of Jesus" (Revelation 14:12).

These Sabbath-keeping people won't deny any of the Bible truths discovered and restored by the Baptists, Presbyterians, Methodists, and Lutherans. They will gather truths from all churches, binding them together in one last-day movement.

Jesus prophesied"

> "And other sheep I have which are not of this fold; them also I must bring, and they will hear My voice; and there will be one flock and one shepherd" (John 10:16).

Jesus is saying, "At the end of time I've got to gather Catholics; they have a lot of truth. I've got to gather those Presbyterians; lots of truth in those Presbyterians. I've got to gather those Baptists; much truth in the Baptists. I've got to gather all my sheep, for there will be one fold and one shepherd. I'll gather them under the banner of Truth.

Revelation talks about God's last-day people. So does Isaiah:

> "You shall raise up the foundations of many generations; and you shall be called the Repairer of the Breach, The Restorer of Streets to Dwell In" (Isaiah 58:12).

There's been a breach in the wall, a breach in the wall of God's commandments. The Antichrist power, the Little Horn power, the papacy, tried to change the law. But God says I'm going to repair that break in the law.

Isaiah goes on:

> "If you turn away your foot from the Sabbath, from doing your pleasure on My holy day, and call the Sabbath a delight, the holy day of the Lord honorable . . . Then you shall delight yourself in the Lord; and I will cause you to ride on the high hills of the earth . . ." (Isaiah 58:13, 14).

Here we see the Sabbath as a symbol of loyalty to God, a part of his law, his Ten Commandments. He asks his people to honor it. That's a way to repair the breach, the break in his law. That's part of the assignment given to God's last-day movement.

Revelation 12:17 describes that last-day movement, the remnant church in this way:

> "And the dragon was engraged with the woman, and he went to make war with the rest of her offspring, who keep the commandments of God and have the testimony of Jesus Christ."

God's Biblical principles, his true doctrines, are restored by the remnant church. This isn't just another denomination. This is a divine movement of destiny.

God is calling people today. He's calling people in all churches, from all faiths and creeds. He wants a remnant that is true to him. He wants a church that believes what the Waldenses believed, that God's Word is true. He wants a church that champions what Martin Luther championed: justification by faith alone. He wants a church that accepts the Baptist truth of baptism by immersion. He wants a church that accepts the Methodist truth of holiness in the Christian life, a church that makes people healthy and whole in every area of their lives, a church that's an Adventist church, awaiting the coming of Christ, a church that's a Sabbath-keeping church, repairing that breach in the wall, restoring all of God's truth.

Friend, I believe Jesus is speaking to you right now. You didn't start to read this book by accident. You may have been a faithful Christian for some time. But now God is calling you to something more. You've discovered new truths. You see the truth of the Bible's Sabbath. You see the truth of God's plan for a last-day people. And God is asking you to do something about it.

You may have concerns right now. You may have worries. You might think, "I may lose my job over the Sabbath."

My father stepped out in faith, and he did lose his job. But God gave him a better one. God does indeed supply all our needs according to his riches.

Friend, I'm a Seventh-day Adventist today not because I was born one. I was born in a wonderful Roman Catholic home. But as I studied the book of Revelation I realized that God was leading me to step out from what man teaches and to follow what Jesus teaches. I had to move beyond human customs and traditions and follow the Bible alone. I listened to these same truths you have been reading in this book—and I had no idea how dramatically these truths would change my life.

But I made a decision. I wanted to be part of God's last-day movement. And I've never looked back. I've never regretted it for a moment. It has opened up for me a wonderful life.

Would you like to say to Jesus, "Lord I want to follow you all the way. I want to make a decision for truth. I'm so thankful I can be part of Jesus' final movement. ❏

22
REVELATION'S LAST APPEAL
THE MYSTERY OF
BABYLON REVEALED

When Pastor Freeman spoke, the 2000 people at Faith Assembly Church listened very carefully, took notes, and nodded in agreement. His sermons lasted an hour, sometimes two. But the congregation hung on every word, and took his messages as authority.

Pastor Freeman had the right credentials. He'd been a professor at Grace Theological Seminary in Indiana. He seemed dedicated, "the genius behind Faith Assembly." He could never be replaced!

Yet this pastor led his congregation into a terrible tragedy. Some 80 people, many of them children, died as a result of following his teachings.

Pastor Freeman didn't lead anyone off to the jungle to commit suicide. He didn't arm his parishioners in some compound and then set it ablaze. No, he simply insisted it was a sin to go to a doctor. He taught that all medicine is evil and satanic, and that every illness or injury can be cured by a positive confession of faith.

Members of the Faith Assembly sect followed this teaching to the letter. No doctor visits. No pre-natal care. They refused immunizations and removed seat belts from their cars.

When people died, it was assumed they didn't have enough faith. The death toll increased. Faith Assembly women were 100 times more likely to die giving birth, than women in the general population—their babies were three times more likely to die.

Finally, Pastor Freeman and other church members were indicted on charges of aiding and inducing reckless homicide. When the news broke people wondered: How could this possibly happen in a Christian church? How could apparently sincere believers follow a man like this?

That question will become increasingly important in the end-time of earth's history. How can we be sure whom we're really following? How can we be sure that we're clinging to the "everlasting gospel" and not some distortion of the gospel?

The book of Revelation reveals truth and exposes error. It is God's safeguard against deception. God does not want us to be deceived. He longs for us to be protected by His truth.

In Revelation, the Apostle John tells the tale of two women. One dressed in pure white represents the purity of the true faith and doctrine. This woman represents the faithful believers who have loved Jesus Christ, kept His commandments, and been obedient to Him down through the ages.

Revelation 17 pictures another woman, but now the opposite picture. Who is this woman in scarlet? What does it mean that she rides on a Beast? What about the name on her forehead, "Mystery, Babylon the Great?" What about the cup in her hands full of wine and abominations?

John, the Revelator, tells us:

> "Come, I will show you the judgment of the great harlot . . . So he carried me away in the Spirit into the wilderness. And I saw a woman

sitting on a scarlet beast which was full of
names of blasphemy, having seven heads and
ten horns" (Revelation 17:1-3).

We know—as shown above and from many other
verses—that in the Bible, a woman symbolizes a church.
The "woman in white" is Christ's bride, the true church.
But just as a pure woman represents a pure church, a corrupt woman represents a corrupt church. The angel calls
the woman riding the Beast a "whore" or harlot. She symbolizes a false or fallen church. Daniel 7:17 and 23 tells us
that a beast represents a king or a kingdom. This woman,
riding and controlling the Beast, dominates the kings or
kingdoms of the earth.

John describes this fallen woman who has left her
true Lover:

> "The woman was arrayed in purple and
> scarlet, and adorned with gold and precious
> stones and pearls, having in her hand a golden
> cup full of abominations and the filthiness of
> her fornication" (Revelation 17:4).

She's a fallen church because she teaches false doctrines, yet she's here described as a rich church with gorgeous display. She's also a large, worldwide church, for
Revelation 17:1 and 15 says she sits on "many waters,"
explained earlier as being many "peoples, and multitudes, and nations, and tongues." She passes around a
wine cup full of false doctrines, and the multitudes
drinking from it become deceived, "drunk with the wine
of her fornication" (verse 2).

God gives many clues to help us identify this false
church, such as Revelation 17:9 and 18, telling us she sits
in a "great city" located on "seven mountains."

But, John says something very interesting about her:

"And on her forehead a name was written: MYSTERY, BABYLON THE GREAT, THE MOTHER OF HARLOTS AND OF THE ABOMINATIONS OF THE EARTH" (Revelation 17:5).

Whoever this woman is, this fallen church, whose colors are purple and scarlet, something significant is written on her forehead, and it is "Mystery, Babylon the Great."

Long before John wrote the book of Revelation, the ancient city of Babylon had been completely destroyed and never rebuilt. For centuries it lay in ruins and had faded into insignificance. But whoever this woman is in Revelation 17, she revives the same pagan teachings that ancient Babylon taught ages ago. She baptizes them and brings them into the Christian church.

"God forbid!" you say. How could principles from pagan Babylon be baptized and brought into the Christian church through this fallen woman, the harlot of Revelation 17?

Truth is stranger than fiction. The Bible urges us to understand her mystery, for written on her forehead is the name "Mystery, Babylon the Great." This means we're going to have to go back and learn something about the ancient city of Babylon in the Old Testament. We'll need to compare its heathen philosophy to what we see in the religious world today. Why? This great, rich church sitting in a city on seven mountains revives and sanctifies the old principles of Babylon!

Revelation 17:2 describes this harlot: "with whom the kings of the earth committed fornication. . ." She has influence over the kings of the earth, great influence over heads of state. They come to her city on seven mountains, and they bow before her, having "lived luxuriously with her" Revelation 18:9.

Some reading these pages may have been drinking the wine of Babylon without even knowing it. Which organ of the body does wine immediately affect? It immediately affects the brain, so people cannot think as clearly.

In 1 Timothy 4:1 and 2 Timothy 4:3,4, Paul warns that in the last days of earth's history false doctrines will be rampant

People who have been taught those false doctrines have difficulty understanding the truth. Indeed, we see that problem all around us today. After the harlot passes out her wine of false doctrines, men and women are deceived and can hardly understand the plain truths of God's Word. It's only the pure, unadulterated Word of God that can sober people up so they can see issues clearly and not be spiritually drunk.

So the Book of Revelation presents a clear contrast. The woman in white of Revelation 12 is God's true church—men and women who love Jesus Christ and respond obediently to keep His commandments. In Revelation 17, we have the system of falsehood revealed. The wine of Babylon, the false doctrines that men and women drink, confuses the mind.

But what does "Mystery, Babylon the Great" mean? Let's study ancient Babylon to learn how Satan would work through paganism to bring the principles of old Babylon into the Christian church under the symbol of the fallen woman of Revelation 17.

What are the first four letters of the word

"Babylon"? They're "baby". Why do we call a baby a "baby"? Because it babbles—it speaks in confused speech.

The Bible says that after the flood, a great tower was built. Was that tower built by man or by God? It was built by man as a "do-it-yourself" salvation project. After the flood, human beings—in defiance of God—built the great Tower of Babel. They wanted to save themselves, without relying on God, if the world were again destroyed by a flood.

In Babylon, Genesis 11:1-9 tells us, God confused their language. The project was going well: brick men were passing bricks, mortar men were putting on mortar—until God confused the language! As a result, the tower was abandoned and people scattered throughout the earth.

So here in the last book of the Bible, "Babylon" is a spiritual term referring to confusion—not the confusion of languages as in old Babylon but religious confusion as the church drifted away from God's Word.

As a variety of false doctrines entered the church, more and more people became confused. Jesus said in John 17:17 that "Your [God's] Word is truth." But the teachings of men bring only confusion, and "Babylon" denotes confusion.

Babylon was an ancient city. If you want to locate the ruins of old Babylon, look on a map about a thousand miles east of Jerusalem and sixty miles south of Baghdad, the capital of Iraq.

If we're going to understand Mystery, Babylon the Great, that false system in Revelation 17, we need to know something about this ancient city of Babylon. How was it built? What did Babylonians believe? And have these beliefs, through a series of compromises, found their way into Christianity and the Christian church?

Let's go back to the founding of Babylon:

> "Cush begot Nimrod; he began to be a mighty one on the earth. He was a mighty hunter before the Lord . . . And the beginning of his kingdom was Babel" (Genesis 10:8-10).

Students of ancient history know that Nimrod was considered to be a god. It's rather interesting, don't you think, that Babylon was founded by a man considered to be a god?

Centuries later, Daniel describes the arrogant pride of Babylon's King Nebuchadnezzar:

> "The king spoke, saying, 'Is not this great Babylon, that I have built for a royal dwelling by my mighty power and for the honor of my majesty'" (Daniel 4:30)?

King Nebuchadnezzar ruled as the god of Babylon. In fact, King Nebuchadnezzar commanded worship after he built that huge image described in Daniel, chapter three. All the Babylonian leaders represented God in the city of Babylon. So Babylon was a great city whose human leaders said they represented God to the people. It was the greatest city of the world, a city that kings came to.

John wrote:

> ". . .The woman [the false church] whom you saw is that great city which reigns over the kings of the earth" (Revelation 17:18).

In the Old Testament, ancient Babylon was also a "great city "that reigned" over the kings of the earth."

Revelation 17 says there would be a corrupt

woman—a harlot symbolizing a false church—who took up residence in the "great city" of Rome. In New Testament times, the Empire that ruled from the city of Rome was a great world power.

In the Christmas story we read every year, Caesar decreed that "all the world should be taxed" (Luke 2:1, KJV). At the time when John penned Revelation in AD 96, he knew as well as anyone that Rome was "that great city which reigns [present tense] over the kings of the earth."

Is there a city in the world today that was built on seven mountains? Indeed, Rome is proverbial as "the city built on seven hills!" Are the colors in that Roman Church purple and scarlet? Indeed, they are. And is there a leader in that church who considers himself to be the prime representative of God, the vicar of God, or God on earth? Indeed, there is.

The apostle Peter could not have been referring to literal Babylon when he wrote in 1 Peter 5:13 that: "She who is in Babylon . . . greets you. . ." In Peter's day no church or any other human institution existed in the desolate ruins of ancient Babylon. He was referring to Rome.

It's easy to see why Jews and early Christians used "Babylon" as a code word or nickname for Rome, for there are many striking parallels between the twin cities of literal Babylon of ancient times and figurative "Babylon" or Rome.

Consider just a few: Both Babylon and Rome were dominant warring powers of their day. Both completely destroyed and devastated the city of Jerusalem. Rome was Babylon all over again. As Babylon's "carbon copy," Rome provides a perfect example of history repeating itself!

Just as the word of Nebuchadnezzar became law rather than the Word of the Bible, so likewise, tradition would take the place of the Bible under the Roman system.

Did that happen? Let's go to the book, *Catholic Belief*, by the Roman Catholic scholar, Father Joseph Faa di Bruno:

> "Like two sacred rivers flowing from Paradise, the Bible and divine Tradition contain the Word of God, the precious gems of revealed truths. Though these two divine streams are in themselves, on account of their divine origin, of equal sacredness, and are both full of revealed truths, still, of the two, tradition is to us more clear and safe" (page 45).

Do you agree that tradition—the customs and practices of man—is clearer and safer than the Bible? "Babylon" is a Bible term that represents confusion. Is it not confusion to say that tradition is "more clear and safe" than the Bible? But Rome dares to hold tradition above the Bible.

Observe the outward manifestations of those who recognize the earthly head of the Roman Catholic hierarchy. How do they speak about him, and how do they act around him? They call him "Holy Father"—a title belonging to God alone.

Christ commanded:

> "Do not call anyone on earth your father [in a spiritual sense]; for One is your Father, He who is in heaven" (Matthew 23:9).

Jesus used the term "Holy Father" when praying in John 17:11, but He used it to refer to His heavenly Father, the almighty God of the universe. For any mere mortal to accept such a title is blasphemy.

But devout Roman Catholics not only refer to the

Pope with exalted titles like "His Holiness," they treat him with a respect that's elevated to reverence. They bow before him, fall on their knees before him, kneel at his feet to kiss his ring, etc. There are many churches in the Christian communion, but in no other instance do we find that the earthly leader or president of the church is bowed down to and, presumably, worshipped.

In strong contrast Peter, supposedly the first Pope, according to Catholic teaching, did *not* accept worship from a fellow mortal when Cornelius fell down at his feet: "As Peter was coming in, Cornelius met him and fell down at his feet and worshipped him. But Peter lifted him up, saying, 'Stand up; I myself am also a man'" (Acts 10:25, 26).

John records his experience with an angel: "And I fell at his feet to worship him. But he said to me, 'See that you do not do that! I am your fellow servant, . . .Worship God'" (Revelation 19:10)!

Note that kneeling at a person's feet is equated with "worship" in the Bible—the inner worship is reflected in the outward action. Note also that Peter and even a heavenly angel refused to allow men to bow down to or worship them—yet both ancient and modern Babylon approve the worship of an earthly leader.

The Bible says Jesus Christ is the only One who can be our Head, the only One who can forgive our sins, the only One before whose nail-pierced feet we should kneel, the only One whose blood was shed to save us.

What else do we discover about Babylon? Only as we understand ancient Babylon can we finally understand the Book of Revelation. Many don't understand Revelation because they don't understand the comparative symbols. All other books in the Bible find their focal point and final culmination in the Book of Revelation. Revelation must not be studied in isolation, like an island to itself, for it ties together all the books of the Bible.

What does "Mystery, Babylon the Great" mean? What does the Old Testament tell us about Babylonian practices?

In Ezekiel, God says:

> "Then your altars shall be desolate, your incense altars shall be broken, and I will cast down your slain men before your idols" (Ezekiel 6:4).

Babylon was the center of idol worship. Anyone walking through Babylon, would see idols everywhere—representing the pagan gods.

Remember God's words:

> "You shall not make for yourself any carved image . . . you shall not bow down to them nor serve them" (Exodus 20:4, 5).

Yet, Babylon was the center of idol or image worship!

Dr. Alexander Hislop, in his classic study, *The Two Babylons,* says: "Babylon was the primal source from which all these systems of idolatry flowed."

"Oh," someone says, "but I don't believe the image is God. I just believe the image represents God." And that is precisely what the second commandment forbids!

Notice, "Thou shalt not make unto thee any graven image, or any likeness of any thing that is in heaven." In other words, the image is a likeness—a representation—of something in heaven that you worship through. "Don't make any likeness of anything that's in heaven above, or that's in earth beneath, or that's in the water under the earth.

Don't bow down to them, nor serve them." But ancient Babylon used images in its worship to represent what was up in heaven.

Historian Henry Thomas Buckle wrote:

> "The adoration of idols that is in Babylon and paganism was succeeded by the adoration of saints" (*The History of Civilization,* Volume 1, page 188).

The worship of the virgin Mary was substituted for the worship of the virgin goddess Diana and other pagan divinities. Yes, the ancient pagans worshipped idols, but often the same idols were used to adore the saints when the pagans came into the Christian church.

We know what God says in the second commandment. But note what Cardinal Gibbons, Catholic Archbishop of Baltimore, said about image worship: "By the images which we kiss and before which we uncover our heads or kneel, we adore Christ and venerate His saints."

In other words, the images are important vehicles of worship. Ancient Babylon had them, modern Rome has them.

But there is more. Here's an amazing statement archaeologists have just uncovered written by Nabopolassar, the king of Babylon, Nebuchadnezzar's father: "At the time Marduk [the chief god of Babylon] commanded me to build the tower of Babel which had become weakened by time and fallen into disrepair [by the time of Nabopolassar, the ancient Tower of Babel was in ruins] He commanded me to ground its base securely on the breast of the underworld, whereas its pinnacle should strain upwards to the skies."

Pagan Babylon had two major teachings that influenced the Christian Church. The first major teaching was that immortal spirits lived in the underworld. The second major teaching was that the sun, the brightest luminary god in the heavens, was to be worshipped. That's why when the temple tower of Marduk was built, it had its roots in the immortal souls or spirits of the "underworld," and it pointed toward the sky.

Note what the heavenly Messenger says to Ezekiel:

> "And He said to me, "'Turn again, and you will see greater abominations that they are doing.' So He brought me to the door of the north gate of the Lord's house; and to my dismay, women were sitting there weeping for Tammuz" (Ezekiel 8:13,14).

They were doing abominations in the Lord's house! And who was Tammuz? Tammuz was the Babylonian god of vegetation.

Why were the women committing abomination in the Lord's house by weeping for this pagan god? They believed that Tammuz died annually when summer came and dried up their crops. But they also believed his immortal spirit descended to the underworld. Therefore, the women wept because the heat was drying the crops, and they wanted the dead god to awake and cause their crops once again to flourish.

So the idea that when people die, they're not really dead—that their soul is immortal and their immortal spirit leaves man at death—can be traced back to ancient Babylon. All of the ancient pagan religions—without exception—had the idea that the soul, or man's essential being, was immortal.

A number of months ago I was inside one of the pyramids in Egypt. The ancient pyramids were memorials and burial chambers for the dead. When Pharaoh died, his servants were slain and buried with him so they could serve him in the spirit world. For the Babylonians and Egyptians believed that when a person died, he wasn't really dead. The Egyptian pyramids were great monuments, great houses for the dead to hold their immortal spirits. But the heathen idea of man's soul being naturally immortal is a pagan doctrine! It comes from Egypt and Babylon, not the Bible.

William E. Gladstone, four-time Prime Minister of Great Britain and a theologian, said:

> "The doctrine of natural, as distinguished from Christian, immortality . . . crept into the Church, by a back door."

How could that happen? What does the Bible say happens to people when they die? The Bible is very clear, as we studied earlier in chapter 14.

The Psalmist wrote:

> "The dead do not praise the Lord, nor any who go down into silence" (Psalm 115:17).

The Bible says the dead don't praise the Lord—but if they were awake and conscious, the saved would be forever praising Him! The words soul and spirit appear in the Bible 1600 times, but never once are they declared to be immortal! The Bible says death is but a "sleep" 53 times. But through Babylonian and Egyptian paganism, through the pagan philosophy of the Greeks, the idea of the immortality of the soul came into the Christian church.

The Bible says the dead don't know anything! They're

unconscious—sleeping a dreamless sleep until Jesus calls them from the tomb. Egypt and Babylon contradict God and say that the dead know everything. But where did those ancient pagans get the false notion of man's "immortal soul?"

The Genesis story tells us that the Great Deceiver told the first lie:

> "And the serpent said to the woman, 'You will not surely die'" (Genesis 3:4).

Satan told Eve in Eden that she wouldn't really die, that she was immortal.

The diabolical idea of an immortal spirit began in Eden, was imbedded in Babylonian and Egyptian paganism, passed to pagan Rome, who passed it on to papal Rome when pagans became quasi-Christians and joined the church. Sadly, this pagan doctrine was also adopted by many Protestants.

Babylon is a great religious power with a mortal leader whose tradition is above the Bible. It's a religious power where the leader's words are accepted over the words of the Bible. It's a city that has images all through it. It's a city that practices the worship of the dead and leads people to worship the immortal spirits of people who have gone on. All of this comes not from New Testament Christianity, not from the Bible, but from Babylon!

Here's Ezekiel speaking again:

> "So He brought me into the inner court of the Lord's house; and there, at the door of the temple of the Lord, between the porch and the altar, were about twenty-five men with their backs toward the temple of the Lord and their

faces toward the east, and they were worshipping the sun toward the east" (Ezekiel 8:16).

What were these worshippers doing with their backs toward God's temple and their faces toward the east? They were worshipping the sun!

In ancient Babylon as well as in ancient Egypt, the idea of sun worship was very, very common. The ancient Babylonian tower temples, called ziggurats, were huge step-like pyramids which had steps to the top of the temples. On the top summit was a flat area where worshipers would hold their hands up to the sun and worship it. They didn't worship the Creator. They mistakenly believed the sun was responsible for life.

Sir James G. Frazer, gives us this statement:

> "In ancient Babylonia the sun was worshipped from immemorial antiquity" (*The Worship of Nature,* Volume 1, page 529).

It's interesting that not only did Egypt and Babylon worship the sun, but the Romans did too. Constantine, the pagan Roman emperor, worshipped the sun. On one side of Constantine's coins was his own picture; on the other side was that of the sun god — *Sol Invictus,* "the invincible Sun."

Later, after he became a nominal Christian, he minted coins with Christ represented on one side, but on the opposite side of the coin he still kept the sun god! It's as if Constantine, still a pagan at heart, wanted to wed paganism and Christianity when he became a Christian.

Arthur P. Stanley wrote: "His [Constantine's] coins bore on the one side the letters of the name of Christ; on the other, the figure of the sun god, as if he could not bear to relinquish the patronage of the bright luminary" *(The*

History of the Eastern Church, page 184).

From time to time people say to me, "Mark, you talk and write about Jesus and His Second Coming, but you've also talked a great deal about the Bible Sabbath. Why?"

Now are you beginning to see why! The Book of Revelation describes a church clothed in purple and scarlet that would perpetuate the ancient pagan principles of Babylon. The entire world would sip the wine of her polluted teachings. Well-meaning Christians would be inebriated with the spiritual intoxication of Rome. Unknowingly, they'd worship the sun god that came down from Babylon and Egypt into pagan Rome, then through papal Rome, and into the Protestant churches.

Unwittingly, they'd accept the doctrine that the soul is immortal. And thus they would worship at the shrine of pagan philosophy. Their minds would be receptive at the time of the end for Satan's almost overwhelming delusion, as he grabs the attention of the world through the phenomenal wonders of spiritualism. Both the ancient Egyptians and the Babylonians believed that the spirits of the dead could come back—if you believe the soul is immortal, who's to say it cannot communicate with the living? Your mind would then be open for the great deceptions in the end-time.

The Book of Revelation leads us from Babylonian errors to God's truth in His Word. I don't want to accept errors that began in Babylon and Egypt, then spread to pagan Rome and later papal Rome, sanctified by a little holy water sprinkled on them as they came into the church.

Lewis Brown says:

"One cannot well refer to those cults of

Babylon and Egypt and the rest as dead religions" (*The Believing World,* page 112).

Babylon and Ancient Egypt are not dead? I thought they were destroyed! He says you can't refer to those cults of Babylon and Egypt and the rest as dead religions! "For the echo of their ancient thunder is still to be heard reverberating in almost every form of faith existing today." Ancient Babylonian image worship is in the church today. Ancient Babylonian sun worship is there. Ancient Babylonian belief in the immortality of the soul is there. Yes, the echo of that thunder is still heard in the church today.

Alexander Hislop, says:

> "To conciliate the pagans to nominal Christianity, Rome, pursuing its usual policy, took measures to get the Christian and pagan festivals [that's the Sabbath and Sunday] amalgamated, and to get paganism and Christianity—now far sunk in idolatry—in this as in so many other things, to shake hands" (*The Two Babylons,* page 105).

In the early centuries, the Pope of Rome united with the pagan leaders and Constantine, and thus the pagan sun day was substituted for the Christian Sabbath, and Satan again believed he had a triumph in the word.

Catholic William Gildea, wrote:

> "The Sun was a foremost god with heathendom. . . . The sun has worshippers at this hour in Persia and other lands. . . . There is in truth, something royal, kingly about the sun, making it a fit emblem of Jesus, the Sun of Justice. Hence the church in these countries

would seem to have said, to 'Keep that old pagan name [Sunday]. It shall remain consecrated, sanctified.' And thus the pagan Sunday dedicated to Balder, became the Christian Sunday, sacred to Jesus" (*The Catholic World,* March, 1894, page 809).

In other words, baptize it. It needs no command of God—no "Remember Sunday to keep it holy"—nothing at all, though it admittedly came through pagan Babylonian sources!

Revelation 17 predicted men and women in the last days would be confused and have great difficulty solving the mystery of "Babyon the Great." We are letting historians help us uncover this mystery.

Arthur P. Stanley observed:

> "The retention of the old pagan name of Dies Solis, for Sunday is, in a great measure, owing to the union of pagan and Christian sentiment with which the first day of the week was recommended by Constantine to his subjects— pagan and Christian alike—as the 'venerable' day of the sun" (*History of The Eastern Church,* page 184).

Dr. Edward Hiscox, author of *The Baptist Manual,* speaking to the Baptist convention, said this:

> "What a pity that it [Sunday] comes branded with the mark of paganism [Dr. Hiscox knew it came from Babylon and Egypt] and christened with the name of the sun god [Dr. Hiscox knew it was named for the sun god] then adopted and sanctioned by the papal apostasy and bequeathed as a sacred legacy to Protestants."

Where did Baptists, Lutherans, Methodists, Episcopalians, and Pentecostals get Sunday? They got it from the papal apostasy. Where did the papal apostasy get it? From the pagan Romans who were worshipping the sun god. Where did they get it? They got it from the pagans in Babylon and Egypt!

The Bible at the time of the end calls men and women back to the true faith, to the pure woman of Revelation 12. It calls them from partaking of the harlot's intoxicating wine of false doctrine.

It's amazing to me that there are over 100 texts in the Bible on the Bible Sabbath, yet someone still asks, "What's wrong with Sunday?" It's amazing to me that the Bible says, "The dead know not anything: and won't get their rewards till Christ returns," yet people say, "My loved one looks down on me from heaven." It's amazing to me that the Bible says, "Thou shalt not worship any graven image," and someone says, "Oh, that doesn't mean images of saints. You can bow down before them"

The wine of Babylon circulates freely today. Men and women are confused. Oh, how thankful I am for God's Word. How thankful I am that the Book of Revelation promises a last-day movement that will gather the honest in heart together.

In contrast to the pagan Sunday, God says in Ezekiel:

> "Moreover I also gave them My Sabbaths, to be a sign between them and Me, that they might know that I am the Lord who sanctifies them" (Ezekiel 20:12).

When the Egyptians were worshipping the sun, Moses was keeping the Bible Sabbath. When the

Babylonians were worshipping the sun, Daniel was keeping the Bible Sabbath. When the Romans were worshipping the sun, Paul was keeping the Bible Sabbath. And today, when the world is confused over this issue and has accepted a pagan philosophy from ancient Babylon and modern Rome, God's people again will be keeping the Bible Sabbath!

God, in Revelation, calls men and women out of the confusion of the last days.

Note John repeating the voice of the angel:

> "'Babylon the great is fallen, is fallen, and has become a habitation of demons . . . For all the nations have drunk of the wine of the wrath of her fornication . . . ' And I heard another voice from heaven saying, 'Come out of her, my people'" (Revelation 18:2-4).

Where does the voice come from? From heaven. If God tells us something from heaven, what should we do? We listen! Are some of Jesus' people in Babylon? Indeed, they are! Many of Jesus' people are in Babylon. Wonderful Catholic and Baptist Christians, Methodist Christians, Pentecostal Christians, Episcopal Christians, and Church of Christ Christians. And other groups! And God calls them "My People!"

Have you been drinking, unknowingly, from the wine cup of Babylon? Have you been even sipping? Are you confused, religiously? Someone says, "You know, I'm a little confused over what I've been reading in this book." Maybe it's because you've drunk the wine of Babylon and God wants to sober you up to hear the truth of God's Word.

The angel says in Revelation 18:4: "'Come out of

her, My people, lest you share in her sins, and lest you receive of her plagues.'" God is calling you out of Babylon with a desperate urgency!

God is calling you out from any system that teaches the errors of old Babylonian and Egyptian philosophy. God is leading you from baptized paganism to a holy Christianity. God is leading you, guiding you from baptized paganism to the truth of the living Word of God.

I agree with Cardinal Gibbons when he wrote:

> "Reason and sense demand the acceptance of one or the other of these alternatives: either Protestantism and the keeping holy of Saturday, or Catholicity and the keeping holy of Sunday. Compromise is impossible" (*Catholic Mirror*, December 23, 1893).

Do you believe that in these issues of paganism in the Christian Church, compromise is impossible? The church baptized Sunday. It came through pagan sources, but the church accepted it. You can accept it only *if* you say tradition is above the Bible. But the Cardinal says, "Compromise is impossible."

But John says:

> "Babylon is fallen, is fallen. . . .Come out of her, My people" (Revelation 14:12; 18:4).

In the end-time, before Jesus returns, He once again will have proclaimed the original truths of Scripture corrupted by Roman Babylon. Once again His church will be led from the traditions of men to the word of God.

When the mighty voice warns, "Babylon is fallen," God doesn't say, "Remain right where you are and compromise for the sake of peace." He calls to His people, "Come out!"

The only way to be safe is to come out! Babylon is fallen! The plagues of God will fall upon Babylon! God is calling you to come out. He says, "Come out of her . . . lest you receive of her plagues" (Revelation 18:4).

So many of you are wonderful Christians, but before you read this book, you never knew how so many pagan teachings came into the church. You never understood how corrupt many church teachings had become. But many of you, sensing the leading of Jesus in your life, have made the decision to follow Christ all the way in baptism, to become part of His last-day church. Not just any church, any denomination, but the remnant church of God, a church leading men and women back to keeping His commandments and teaching Scriptural truths again.

God brought you to this moment of destiny in your life. God loves you more than you can comprehend. He wants you on His side—and by His side. He wants you united with Him so He can spend eternity with you. Tell Him that is where you want to be. ❏

23

REVELATION'S MARK OF THE BEAST EXPOSED

S ome people are so afraid of it they try to avoid
having a social security number.

Some people think about it whenever they go
through the grocery store check out. That machine scanning those bar codes, permitting them to buy groceries,
what could be behind it all?

Some people worry about it whenever they give personal information to some distant data-crunching computer.

Our topic, the mark of the beast, has inspired a great
deal of speculation, and a flury of strange ideas.

But the fact remains it's one of the vital subjects in
the book of Revelation. Intense interest in the subject is
has been building for decades. We see the phrase "mark
of the beast" and the mysterious number associated with
it, 666, displayed everywhere, from movie marquees to
paperback book covers.

And we have many questions. Is the beast a person?
Is the beast a system or some organization? Who is the
beast? What's the mark? What does 666 mean? And how
can I avoid that mark?

God does not leave us in the dark. The book of
Revelation will give us some clear answers. John wrote:

> "Then I stood on the sand of the sea. And I
> saw a beast rising up out of the sea, having
> seven heads and ten horns, and on his horns

ten crowns, and on his heads a blasphemous name" (Revelation 13:1).

Although this beast may appear ghastly at first, remember we're dealing with symbols. Today we speak of America as an eagle and Russia as a bear. Those are symbols that represent nations, powers in the world.

Revelation is describing here a great power which rises up out of the sea.

We learned in chapter 15 that the "sea" or "waters" represent nations, or people.

The beast has seven heads and ten crowns. It covers seven historic periods, with ten kingdoms supporting it. Since it is speaking blasphemy, or words against God, it is apparently a religious power. The description continues:

> "Now the beast which I saw was like a leopard, his feet were like the feet of a bear, and his mouth like the mouth of a lion" (Revelation 13:2).

Here is pictured a composite beast. John uses the same symbols that Daniel used in his description of great world powers. He symbolized Babylon as a lion, Medo-Persia as a bear, Greece as a leopard, and the Roman Empire as a dragon-like beast.

This beast of Revelation 13 succeeds this outline of world history. We're going to look at seven clues which identify the beast power.

CLUE NUMBER ONE

Look at the last part of Revelation 13:2.

> "And the dragon gave him his power, his throne and great authority."

Whoever the beast is of Revelation 13, where does he get his power from? The dragon. Where does he get his throne of government from? The dragon. Where does he get great authority from? The dragon. And who does the dragon represent? Pagan Rome.

But someone says, I thought the dragon was a symbol of Satan? It is. But Satan always has to work through some earthly institution. So, in Revelation 12:9, it identifies the dragon as Satan. But Satan works through human agencies. In Revelation 12, the dragon working through pagan Rome, attempted to destroy Jesus, the man child. A Roman official tried to kill baby Jesus. A Roman governor condemned Jesus. A Roman executioner crucified Jesus. A Roman emblem sealed Jesus' tomb. And a Roman guard watched that tomb. So, in Revelation 12, the dragon represents Satan working through pagan Rome to destroy Jesus.

After pagan Rome fell apart, pagan Rome gave its government or its seat of authority to somebody. Who did the pagan Roman government give its seat of authority to?

Professor Labianca, professor of history in a university in Rome says: "To the succession of the Caesar's came the succession of the pontiffs in Rome."

Constantine, seeing that the Roman empire was falling apart, moved his headquarters to Constantinople. And he gave his seat of government in Rome to the pope of Rome.

Arthur P. Stanley describes the shift from a political power to a religious hierarchy:

> "The popes filled the place of the vacant emperors of Rome, inheriting their power, prestige, and titles from paganism . . . The papacy is

> but the ghost of the deceased Roman Empire, sitting crowned upon its grave" (*Stanley's History,* page 40).

Pagan Rome gave its authority over to papal Rome. That's the first clue identifying the beast.

CLUE NUMBER TWO

This power in Revelation 13 would become primarily a worldwide religious power, as well as a political power. Revelation 13:8 says,

> "All who dwell on the earth will worship him, whose names have not been written in the Book of Life of the Lamb slain from the foundation of the world."

All who dwell on earth will worship him—a universal power that initiates worship. A universal religious power that transcends geographical boundaries. This is the second clue to the identity of the beast.

CLUE NUMBER THREE

The power is described in Revelation 13:5, "as a mouth speaking great things and blasphemies"

Remember that Christ himself was accused of blasphemy. Why? Because he claimed to be one with God. If Jesus hadn't been divine he would have been guilty of blasphemy.

Compare the following documents:

> "The Pope is of so great dignity and so exalted that he is not a mere man, but as it were God, and the vicar of God" (Extracts from Lucius Ferraris, "Papa II" (art.), *Prompta Bibliotheca,* vol. 6 pages 25-29).

Ferraris is quoting an encyclical letter:

"We hold upon this earth the place of God Almighty" (*Encyclical Letters of Leo XIII,* page 304).

These claims give us clue number three as to the identity of the beast.

Another part of this identity of the beast as a power who speaks blasphemies, is his claim to forgive sins.

When Jesus said he forgave a certain man's sins, the Pharisees were furious. They claimed that Jesus spoke blasphemy. Mark 2:7 records their response: "Why does this Man speak blasphemies like this? Who can forgive sins but God alone?"

For a change, the Pharisees were correct! Only God can forgive sins. The Pharisees just couldn't grasp the concept that God, in the person of Christ, was among them.

Read for yourself the claims of the Roman Church:

"Seek where you will, through Heaven and earth, and you will find but one created being who can forgive the sinner . . . That extraordinary being is the priest, the Catholic priest" (*The Catholic Priest,* pages 78, 79).

"God Himself is obliged to abide by the judgment of His priest, and either not to pardon or to pardon, according as they refuse or give absolution . . . The sentence of the priest precedes, and God subscribes to it" (*Dignity and Duties of the Priest,* Vol. 12, page 2).

According to Biblical definitions this is blasphemy, a counterfeit system of forgiveness. It's not the gospel of grace. It's putting something between ourselves and the one true mediator, Jesus Christ. Only God can forgive sins. It was true then. It is true now. No earthly religious leader has the right to interpose himself between our souls and God.

CLUE NUMBER FOUR

Revelation 13:7, again, speaking of the beast:

> "And it was granted to him to make war with the saints and to overcome them."

Making war with the saints, sounds like persecution.

Has the Roman church ever persecuted dissenters? Here's a conservative estimate. Christians martyred by the state church during the Dark Ages number over 30 million. Whole communities were wiped out for no other crime than "heresy." They dared to believe something other than what the church taught.

Interestingly enough, the Roman Church admits to the persecution it inflicted:

> "The Church has persecuted. Only a tyro in church history will deny that" (*Western Watchman,* December 23, 1908).

But even more disturbing is a statement from a Catholic textbook.

> "The church may by divine right confiscate the property of heretics, imprison their persons and condemn them to the flames . . . In our age the right to inflict the severest penalties, even death, belongs to the church . . . There is no graver offense than heresy. . . therefore it must be rooted out" (*Public Ecclesiastical Law,* vol. 2, p. 142).

It's possible to believe in our hearts that we are carrying out the work of God—and yet do terrible things to other people. But this is not the work of Christ. This is the work of the beast who makes war with the saints.

CLUE NUMBER FIVE

This clue relates to a time prophecy:

> "And he was given a mouth speaking great things and blasphemies, and he was given authority to continue for forty-two months" (Revelation 13:5).

Forty-two months. Remember that a day stands for a year in Bible prophecy (Ezekiel 4:6); thus, 42 months, or 1260 days, equals 1260 years.

Does this period of time fit in with the history of the Roman Church?

We know from history books that 538 AD is an important date for Catholics. In that year the three powers in conflict with the papacy were conquered, securing the pope's position as a religious-political leader. In that same year the decree of Justinian, the Emperor, went into effect making the bishop of Rome the head of all the churches, the definer of doctrine, and the corrector of heretics.

This decree marked the beginning of papal supremacy in 538 AD.

Let's add 1260 years to 538 AD. That's when we should expect to see as foretold by John's description of the end of this period of papal supremacy, one of the heads of the beast that had been mortally wounded."

Adding 1260 years to 538 AD we come to the year 1798. What happened to the papacy in that year?

Papal power was indeed seriously wounded, in 1798. Napoleon sent General Berthier to Rome in not such a friendly visit! He took the pope captive. Notice the historical account:

> "The murder of a Frenchman in Rome in 1798 gave the French an excuse for occupying the Eternal City and putting an end to the Papal temporal power. The aged Pontiff himself was carried off into exile to Valence . . . The enemies of the Church rejoiced. The last Pope, they declared, had resigned" (*Church History,* page 24).

The 1260 years fit. Had Napoleon consulted Scripture, however, he would have realized that the papal system was not finished, only wounded. And as Revelation 13:3 tells us, that deadly wound would be healed. *In fact, all the world would marvel at its healing and follow the beast.*

Those later events, set the stage for the dramatic role of the papacy in the last days.

CLUE NUMBER SIX

Look at Revelation 13:18:

> "Here is wisdom. Let him who has understanding calculate the number of the beast, for it is the number of a man: His number is 666."

In the Bible the number seven represents perfection, completeness. The number six, on the other hand, is a symbol of imperfection, representing human error, incompleteness. The number six stands for rebellion rather than obedience.

So what does a triple six represent? Something very

wrong. One could say it pictures a triple union of error—the union of the dragon, beast, and false prophet. These three figures come together in the book of Revelation in an unholy alliance. What is pictured is a powerful confederacy under the Pope of Rome.

"Here is wisdom. Let him that had understanding count the number of a man, and the number is 666." Clue number six, the official title of the papacy, adds up to 666.

Here is something fascinating. The official symbol of the papal authority is the papal tierra. This triple crown indicates the belief the pope is the lord of heaven, earth and lower regions. An inscription once found on the papal tierra is VICARIUS FILII DEI.

The Catholic publication, *Our Sunday Visitor,* says:

> "The official title of the papacy is Vicarius Filii Dei or Vicar of the Son of God."

Since this is a Roman title, we would expect to use Roman numerals to calculate it.

V = 5	F	D = 500	112
I = 1	I = 1	E	53
C = 100	L = 50	I = 1	501
A	I = 1	501	666
R	I = 1		
I = 1	53		
U = 5			
S			
112			

CLUE NUMBER SEVEN

This clue relates to how the beast will use his power to force compliance. Look at Revelation 13:16,17:

> "And he causes all, both small and great, rich

> and poor, free and slave, to receive a mark on
> their right hand or on their foreheads, and that
> no one may buy or sell except one who has
> the mark or the name of the beast, or the
> number of his name."

This is the mark of course that has been the focus of so much attention, and a lot of wild speculation in the past few years. Is it related to bar codes or to driver's licenses? Is someone going to try to plant a computer chip in your head?

Remember, that Revelation is a book of symbols. The mark of the beast is a symbol of rebellion against God, disloyalty to the government of God.

Revelation 13 and 14 make it clear that those who ally themselves with the beast will receive this mark. That's one group. But another group emerges in the end-time. They receive a very different kind of mark. Look at Revelation 7:2, 3:

> "Then I saw another angel ascending from the
> east, having the seal of the living God. And he
> cried with a loud voice to the four angels to
> whom it was granted to harm the earth and the
> sea, saying, "Do not harm the earth, the sea, or
> the trees till we have sealed the servants of our
> God on their foreheads."

This a group which receives the protective seal of the living God. Who are they? God's faithful people. The remnant. Revelation 14:12 points them out:

> "Here is the patience of the saints; here are
> those who keep the commandments of God
> and the faith of Jesus."

Two groups in the last days. Two different marks. The mark of the beast and the seal of the living God.

What's the issue here? The focus of the controversy in the last hours of this earth's history will center on humanity's response to God's commands. It's the seal versus the mark. God's true sign of authority versus Satan's counterfeit.

Government seals usually contain three essentials—name, title and territory of ruler and government. We know the seal of the president of the United States, for example, and what it looks like. It has the name, the title and the territory.

The crucial components of God's seal are the same—name, title and territory. And those components are found in God's law, in the very heart of the Ten Commandments. The fourth commandment actually contains the seal of God's authority. It gives his name, title and territory:

> "Remember the Sabbath day, to keep it holy. Six days you shall labor and do all your work, but the seventh day is the Sabbath of the Lord your God. In it you shall do no work . . . For in six days the Lord made the heavens and the earth, the sea, and all that is in them, and rested the seventh day. Therefore the Lord blessed the Sabbath day and hallowed it" (Exodus 20:8-11).

Notice the components of God's seal, right here in the heart of his law:

◆ He gives his name — the Lord your God.
◆ He gives his title – creator
◆ And he gives his territory — heaven and earth.

In this way, the Sabbath command serves as a seal, a seal of God's authority.

The final controversy between Christ and Satan will center on God's creatorship and rulership. Satan has refused to acknowledge God as sovereign over creation. And that hostility has contaminated planet Earth. Satan has tried to get men and women to reject God's rulership in their lives.

The Sabbath command plays a key role in this controversy. It is a symbol, a seal, of God's authority over us as Creator and Redeemer. It has been a special sign for God's people since the beginning of time. It will be a special sign in the end-times.

God calls the Sabbath his sign, his mark of authority. Now think about this. What does the beast power claim as its mark of authority? Let's look at some Catholic publications for an answer:

> "Sunday is our mark of authority . . . The church is above the Bible, and this transference of Sabbath observance is proof of that fact" (*Catholic Record,* Sept. 1, 1923).

Read this from Father Enright, former President of Redemptorist College:

> "The Bible says, remember that thou keep holy the Sabbath day. The Catholic Church says, No! By my divine power I abolish the Sabbath day, and command you to keep holy the first day of the week. And lo! The entire civilized world bows down in reverent obedience to the command of the holy Catholic Church."

Do you see what the issues are? The issue in the final days focuses on worship: true worship or false worship. Worship on the true Sabbath or accepting a counterfeit Sabbath.

Now let me be very plain. The mark of the beast is the mark of papal authority in the changing of the Sabbath from Saturday the seventh day to Sunday the first day. *But nobody has the mark of the beast today.* Some day soon church and state will unite enforcing the counterfeit Sabbath; no one will receive the mark of the beast until religious legislation is passed enforcing the substitute Sabbath and people everywhere will be forced to make a decision.

The Bible predicts a coming confederacy of religions attempting to unite church and state. Indeed the Bible says, that confederacy will cause all, both small and great, rich and poor, free and enslaved, to receive a mark on their right hand or in their foreheads. What does it mean a mark on their right hand or in their foreheads? The forehead is a symbol of the mind. So, you are either intellectually convinced in your mind or you are forced to obey, the hand being a symbol of passive acceptance. So, people either intellectually accept the church-state union and counterfeit law, or they are forced to accept it. The issue is worship, true and false worship, that focuses on the very law of God, the very thing that makes God, God.

Indeed, our historic freedoms will be challenged. But God will have a group of people who say, "For me it's the Bible and the Bible only. I want to be done with the traditions of man." In the days of Peter, when the religious leaders united with the Roman state powers, Peter was thrown in prison. They denied Peter the privilege of preaching the truth. And Peter replied, "We ought to obey God rather than man" (Acts 5:29).

◆ God says, the issue is worship.
◆ God says, a religious political power has changed the Sabbath.
◆ God says, this is more than a matter of days. It's a matter of authority, of loyalty, of obedience. It's a matter of a massive conflict between good and evil; a conflict between Christ and Satan.

And Christ says to you today, flee from false worship, because soon church and state will unite to undermine our freedoms.

Everyone of us one day will make a decision for Christ or the Evil One. Even today, we are making a decision to stand with the people of God or the popular churches. God says to you, "make a decision to follow Me."

The road of life goes only one of two ways: the true Sabbath or the counterfeit Sabbath. So many people that have never known these truths are hearing God's call. So many wonderful Sunday-keeping Christians, now understand the issues. They're making decisions to follow Christ. In the days of their ignorance, God winked. But now he's making His final appeal.

You are free to make your own decision. Don't waste your freedom. ❏

24
REVELATION DESCRIBES THE UNITED STATES IN PROPHECY

The vote was deadlocked on July 2, 1776. Should this band of colonies declare their independence from mother England? The Continental Congress debated all that day. The Delaware delegation had three votes. There were two delegates present and one voted for independence. The other voted against it. The third delegate was at home on his farm. And he was marooned there because of a very heavy rainstorm. But he got word that the congress was deadlocked. And his vote might decide the future.

And so, on horseback, he rode all night through the mud and through the rain. He came to the Continental Congress to cast the deciding vote.

As legend has it, there was a little boy who was looking through the crack in the door watching those delegates. His grandpa had assigned him to do that because grandpa was the bell ringer. And grandpa was standing with a great rope at the bell tower ready to ring the bell if the declaration was signed. As the lad looked through the door, he saw quill pens signing that declaration. He heard the shuffling of feet. And his grandpa was quite pessimistic. He kept walking back and forth, saying they will never sign it.

But then the delegate from Delaware arrived to cast the deciding vote. The little boy ran over and shouted, "Ring grandpa, ring for liberty."

The United States has always pictured itself as the place where freedom rings, where liberty is cherished. It has become a stronghold of democracy in the modern world.

And since it has played such a key role in history as a world power, you can't help wondering, "Does the United States play a role in the book of Revelation? Is it pictured there in any way?"

The issues of liberty and human conscience loom large in the end-time drama which Revelation highlights. Will this particular country still be ringing the liberty bell in those last days?

Look at Revelation 13:11. John has just pictured the rise of the beast, the papal power, and prophesied its history, predicted its role in the end-times. Now he introduces a second beast:

> "Then I saw another beast coming up out of
> the earth, and he had two horns like a lamb."

What clues do we have to identify this lamb-like beast? Clue One: we'll note *where* this beast arises. This second beast, separate and distinct from the first beast, arises from the earth.

Daniel 7:17 says, beasts represent kings or kingdoms. So, this second beast in Revelation 13, is a kingdom, a nation. And it arises from the earth. Now where did the first beast of Revelation 13 come from? The first beast rose out of the sea. All the other beasts (that is, nations), that we have studied have come up out of the sea.

Remember, Revelation 17:15 tells us the sea represents peoples, nations and tongues. If that's the case, what do you think the earth would represent? An unpopulated area.

What do we have so far? This beast, this nation rose out of an unpopulated area, an unsettled, wilderness area.

That rings a bell! The United States would fit.

A prominent writer described the rise of the United States:

> ". . . the mystery of her coming forth from vacancy . . . Like a silent seed we grew into an empire" (*G.A. Townsend, The New World Compared With the Old*, page 635).

A European journal in 1850 wrote of the United States as an empire that was "emerging . . . amid the silence of the earth, daily adding to its power and strength" (cited in Uriah Smith, *Daniel and the Revelation,* page 578).

Clue Two: Let's focus on the time period in which this second beast arose.

Revelation 13:10 describes the first beast as going "into captivity." The very next verse, speaks of the rise of the second beast. This second beast arose about the same time as the first beast was taken captive, the time it received that wound in its head, (verse three).

In the last chapter we learned that the first beast, the papacy, received a serious wound in 1798. That's when the pope was taken captive by the French. Papal supremacy was broken.

So, we can say that this second beast arose to prominence in the late 1700s. Does that fit the history of the United States? Yes it does. In 1798 this new country was emerging as a nation to be reckoned with.

When we scan history we discover that only one world power was "coming up" in 1798—the United States of America.

Clue Three: Let's look at how this second beast, this nation, rose up. Revelation 13:11 tells us that this beast which rose out of the earth had two horns like a lamb.

It's like a lamb. What does that mean? A lamb represents youthfulness. This is not an old beast. It's a baby lamb, a new power arising among older nations.

What significance do these two horns have? Horns are a symbol of authority. Horns are a symbol of power.

Now, Clue Four: This prophecy is talking about a democracy. Why? A democracy—horns are a symbol of power. On these horns, there are no crowns. Remember the first beast? There were crowns on the horns. Crowns on the horns indicate kingly power in prophecy. But here, no kingly authority. This is in contrast to the first beast in Revelation 13:

> "Then I stood on the sand of the sea. And I saw a beast rising up out of the sea, having seven heads and ten horns. And on his horns ten crowns" (Revelation 13:1).

But, on the second beast, that's rising up around 1798, in an unpopulated area of the world, that's quickly achieving worldwide prominence, that's separate from the old world of Europe, there is another power coming up but there are no crowns on its horns.

This suggests a democratic form of government, a tolerant form of government. This nation, symbolized by a lamb, contrasts with those oppressive beasts in the book of Revelation.

Clue Five: Revelation also suggests that this lamb-like beast has world-wide influence. It causes the earth and those who dwell in it to worship "the first beast" power (Revelation 13:2).

The United States didn't fit that picture a century ago. But now it certainly does. Its influence is indeed global. It impacts people everywhere financially, politically and culturally.

So let's review the five clues about the second beast, the lamb-like beast of Revelation 13. We know that its "coming up" would take place around 1798. It would arise in a relatively unpopulated area. It would be a nation, but a young one. It would have no crowned head, no kingly authority. Yet, it would rise to a position of worldwide power and influence.

John the Revelator has pinpointed the rise of the United States of America; our nation fits the prophecy precisely.

It's exciting to know that this country has a role to play in the final end-time drama. The nation that rose to champion religious and civil liberty has a spotlight thrown on it.

But what role exactly will the U.S. play? Let's look at the evidence in Revelation 13:11. I'm afraid that the picture becomes grim rather quickly. This beast that had two horns like a lamb, begins to speak "like a dragon."

Obviously something happens to this nation. It started out as a lamb, but eventually it will speak like a dragon. How does any nation speak? A nation speaks through its legislative bodies. The elected officials of any nation speak for that nation as they pass laws. Revelation 13 describes the change from speaking as a lamb, that is to say, laws that allow freedom, to speaking as a dragon, that is to say, laws that are coercive.

But the picture gets even darker. Read this amazing declaration in verse 12:

"And he exercises all the authority of the first

> beast in his presence, and causes the earth and
> those who dwell in it to worship the first beast,
> whose deadly wound was healed."

Look carefully at what this is saying. The second beast actually causes those who dwell on the earth to worship the first beast. Translation: The United States will cause people in the world to worship papal principles. Church and state, which have been kept apart for so long, will unite to enforce religious practices. The strong arm of the state will be used to coerce in a way similar to papal practices through the centuries. Protestant America will reach across the ocean and join hands with the papacy in a new, very dangerous, alliance of church and state.

What is the sign of papal power? Sunday worship. That's their claim. It's the day which the Roman Catholic Church has declared holy.

You may wonder, how could something like that ever happen? It seems impossible.

Wait, there's more. Look at Revelation 13:13, 14. Speaking of the second lamb-like beast, John says:

> "He performs great signs, so that he even
> makes fire come down from heaven on the
> earth in the sight of men. And he deceives those
> who dwell on the earth by those signs which he
> was granted to do in the sight of the beast."

How are people deceived? How can a country like the United States give its allegiance to the beast of Revelation 13? Because of the miracles and wonders that soon will take place.

Many people assume that any miracle is God's doing, that any miracle confirms someone's claims to truth.

God indeed performs signs and wonders as He thinks best. Sometimes miracles accompany the work of God. But Satan too can work miracles. He can perform counterfeit signs and wonders.

Speaking of the last days, Jesus gave this warning to his followers:

> "For false Christs and false prophets will arise and show great signs and wonders so as to deceive, if possible, even the elect" (Matthew 24:24).

Spectacular signs and wonders are not necessarily a sign of divine favor. They can be an effort of our enemy to deceive.

And people who would rather have a sensational sign than the simple, straightforward truth of God's Word, are setting themselves up for a fall. They will be deceived by the razzle-dazzle of a sinister power.

John reminds us:

> "For they are spirits of demons, performing signs, which go out to the kings of the earth and of the whole world, to gather them to the battle of that great day of God Almighty" (Revelation 16:14).

Kings are going to be deceived—great men, politicians, statesmen—will be taken in by the wonder-working power of the Great Deceiver.

That wonder-working power enables the lamb-like beast to cause all to worship the first beast. That's what will enable the United States to enforce allegiance to the papal principles. Men and women will unite around the beast's sign of authority and enforce Sunday worship.

Does it sound hard to believe?

Think about how powerful this might be: a revival sweeping across the country, featuring great miracles, great wonders. Think of how easy it would be to rally around what appears to be the work of God, what appears to be the last chance to save our country from moral ruin.

Miracles happen. A spirit of unity prevails. People want to push the revival as far as it can go. They will want something that can unite us all, some symbol, some symbol of our common worship.

At first glance, the proposal seems so logical: Let's all unite and worship on Sunday, in one spirit of brotherhood. Wouldn't that unite our troubled nation and make it truely one nation under God?

Does this sound far-fetched? Some religious leaders already have boldly suggested that a common day of worship may be a partial solution to our recurring energy crisis. They've suggested that, by forbidding all driving on Sunday, except to church, we could save up to 15 percent of our gasoline supply.

Read what the then editor, Harold Lindsell, proposed for the purpose of conserving energy—that "all businesses, including gasoline stations and restaurants, should close every Sunday" *Christianity Today* (May 7, 1976).

Lindsell expressed his conviction that such a move would satisfy both natural laws and the "will of God for all men." He sensed that it was highly unlikely that Sunday would voluntarily become a day of rest. So he further suggested that one way to accomplish this would be "by force of legislative fiat through the duly elected officials of the people."

Some time ago, the U.S. Supreme Court ruled that in some instances, Sunday laws may be enforced, not on the basis of religious considerations, but in the interests of safeguarding the health and welfare of the American people. The late Justice William O. Douglas disagreed and stated the following in his dissenting opinion to the majority decision of the court:

> "It seems to be plain that by these laws, the states compel one, under the sanction of law, to refrain from work or recreation on Sunday because of the majority's views on that day. The state by law makes Sunday a symbol of respect or adherence."

America can and will enforce Sunday observance. Swept up by the momentum of a false revival and a national crisis, thousands will rush under that banner, thousands will call for the state to enforce religious principles.

Are you aware that in the United States of America, right now, there is a movement to redefine religious liberty? Chief Justice William Renquist wrote recently that the wall of separation between church and state is a metaphor based on bad history. This is a United States supreme court judge. The metaphor, he said, has proved useless as a guide and should be frankly abandoned. Even today there are those who are reevaluating the entire issue of the wall of separation between church and state. The *St. Louis Dispatch,* October 29, 1991, made this interesting observation:

> "As the second century of the bill of rights draws to a close, the supreme court is redefining what religious liberty will mean in the third century. Broadly, the court's new approach helps conventional religions while hurting unconventional ones."

Now, notice what this judgment is saying. It is saying

that the court is moving in this direction, of redefining what an acceptable religion is. And if you happen to fall into that conventional religion you can have the stamp of approval.

Events are moving us toward that day when the lamb-like beast will roar like a dragon. Let's look at one more characteristic of this second beast does:

> "He deceives those who swell on the earth. . . . telling those who dwell on the earth to make an image to the beast who was wounded by the sword and lived. He was granted power to give breath to the image of the beast, that the image of the beast should both speak and cause as many as would not worship the image of the beast to be killed" (Revelation 13:14, 15).

Let's try to understand this phrase: "make an image to the beast."

An image of anything is something that looks like something else. If a little boy is his Dad's "spittin' image," he looks just like his Dad.

Remember, we're dealing with symbols in Revelation. This image of this beast won't be some literal image, a statue or idol. It will be a replica, a repeat performance of what the beast did before, of what the papal power did during the Dark Ages.

At the height of its power, the papacy clothed itself with civil power; it had the authority to punish dissenters, confiscate goods, imprison people and even execute them. It created a union of church and state.

So what will an image of the beast, an image of the papacy be? It will be another union of church and state. It will be another ecclesiastical establishment clothed with civil power. It will be another power trying to enforce its religious claims.

Think about this scenario. Think about a nation ripped apart by crime, riddled with lawlessness. Think about a people who are in anguish because moral principles seem to have gone out the window. Kids are mowing down other kids in our schools. Violence and obscenity and abuse multiply around us. We can't win the war on drugs.

People will be crying out for answers, demanding solutions. And our most instinctive reaction is this: "there ought to be a law." Well-meaning Americans will band together to pass laws to save our country. They will think they can rescue the country by enforcing morality. We've got to make our nation Christian again, they will say. A good motive but a bad procedure. The temptation is to pass laws forcing people to do by civil power what the church has failed to do by persuasive teaching and preaching.

Think of how powerful this new power will become when legislative initiatives are backed by a false revival sweeping the country, backed by signs and wonders.

Liberty magazine quoted a contemporary evangelical leader who said, "If Christians unite, we can do anything. We can pass any law or any amendment and that's exactly what we intend to do."

Pat Robertson wrote recently:

> "The next obligation that a citizen of God's world order owes is to himself. 'Remember the Sabbath day to keep it holy' is a command for the personal benefit of each citizen. . . . Higher civilizations rise when people can rest, think and draw inspiration from God. Laws in America that mandated a day of rest (Sunday laws) have been nullified as a violation of the

separation of church and state. . . .As an out-
right insult to God and his plan, only those
policies that can be shown to have a clearly
secular purpose are recognized." (*The New
World Order,* page 236).

Do you see his reasoning? He is saying we have out-
lawed the Sunday laws. But if we're going to bring this
whole nation back to God, we have to worship God
together. Therefore, it is logical in a time when moral
values are waning, in a time of crisis, to unite on that
point we have in common, which is Sunday among all the
Christian churches.

Let me tell you about a man named Milton Schustek,
a dear friend. He lived in Czechoslovakia during the
years of Soviet domination, during years of great religious oppression. He told me this story.

When the communists took over his country, he
wanted to be free to worship on the Sabbath. He wanted
to be free to read his Bible. He wanted to continue his
work as a minister.

But the Communists had other ideas. They were
determined to turn all ministers into laborers. Milton
knew that they wanted to send him as far away from his
congregation as possible, far away to the coal mines.

But he got an idea; he figured out a way that he might
be able to stay close to his pastoral work in the city of
Prague. One job in that city nobody wanted. Nobody
wanted to clean out the sewers. Nobody wanted to climb
into those narrow, filthy culverts and clean them, hundreds
of feet under the city.

Milton decided to go see communist officials about
that job. But first he got down on his knees and prayed.
"Jesus," he said, "I want to worship you every Sabbath.

Please help me to keep your law and to be honest and faithful to you."

Milton was ushered in to see the local official. Milton said to her, "I understand you want to ship me to the mines to work. Let me tell you something. My grandfather worked in the mines and my father worked in the mines and I'm willing to work in whatever mine you send me. But I have a suggestion. You need someone to do the worst job you have. I know about it. It's climbing down into those sewers. And I'm willing to do it. Why don't you assign me to clean the sewer pipes of Prague. I'd be happy to do it, because that would give me the privilege of worshipping my God here."

Something touched that Communist official's heart. She looked down at her desk. Then she looked up at him and said, "Pastor, I'm not a godly woman. I'm just trying to fulfill work assignments. But I'll let you worship your God. Go and clean the sewer pipes."

I'll never forget the look on Milton's face as he was telling me this story. He admitted it was a very tough job, very dark, very stressful. But every day it was worth it, he said, "I could worship my God in loyalty, in truth."

Yes, God has his faithful people in every age. They are lights shining in a dark place. And I'd like you to take your stand among those faithful people. Don't worry about the obstacles you may face. Don't worry about the challenges your commitment may bring. Milton Schustek was willing to serve God at any cost. And God took care of him, and He will take care of you too.

Perhaps in reading these pages, you hear God speaking to your heart. You know that God is leading you to make a decision. But you're concerned about your relatives. You are concerned about your husband. You are concerned about your wife. You are concerned about the church that you're a member of. You are concerned about what people in your neighborhood or social circle are going to think. You can't see how it's possible for you to step out and follow Christ because of the pressure from other people around you.

If it's a decision you want to make but you're really struggling—please, ask for extra power from God. Your husband cannot make this decision for you. Your wife cannot make this decision for you. Your parents cannot make this decision for you. Your neighbors can't make it for you. If you say, "Lord, I'm struggling. I need your power." Jesus won't let you down. You will be a different man, a different woman. You'll sense that the assurance of God is in your heart, that you can make this decision. And God will give you the power to be firm and joyful when you join His loyal family. ❏

25
REVELATION'S SPIRITUAL REVOLUTION FOR A NEW MILLENNIUM

In the summer of 1993, the annual "Crucifix at the River" festival began in the Philippines. Crowds gathered at a little town north of Manila for nine days of festivities. But what began as a colorful religious spectacle ended in a tragedy. It ended with hundreds of bodies laid out in a makeshift morgue in the center of town.

This is what happened. More than three hundred worshippers crowded on the three barges of a shrine that was to float down the river. The shrine carried a three-tiered altar and a wooden crucifix.

Unfortunately, as the shrine drifted downstream people began to swim out and try to climb on board. It was already packed. Marshals did their best to toss people back into the water. But more and more people climbed on until the overloaded shrine began to sink. People panicked. The current had grown swifter and the barges keeled over. Over three hundred people drowned.

Now its impossible for any of us to pass judgment on the faith of those worshippers at the festival but when I read of this tragedy, this thought passed through my mind—what a graphic illustration of what happens when we cling to the wrong thing.

These peoples' religious boat sank. In a time of crisis it could not sustain them. They were simply clinging to the wrong thing in the name of religion.

Could it be that some of us are clinging to the wrong thing in the name of religion? Let me speak to you very plainly. More than 1800 different denominations, creeds, and religious groups are in America today. New churches are rapidly springing up across the country. Materialism has not satisfied the restless longings of the 21st-century seekers. Our insatiable desire for pleasure has not met the needs of the heart. Our soul-needs often go unmet. Deep within the fabric of our beings there is this inner longing to know and discover truth. For this reason there is a turning toward religion.

For many, an inner compulsion is calling them back to the purity of New Testament Christianity. It's a hunger for genuine Christianity. Many long for something solid which won't sink when we cling to it.

Throughout the centuries God has always had a people He called His own. God appeared to Abraham in the wilderness and said, "Do not go down to Egypt; dwell in the land of which I shall tell you." Genesis 26:2. Then God explained why He chose Abraham: "Because Abraham obeyed My voice and kept My charge, My commandments, My statutes, and My laws" (Genesis 26:5). Abraham was obedient to God and God chose him to preserve His truth.

In Deuteronomy 11:1, God instructs His people, "Therefore you shall love the Lord your God, and keep His charge, His statutes, His judgments, and His commandments always."

Throughout the Old Testament and into the New, God's people—His church—were a special, called-out people. The apostle Peter describes them this way:

> "But you are a chosen generation, a royal priesthood, a holy nation, His own special

people, that you may proclaim the praises of
Him who called you out of darkness into His
marvelous light" (1 Peter 2:9).

So the question is, How does the average person sort
out the claims and counter claims of all these religious
organizations? With so many conflicting theories and doctrines, are you certain that what you have put your faith in
won't let you down? Will it support you in a crisis?

Here is a safe principle: You do not go to the church
to find the truth, you discover the truth to find the church.

Paul defines the church this way:

"I write so that you may know how you ought
to conduct yourself in the house of God, which
is the church of the living God, the pillar and
ground of the truth" (1 Timothy 3:15).

This is one of the clearest definitions of the church
in all the Bible. The church is not merely a social institution where people assemble to feel good. The church is
not some organization built on human tradition. The
church is the custodian of, the protector of, the preserver
of, the proclaimer of God's truth.

John Milner sums up our dilemma in these words:

"There is but one inquiry to be made, namely,
which is the true church . . . By solving this
one question . . . you will at once solve every
question of religious controversy that has ever
been or that ever can be agitated. *The End of
Religious Controversy,* page 95.

Where do you start in the quest for truth? So many
denominations, so many truth claims! Maybe you've
asked yourself, "Why doesn't God make it easier to sort
it all out so we can clearly identify his last-day church?"

According to Scripture Jesus never intended that there should be such confusion, such a profusion of churches. Just before his crucifixion, Jesus prayed this for his followers, that "they all may be one, as You, Father, are in Me, and I in You" (John 17:21).

In this prayer for the unity of the church, Jesus prayed that His church be united in truth. Jesus Himself said:

> "Sanctify them by Your truth. Your word is truth" (John 17:17).

Earlier to His disciples He underlined the significance of His truth in these words, "And you shall know the truth, and the truth shall make you free" (John 8:32). The truth is liberating. It frees you from error. Christ didn't want divisions in the church.

But Paul was a realist. He warned about wolves coming among God's flock of sheep. He spoke of men arising, speaking "perverse things" and drawing followers away— "Also from among yourselves men will rise up, speaking perverse things, to draw away the disciples after themselves" (Acts 20:30).

Look at church history and you'll see this is exactly what happened. After the establishment of the New Testament church, false teachers arose.

Some members accepted their heresies. They formed splinter groups and cults. Others were confused. Disciples were drawn away; Christianity splintered— even within the first hundred years! But through it all God maintained a core church which remained faithful to the teachings of Christ.

In the book of Revelation God revealed to his prophet John important principles about the true church in the last days, and about false churches. He revealed that apostasy and religious confusion would exist in earth's last days. In previous chapters, we studied John's panoramic view of the history of the church from the time of Christ's birth to the end of the world.

The chapter is written in symbolic language. It pictures a woman in white, clothed with the sun, standing on the moon with a crown of twelve stars on her head, crying out to be delivered in childbirth. As we've seen before, this woman represents God's people, his church. The apostle Paul used the same image:

> "I have betrothed you to one husband, that I may present you as a chaste virgin to Christ" (2 Corinthians 11:2).

Revelation chapter 12 also pictures an evil enemy lying in wait. He wants to destroy this woman's child at birth:

> "And the dragon stood before the woman who was ready to give birth, to devour her child as soon as it was born" (Revelation 12:4).

The identity of the dragon is clear: He is the same dragon who made war in heaven—"that serpent of old, called the Devil and Satan" (Revelation 12:9).

This great struggle between good and evil originated in heaven. That's where Satan, desiring to be like the Most High, stirred up one-third of the angels in an attempt to overthrow God's kingdom. The evil angels and Satan were thrown to earth. And this is where the battle has continued. After Adam and Eve gave in to Satan's lies he was able to get a foothold on this planet.

Centuries later Satan tried to take the life of Jesus, the man child of Revelation, as soon as he was born in Bethlehem. Satan continued his attacks on Jesus throughout his ministry. He desperately wanted to block God's plan to save a fallen world.

When Christ's body hung limp on the cross, apparently forsaken by God and man, Satan thought he had won the battle. But the empty tomb proved that all his schemes had been in vain. Christ returned victorious to his heavenly Father. It happened just as John had been shown: "And her child was caught up to God and to His throne" (Revelation 12:5).

Satan had failed to destroy God's Son. So he turned his wrath on the woman—on the Christian Church. All but one of Christ's disciples died a martyr's death. Paul was beheaded outside the walls of Rome. Later thousands of believers were tortured and thrown into dungeons. Many sealed their loyalty with their blood.

As long as the apostles were alive, the church stood firm and true. But something happened with later generations. Believers compromised; their commitment wavered. Apostasy plagued the church.

In the fourth century, Emperor Constantine tried to hold the Roman Empire together by uniting pagans and Christians in one system of worship. The good news was that Christians were no longer persecuted; they weren't outcasts. The bad news was that the church incorporated pagan beliefs and practices and thus the great majority found little reason to die for anything.

The church was no longer like that pure woman. During this time of great compromise, however, many Christians did remain faithful to God's truths. They protested against the corruption in the church. But Roman Emperors sided with the established church. In fact they issued edicts enforcing conformity to the Roman Catholic Church.

Archibald Bauer writes:

"Great numbers were driven from their habitations with their wives and children, stripped and naked . . . many of them inhumanly massacred" (*The History of the Popes,* vol 2, page 334).

God's faithful followers were bitterly persecuted by the official church as prophesied in Revelation 12:6:

> "Then the woman fled into the wilderness, where she has a place prepared by God, that they should feed her there one thousand two hundred and sixty days."

John predicted that the persecution was to last 1260 days. As we studied earlier, according to prophetic time, a day equals a year (Ezekiel 4:6, Numbers 14:34). Using this day/year principle in prophecy, the 1260 symbolic days of Revelation 12:6 are actually 1260 years. History confirms this prophecy with incredible accuracy.

Look at exactly when this reign of intolerance began. When were those who protested the errors of the state church persecuted? When did it start? In AD 538, the Roman emperor Justinian declared the bishop of Rome to be "the head of the church, the true and effectual corrector of heretics." That decree came shortly after Justinian ordered the Roman general, Belisarius, to destroy the three religious powers that opposed the church in Rome. Heresy was crushed by the sword. It was decreed that the church in Rome alone could interpret Bible truth. All other interpretations were heretical; they needed to be stamped out.

Faithful Christians who cherished the essential truths revealed in God's Word found that they had to flee in order to survive. It was just as John prophesied, "The woman fled into the wilderness."

The Waldenses, Albigenses, Huguenots and others fled

to the Alps in northern Italy and southern France. They hid in secluded valleys, remote caves and high mountains. They were hunted down like criminals. Many were killed because they would not give up the teachings of Jesus.

During the Dark Ages millions of believers were cruelly persecuted. They gave up their lives rather than compromise their faith. Some historians estimate that as many as 50 million were slain.

The reign of intolerance lasted for centuries. But God's truth managed to triumph once again. The Bible, long chained to monastery walls and cathedral pulpits, was translated into the common language. Ordinary believers began to discover what Scripture really taught. Courageous reformers boldly proclaimed God's Word.

These reformers were hunted and persecuted. But the fires of the Protestant Reformation would not be put out. Other reformers uncovered more and more lost truths from the Word of God. But this only aroused further the fury and wrath of Satan.

How long did the reign of intolerance last? Let's look for an ending point. When was the absolute power of the church broken? In 1798 the Pope was taken prisoner by Napoleon's general, Bertheir.

1798 marks the end of the reign of intolerance and persecution. As we've seen, 538 AD marked the beginning. How many years are between 538 and 1798? 1260 years exactly. Revelation's prophecy was exactly fulfilled.

This prophetic time period came to a close at the end of the eighteenth century. At that time began many missionary ventures around the world. New truths were being discovered. The Bible calls these "last-day" Christians who followed truth as it unfolded—His "remnant."

God's remnant is the last true body of believers on

earth. It's a bit like a fabric remnant, the last part of the original. These are the final survivors of the war behind all wars. These are the faithful children of the pure woman besieged by the dragon.

How do we identify this remnant? What sets it apart? John gives us two important clues. Here John describes God's followers at the end of time:

> "And the dragon was enraged with the woman, and he went to make war with the rest [remnant] of her offspring, who keep the commandments of God and have the testimony of Jesus Christ" (Revelation 12:17).

It's end-time. God has a church. He calls it His bride—the pure woman of Revelation 12 at the end of tiime. The devil is angry and makes war with God's people. Just as he tried to destroy Jesus, he attempts to destroy the church.

Here is God's description of His bride—His true church. At first glance you'd think most any church would fit it. But let's look more closely. Do all religions today really "keep the commandments of God?" Or do some pay lip service to God's Ten Commandments, while ignoring the specifics of those commands?

Look at the second commandment for example. It states very clearly, "Thou shalt not make unto thee any graven images." But look around you. You will find that many congregations are accustomed to bowing before icons of wood and gold and glass.

Think of the fourth commandment. This is perhaps the most ignored of all:

> "Remember the Sabbath day, to keep it holy.
> Six days you shall labor, and do all your work,

but the seventh day is the Sabbath of the Lord
your God" (Exodus 20:8-11).

The seventh day is God's Sabbath. Take a look at any
calendar. You'll immediately see that the seventh day of
the week is Saturday. It's not Sunday. But drive by any
number of churches in your neighborhood on Saturday
and you'll find empty parking lots.

Remember, one of the distinguishing characteristics
of God's true church is obedience to his commandments,
to all ten of them. That includes the fourth, which
instructs us to keep the seventh day holy.

Most Protestant churches do agree with nine of the
commandments. The difference of opinion and practice is
over the fourth.

God's last-day church strives to follow all of God's commandments. That's something we should pay attention to.

But let's look at the other characteristic mentioned in
Revelation 12. God's church, it says, will also have the
"testimony of Jesus." What is that? Revelation 19:10 tells
us: "the testimony of Jesus is the spirit of prophecy."

God's last-day church will have the gifts of the Spirit,
including the spirit of prophecy. The gift of prophecy is
one of God's last-day marks of His true church.

Paul portrays God's last-day church this way:

> "Even as the testimony of Christ was con-
> firmed in you, so that you come short in no
> gift, eagerly waiting for the revelation of our
> Lord Jesus Christ" (1 Corinthians 1:7).

Remembering the true Bible Sabbath and a church
which has been guided by the gift of prophecy fits the
identifying characteristics of God's true church.

But there is more. Scripture gives us other guidelines

as well in seeking the true church, God's special last-day church for example. Jesus issued this command:

> "Go therefore and make disciples of all the nations, baptizing them in the name of the Father and of the Son and of the Holy Spirit, teaching them to observe all things that I have commanded you; and lo, I am with you always, even to the end of the age" (Matthew 28:19, 20).

Baptism by immersion—true Bible baptism—is a sign of God's true church. God's true church has a purpose—it is a worldwide mission movement, reaching the world with the Gospel.

Revelation 14 sheds more light on this issue. It pictures three angels "flying in the midst of heaven" to deliver God's last message to earth. This is a message which God's last-day church is to proclaim. The three angels deliver three messages. The first emphasizes two great truths to be shared with every human being:

> "Fear God and give glory to Him, for the hour of His judgment has come; and worship Him who made heaven and earth" (Revelation 14:7).

Judgment and worship. Two crucial components of the message of God's last-day church. God's remnant will be calling men and women to recognize God as Creator and to worship him on that great memorial of creation, the seventh day. And they will be teaching that the judgment hour has come. In the light of this judgment, God calls His people to place Him in the center of their lives. He calls them to give glory to God in the way they live. God's true church urges people to present their bodies to God as a living sacrifice. It urges them to give up alcohol, tobacco, drugs and unclean foods. It calls them to live lives of moral plenty.

God has an urgent message for today. It's a message that paves the way for Christ's Second Advent. God's true church pulsates with an advent consciousness. It believes and preaches with power that Jesus is coming soon.

The second message, given by the second angel in Revelation 14 is this:

> "Another angel followed saying, 'Babylon is fallen, is fallen, that great city, because she has made all nations drink of the wine of the wrath of her fornication'" (Revelation 14:8).

This message calls for God's true people to separate themselves from Babylon, from false religion, from corrupt religion. It calls them to have no part with apostasy, with anything that would distort the gospel and obscure the truth about Jesus our Savior. It calls believers from law-breaking to law-keeping. It appeals to them to unite with the faithful remnant.

The third message, given by the third angel is a very solemn one:

> "If anyone worships the beast and his image, and receives his mark on his forehead or on his hand, he himself shall also drink of the wine of the wrath of God" (Revelation 14:9, 10).

This is a message of warning as earth plummets toward the end-time, toward the final judgment. God's last-day church must share that message of warning. It must speak clearly about what worshipping the beast and his image means. God's last-day church will be a bold movement, calling for commitment, crying out for change, pointing to the Bible, warning of judgment, upholding the commandments.

Commitment to such a body of Christians is not to be

taken lightly. But it produces great peace of mind. It produces a profound satisfaction in following God's truth wherever it leads. As Jesus said "If you know these things, happy are you if you do them" (John 13:17).

Here is the summary of how to recognize God's true church.

1. God's true church will recapture the pure faith of the disciples.
2. God's true church will have the dual characteristics of
   a. Keeping God's commandments and
   b. Being guided by the gift of prophecy.
3. God's true church will be a worldwide mission-driven movement.
4. God's true church will call people to total commitment to Christ in light of His soon return. This commitment will be manifested in genuine Bible baptism.
5. God's true church will especially lead people to accept and practice the long-neglected sign of the Creator—the Bible Sabbath.
6. God's true church will encourage people to give glory to God by dedicating their bodies to Him as well as their minds. It will lead them to uphold the Biblical principles of health.
7. God's true church will make a final appeal in light of the urgent times we live in to leave falsehood and accept truth.

Let me share with you my personal testimony. I was not brought up in a Bible-believing, Sabbath-keeping church. I was not brought up as a Seventh-day Adventist. I was raised in a lovely Roman Catholic home. Deep within my heart I longed for truth. Like most Catholics, I was baptized as an infant, attended mass on Sunday, believed in purgatory, the immortal soul, accepted images in the church, ate pork, and had little sense of the soon return of our Lord. For years I served on the altar at mass with the priests as an altar boy.

But something was tugging at my heart. I was spiritually restless. My father accepted God's truth and urged me to begin studying the Bible. The more I studied, the more convinced I became that God was leading me to accept all of His truth.

The issue boiled down to simply this, "Would I accept a church based on man's ideas or would I accept a divinely established movement of destiny based on the Bible?"

Would I accept the Bible and the Bible only as my basis of faith? God's church is not in the majority. You can never base truth on a majority vote. God's church is not the most popular because truth rarely wins a popularity contest. God's church is not the most spectacular or ornate because God values truth more than architecture.

I value the words of the American writer, James Russell Lowell, "Truth forever on the scaffold. Wrong forever on the throne. But that scaffold sways the future, and beyond the dear unknown standeth God watching over His own."

God is calling you to make a decision for truth. He has not left you alone. He will lead you. He will strengthen you. He will encourage you. He will empower you. Let Him do all this for you! ❏

26
REVELATION'S PROPHETIC MOVEMENT AT END-TIME

We are witnessing a phenomenal explosion of interest in psychic phenomena today—great fascination with the occult and with astrology. More than 2000 of the nation's leading newspapers carry astrology columns. Go to any bookstore and you'll find scores of books on so-called supernatural revelations. Some have become bestsellers recently.

Ruth Montgomery's book, *Gift of Prophecy,* on the life of Jeanne Dixon sold more than a million copies. *The Sleeping Prophet,* a book on the life of psychic Edgar Cayce, continues to generate phenomenal sales.

As we come to the crisis hour of earth's history, men and women everywhere are looking for answers outside themselves. They want some way to deal with frustration, hopelessness and despair. Humanity is crying out for a voice, an authoritative voice, from outside normal human experience. People want a voice that speaks with certainty.

But of course this desire brings with it certain risks. Plenty of voices have spoken with great certainty—and have led people off a cliff. How do we know which ones to listen to? How can we be sure a prophet or a voice from beyond is genuine?

After all, Jesus predicted that many false prophets would rise in the last days: "For false christs and false prophets will arise and show great signs and wonders to deceive, if possible, even the elect" (Matthew 24:24).

Jesus also gave us this warning:

> "Beware of false prophets, who come to you in sheep's clothing, but inwardly they are ravenous wolves" (Matthew 7:15).

How right He was! False prophets and astrologers and psychics are all around us today. They are a sign of the last days. Satan has attempted to counterfeit the genuine gift of prophecy by raising up false prophets.

Doesn't the existence of a counterfeit indicate that there must be a genuine? How many of you have ever seen a three-dollar bill? Nobody makes those. Why not? No counterfeiter in the country would bother making a three-dollar bill. Counterfeiters imitate the real thing.

Does the Bible actually predict the manifestation of the gift of prophecy in these last days? Or did the gift of prophecy cease in Bible times?

Paul gives us some help:

> "And He Himself gave some [gifts] to be apostles, some prophets, some evangelists, and some pastors and teachers, for the equipping of the saints for the work of ministry, for the edifying of the body of Christ, till we all come to the unity of the faith and of the knowledge of the Son of God, to a perfect man, to the measure of the stature of the fullness of Christ; that we should no longer be children, tossed to and fro and carried about with every wind of doctrine, by the trickery of men, in the cunning craftiness by which they lie in wait to deceive, but, speaking the truth in love, may grow up in all things into Him who is the head—Christ" (Ephesians 4:8, 11-15).

Here Paul tells us that when Jesus ascended to heaven, he gave special gifts to men. Among those gifts was the gift of prophecy. It's purpose, according to this passage, was to perfect a people and prepare a church for the coming of Christ. The gift of prophecy will remain in God's church until we come to the unity of the faith, to the measure of the stature of the fullness of Christ. That continual need for the gifts doesn't end until Jesus returns.

That is why Paul wrote these words:

> "So that you come short in no gift; eagerly waiting for the revelation of our Lord Jesus Christ" (1 Corinthians 1:7).

Jesus promised that the gift of prophecy would be revived in the last generation. Knowing this, Satan has raised up false prophets to deceive many.

This leads us to a very important question. How can you tell the difference between a true and a false prophet? What are the Biblical tests for the true gift of prophecy?

Interestingly enough, Jesus has given us very plain answers to those questions. No one needs to be deceived. The Bible outlines clearly the tests of a true prophet. And those tests expose the fraudulent claims of false prophets.

So let's look at Biblical principles that teach us how to recognize the authentic gift of prophecy.

Before sin entered the world, God communicated with human beings face to face. Sin broke that personal communication. Isaiah puts it this way:

> "Your iniquities have separated you from your God; And your sins have hidden His face from you, So that He will not hear" (Isaiah 59:2).

Sin separates us from God. But God didn't abandon us to our fate. He chose another method of communication:

> "If there is a prophet among you, I, the Lord,
> make Myself known to him in a vision, And I
> speak to him in a dream" (Numbers 12:6).

Prophets speak for Him, linking heaven and
humanity. Prophets receive messages in two basic ways:

1. An angel brings them a vision or a dream
   (Revelation 1:1).
2. The Holy Spirit impresses their minds, revealing
   heaven's truth to them (2 Peter 1:21).

True prophets don't teach their own ideas. They are
heaven's messengers. Their messages reveal God's will.
Since they've received a message from heaven, they can
speak with certainty and conviction.

The Bible also tells us that there are two kinds of
prophetic messages. The best known are the written revelations which form the books of the Bible, the revelations given to Moses, Daniel and John, for example.

In addition God has spoken through other prophets,
people whose writings were not preserved or people who
gave only oral messages. Enoch, Elijah and Elisha, for
example, did not contribute to the written Bible. But they
served as God's prophets.

In Acts 11:27 we find that a prophet by the name of
Agabus went to Antioch and predicted a great famine
throughout the world. Agabus is called a prophet. But
there is no book of Agabus in the Bible. There is no book
by John the Baptist either; none of his sermons are
recorded. Yet Jesus said there was never a greater prophet
than His cousin, John.

Throughout the ages God has had prophets who
played special roles in His plan, women as well as men.
We read of Deborah, a prophetess in Old Testament times
and Anna, a prophetess in the New Testament. The book

of Acts mentions the four daughters of Philip who served as prophetesses to the church. But they didn't write anything in the Bible. Paul tells us:

> "And God has appointed these in the church: first apostles, second prophets" (1 Corinthians 12:28).

The Bible predicts that in these last days the prophetic gift will be restored. This gift will be found within God's true church. That's what the book of Revelation tells us. Revelation focuses on last day things, and tells us what will characterize God's last-day church:

> "And the dragon was enraged with the woman, and he went to make war with the rest of her offspring, who keep the commandments of God and have the testimony of Jesus Christ" (Revelation 12:17).

This verse is part of a brief history of the church from before Christ's time to the time of the end. Chapter 12 predicts that the church would be persecuted during a 1260-year-period and that it would flourish again at the end of time. And then, verse 17, identifies these two characteristics of God's last-day people. They keep the commandments of God and they have the testimony of Jesus.

John tells us very plainly: "the testimony of Jesus is the spirit of prophecy" (Revelation 19:10). *The prophetic gift will be restored in God's last-day church.*

How, can we identify this last-day church which has been predicted to rise in these last days?

The greatest religious movement of the nineteenth century was the Advent movement of 1844. Many believers who'd studied Daniel's 2300-day prophecy expected the Lord to return in 1844. The movement was made up of Baptists, Methodists, Congregationalists, Catholics and many others. Their message of the soon return of Jesus united them. They were deeply motivated to prepare their minds and hearts to meet Jesus. Unfortunately other religious leaders resented the Advent movement, and so these "Adventists" were often unable to remain in their former churches.

Popular churches rejected the teaching of the near Advent. Those who accepted it either voluntarily left their churches or were disfellowshipped. But they were united in their common devotion to the soon-coming Christ.

In December of 1844 a deeply spiritual young woman at 17 was given her first vision. Ellen Harmon, later to become Mrs. Ellen G. White, saw the Advent people traveling an elevated road to heaven with a brilliant light illuminating the pathway. Her messages greatly encouraged the small, scattered group of Adventists. Later they would form the Seventh-day Adventist denomination.

From 1844 until her death in 1915, Ellen White received more than 2000 prophetic visions and dreams. She wrote more than fifty books and lectured to tens of thousands on three continents. With amazing accuracy and insight, she wrote on subjects like education, nutrition, the life of Christ, practical godliness, general health, medical practice and the coming world crisis.

In his book, *California, Romantic and Beautiful,* George Wharton James wrote about Ellen White. She lived her last years in California and her influence was especially felt in that state. Wharton wrote:

> "This remarkable woman, though almost entirely self-educated, has written and published more books in more languages which

circulate to the greater extent than any other woman in history" (page 319).

Ellen White was prolific, and influential. But did she pass the tests of a true prophet? The Bible gives us six specific tests. How does Ellen White measure up? It's important to test everything by the Word of God.

FIRST TEST

The first test involves accuracy. A true prophet must be 100 percent accurate. Bear in mind that some prophecies are conditional. That is, their fulfillment depends on how people respond to them. But prophecies that have no conditions attached must be accurate. A true prophet doesn't guess about the future. He or she foretells what God reveals to them. Jeremiah wrote:

> "As for the prophet who prophesies of peace,
> when the word of the prophet comes to pass,
> the prophet will be known as one whom the
> Lord has truly sent" (Jeremiah 28:9).

Have you ever wondered what the prophetic accuracy is of some of the psychics of our time? How did Jeanne Dixon fare? A leading newspaper did a careful survey recently. It concluded that she was accurate—30 percent of the time.

Let's assume she was right 60 percent of the time. Do we then assume that God was wrong 40 percent of the time? Do we have to assume that prophetic revelations from heaven are so obscure that even a gifted prophet can understand them only 60 percent of the time?

What about Ellen White? What is her percentage of prophetic accuracy? Let's look at some of her predictions.

A century ago she warned about the dangers of too much fat and sugar in the diet.

Almost 70 years before the surgeon general's report on smoking and health, she warned, "tobacco is a slow, insidious, but most malignant poison." It wasn't until 1964 that science linked tobacco with cancer. Yet this divine warning was given more than 70 years in advance.

Ellen White discussed the important effects of pre-natal influence during pregnancy and cancer as a germ long before scientific research caught up with her.

Ellen White's statements on health and disease prevention were decades ahead of their time. I think it's exciting to see God revealing prophetic insights that benefit humanity. Medical science today is validating the gift of prophecy.

More than a century ago, Ellen White predicted an explosion of interest in the occult, psychic phenomena and astrology. Today spiritualism is leaping across denominational boundaries, emerging as the dominant religious force that will one day unite all churches.

SECOND TEST

At times, keen observers of human nature can make some predictions that come true. And yet, their teachings may not be in harmony with biblical principles. One of the great tests of the true gift of prophecy is whether or not the prophet's life and teachings are in harmony with the Scriptures. Moses warned:

> "If there arises among you a prophet or a dreamer of dreams, and he gives you a sign or a wonder, and the sign or the wonder of which he spoke to you comes to pass, saying, 'Let us go after other gods which you have not known, and let us serve them,' you shall not listen to the words of that prophet or that dreamer of dreams . . . You shall walk after the Lord your God and

fear Him, and keep His commandments, and obey His voice, and you shall serve Him and hold fast to Him" (Deuteronomy 13:1-4).

A true prophet must live and teach in conformity to the principles of the Bible. A true prophet will never try to replace or distort what God has already revealed in his Word.

What was Ellen White's attitude toward the Bible? Does she pass the test? Did she consider her writings a second Bible? She wrote:

"In our time there is a wide departure from their [Protestant Reformers] doctrines and precepts, and there is need of a return to the great Protestant principle—the Bible, and the Bible only, as the rule of faith and duty" (*The Great Controversy*, pages 204, 205).

The writings of a true prophet always agree with the Bible. You can read the entire writings of Ellen White and you will not find a single contradiction to God's Word. Her writings complement the Bible. In a sense they function like a telescope. They don't put more stars in the sky. They just make clearer and more bright the ones already there. Ellen White's writings magnify and bring out the precious gems of truth in Scripture.

THIRD TEST

A true prophet always exalts the law of God. He or she always calls people to obedience. Listen to Isaiah:

> "To the law and to the testimony! If they do not speak according to this word, it is because there is no light in them" (Isaiah 8:20).

That's clear. Prophets uphold God's moral principles; they don't undermine them.

Obediance to God's will is something that Ellen White consistently emphasized. For more than 70 years she called people back to obedience to all ten commandments, including the Sabbath, always within the context of God's grace empowering the life.

This was the calling of Old Testament prophets that we see over and over again. They were raised up in periods of apostasy to call men and women back to God, back to his commandments, back to His principles of life. Elijah called Israel back from idolatry, back from sun worship. Nehemiah called for a reform in Sabbath-keeping. In the New Testament, John the Baptist challenged Herod to repent of his adultery.

Every Biblical prophet exalted God's law. And that's what Ellen White did. She did it in her speaking and in her writing.

Sometimes false prophets seduce believers because they make dazzling predictions or have a powerful presence. But their relationship to God's law and to the teachings of Jesus doesn't stand up to the light of truth.

FOURTH TEST

Remember that Revelation 19:10 equated the gift of prophecy with the testimony of Jesus. The two are interchangeable. So we have to say that a true prophet witnesses to Jesus Christ. The central focus of a prophet's ministry today should be Jesus Christ.

Many so-called prophets today end up exalting themselves more than Jesus. What about Ellen White?

An official in the Library of Congress in Washington D.C. was asked which book in that vast library was the best one on the life of Christ. He gave this answer: "My preference or choice would be guided by what I wish to get from the book or books to be read, but let me put it this way: I would put *The Desire of Ages,* by Ellen G. White first for spiritual discernment and practical application."

Ellen White exalted Jesus in so many insightful ways. Her books, *The Desire of Ages, Christ's Object Lessons, Thoughts From the Mount of Blessings,* and *Steps to Christ* throw a wonderful spotlight on the life and teachings of the Savior.

Ellen White passes this test with flying colors. Throughout her ministry, she magnified the name of Christ. In her book *Gospel Workers* she wrote:

> "Lift up Jesus, you that teach the people, lift Him up in sermon, in song, in prayer. Let all your powers be directed in pointing souls, confused, bewildered, lost, to 'the lamb of God'" (page 160).

FIFTH TEST

This involves physical phenomena associated with prophecy in the Bible. Three physical criteria distinguish the genuine gift:

A. Prophets experience day-time visions with their eyes open—their eyes remain open throughout the vision. Numbers 24:4

B. In vision, prophets have no physical strength. Daniel 10:8.

C. Prophets, in vision, do not breathe. Daniel 10:17.

Let's look at how observers described Ellen White in her visions. She was sometimes examined by physicians while in this state. Eye witnesses confirmed that her eyes remained open throughout her visions, and that she retained no strength, and that her breath ceased.

Dr. Drummond was a physician who found himself rather skeptical about what people were saying about

Ellen White. At one point he even declared that he could hypnotize her and give her a vision. One day Ellen White was caught up in a vision while in this man's presence. Dr. Drummond stepped forward and examined her thoroughly. After a bit he turned pale. "She doesn't breathe," he exclaimed. His examination convinced this physician that the visions were from God.

Sometimes the visions of Ellen White lasted for hours, sometimes for only a few minutes. But the physical phenomena surrounding her visions give evidence that they were supernatural.

SIXTH TEST

Jesus gave us a very simple, yet profound test:

> "Therefore by their fruits you will know them" (Matthew 7:20).

A true prophet is known by the results of their ministry. What is the impact of their ministry in people's lives? We can look back and evaluate the impact of Ellen White's ministry.

Look at the world-impact of the Seventh-day Adventist Church alone. As a result of God's messages through Ellen White, the church has established over 500 hospitals, dispensaries and clinics throughout the world. Some years ago a millionaire named Charles Kettering received treatment at one of these hospitals. He was so impressed with the caring service he received that he gave ten million dollars to start a new Adventist-operated hospital near his home in Ohio.

The world-famous Seventh-day Adventist medical center at Loma Linda University was established as a direct result of Ellen White's visions. At first the Council on Medical Education tried to persuade the new medical college not to apply for accreditation. An adequate staff wasn't really available. The school insisted however, and was given the lowest rating of "C." It wasn't long, however before the school received full accreditation and its graduates were welcomed everywhere.

In recent years the United States government has sent the Loma Linda Heart Team to various countries on good-will tours. The medical center has become one of the most advanced heart-transplant facilities in the world.

Because of the guidance of Ellen White, Seventh-day Adventists have become a world-wide presence, and yet a very unified presence. The church ministers in more countries than any other Protestant denomination. In the 1870s Ellen White advised that the time had come to establish overseas mission centers. She felt these could proclaim the last-day message of the three angels in Revelation 14 with greater intensity. As a result, the first Seventh-day Adventist foreign missionary sailed out of Boston harbor in 1874. In a little more than a hundred years our work has grown so that now the sun never sets on the mission of Seventh-day Adventists.

In a time when most churches are cutting back on their mission budgets, Seventh-day Adventists are moving forward. A few years ago some 100,000 people in the Kasai area of Zaire approached Seventh-day Adventist leaders and asked, "Can you send teachers to instruct us? We want to become Adventists." Thousands have been baptized, and thousands more are preparing for baptism.

A number of years ago, in the vast desert wastes of Bechuanaland, South Africa, lived a primitive bushman named Sukuba. He lived an isolated life as a member of a nomadic people. One winter night he crept into his shelter and prepared to sleep.

But suddenly the night became brighter than day. A shining being appeared to him and told him to find the people of the "Book." He must find the people who worshipped god.

Sukuba wasn't sure what that meant. What book? How could he read it if he found it?

The language of the bushman contained clicks and guttural sounds that were quite unlike the language of other African tribes. It has never been reduced to writing. But this "Shining One" as Sukuba called the angel who appeared to him, had said, "The Book talks. You will be able to read it."

Sukuba travelled for days with his family, in search of the book. He reached the hut of some Bantu farmers and asked if they knew of the people with the Book.

The tribesman was startled to hear the bushman speaking his Bantu language somehow. He immediately took Sukuba to his paster. The pastor was deeply moved by Sukuba's story. And he said, "Your journey is over."

Sukuba was very happy. But that night the Shining One appeared to him again. He said that these were not the people he was looking for. He must find "the Sabbath-keeping church and Pastor Moye." Pastor Moye would have a Book and also "four brown books that are really nine."

The next day Sukuba prayed for a sign. He needed some direction for his journey. When he did, a cloud appeared in the sky. Sukuba set off after it and followed it for seven days. It disappeared over a certain village. There Sukuba asked for Pastor Moye and was quickly directed to his home.

After Sukuba told his story in the local dialect, Pastor Moye brought out his worn Bible. "That is it!" Sukuba exclaimed. "That is it! But where are the four books that are really nine?" Well, as it turned out, Ellen White, years before, had written nine volumes of instruction to God's church called *Testimonies to the Church.* And these were later combined into four books.

Sukuba's search was over. He had found the people of the Book. He had found a Sabbath-keeping people, a people blessed with the prophetic gift. Eventually he and his family accepted Christ and were baptized. He became a missionary to his own people.

God is working in marvelous ways today to lead men and women to His true church. The fact that you are reading this book is no accident. Like Sukuba, you are being guided. God is guiding you into his truth. God is giving you courage to face the future.

Perhaps you've been searching for truth for years. I believe your search has ended. You've been divinely guided to this destination. You, like Sukuba, can exclaim, "This is it! God's church!"

Don't you want to join those who keep the commandments of God and have the testimony of Jesus? Don't you want to join God's last-day people? Consider this commitment carefully. It could be the most important decision of your life. ❑

27

REVELATION'S GREAT
END-TIME MOVEMENT

Have you ever gone through a time of great disappointment? A time of failure? I want to talk to you about what God does with our disappointments, how He can create something great out of something terrible, and how He can give us new beginnings. That can happen for God's people as a whole. That can happen for individuals. God is indeed a God of new beginnings. And people who understand that can make a big difference in this world.

I believe God is a God of new beginnings. I believe he can deal with our greatest disappointments and can turn tragedy into triumph.

I'd like to show you how He does that. Throughout the history of His church, God has turned tragedy into triumph, disappointment into rejoicing.

Let's look at the tenth chapter of Revelation. The chapter opens with a glorious angel coming down from heaven, clothed with a cloud. His face shines like the sun and a rainbow stretched over his head. This is another dramatic scene in the book about end-times. It's setting the stage for another important end-time event.

Let's look at verses 2-4:

> "And he had a little book open in his hand. And
> he set his right foot on the sea and his left foot
> on the land, and cried out with a loud voice, as
> when a lion roars. And when he cried out, seven

thunders uttered their voices. Now when the
seven thunders uttered their voices, I was about
to write; but I heard a voice from heaven saying
to me, 'Seal up the things which the seven thunders uttered, and do not write them.'"

What does this symbolism refer to? What little book
could this be? What Bible book was sealed up? Daniel
clearly explains that his prophetic book would be sealed
until the time of the end:

"But you, Daniel, shut up the words, and seal
the book until the time of the end. . .Go your
way, Daniel, for the words are closed up and
sealed till the time of the end" (Daniel 12:4,9).

The book of Daniel fits this picture well. It is a book
of apocalyptic prophecy, like Revelation, the only such
book in the Old Testament. It is a book full of symbols, of
symbolic beasts, like Revelation. But its meaning would
be understood only as the end-time age opened. Its
prophecies are aimed at the end-time. So in that sense,
their meaning was sealed to previous generations.

The sealed book of Daniel would be unsealed and
undersood at the time of the end.

Now look at John's announcement:

"But in the days of the sounding of the seventh angel, when he is about to sound, the
mystery of God would be finished, as He
declared to His servants the prophets"
(Revelation 10:7).

The days of the sounding of the seventh angel refers
to the end-times. In that time, "the mystery of God would
be finished."

How was this prophecy of Revelation 10 fulfilled? In

the 1840s, just as Daniel's time prophecies were coming to an end, faithful Bible students began restudying these amazing predictions. Godly men and women in that movement did indeed unlock the mysteries of the book of Daniel, and of Revelation. They saw how the symbols and the prophecies pointed to the time of the end.

Now back to Revelation 10. A voice from heaven speaks to John the Revelator. This voice asks him to go take that book from the hand of the angel. And John responds:

> "And I went to the angel and said to him, 'Give me the little book.' And he said to me. 'take and eat it; and it will make your stomach bitter, but it will be as sweet as honey in your mouth.' And I took the little book out of the angel's hand and ate it, and it was as sweet as honey in my mouth. But when I had eaten it, my stomach became bitter" (Revelation 10:9,10).

What is this all about? Let's look at those Bible believers who unlocked the mysteries of the book of Daniel, the people who re-discovered the Second Coming prophecies.

They were thrilled to discover that Jesus was coming again soon, that they were living in the end-times. Those prophecies in the book of Daniel were indeed sweet in their mouths, sweet as honey. It was wonderful to see understand how all of God's truth fit together.

But they made a serious mistake. They tried to set a date for the return of Jesus Christ: October 22, 1844. Jesus had said that no one knows the precise day or hour of his return. But these earnest people set a date anyway not realizing what really was to happen on October 22.

They waited for Christ to appear on that day with intense expectation. And when Christ didn't return they were crushed. They were bitterly disappointed. Now those prophecies, once so sweet in their experience, seemed terribly bitter in their stomachs. The sweetness of discovery was gone. The bitterness of disillusionment threatened to snuff-out their faith.

So what did God do to these people who misunderstood prophecy? To these people who looked like fools in the eyes of the world? Did he abandon them?

No, God kept revealing things. God kept nudging them closer to the truth. These people had to grow. They had to give up some cherished assumptions. And God helped them do that. He helped them see how they had misapplied certain time prophecies. He helped them understand how certain events in the heavenly sanctuary prepare the way for the end-times, and for the return of Christ. Yet through their misunderstanding of prophecy, God had focused the attention of the world on the second coming of Christ.

What happened to these people who were bitterly disappointed? They grew into an Advent movement that spread all over the world, one of the greatest missionary movements in modern times.

Look how John described what happened to this disappointed group:

> "And he said to me, 'You must prophesy again about many peoples, nations, tongues and kings'" (Revelation 10:11).

Yes, there was bitter disappointment. But the call to prophesy would come again. This enlarged message would now go out to the whole world.

That is what happened to the great Advent Awakening. The bitter disappointment led to a new beginning. That's what God does very well—He gives us new beginnings. Remember, this is exactly what happened at the first coming of Jesus. The disciples thought Jesus would come to establish an earthly kingdom. They thought He was going to defeat their enemies. They expected triumph not a cross. At the crucifixion the disciples lamented, "But we were hoping that it was He who was going to redeem Israel" (Luke 24:21).

When Christ died on the cross, the disciples were bitterly disappointed. Out of the disappointment of 31 AD, God raised up the New Testament Christian church. God gave the disciples a new beginning—a powerful new beginning—a Spirit-filled, new beginning. In 1844, God did it again. Out of the disappointment of the early advent believers, God has raised up a movement to move the world.

Do you realize that this new beginning is the most exciting thing that is happening on the planet today? The message of Christ's soon return is being proclaimed all over the world.

People from the most unlikely places, people from vastly different cultures, are all making the same discovery. And that discovery is going to change the face of our planet.

I want to give you a glimpse of that force at work in the midst of the Seventh-day Adventist movement. Adventists have always believed the proclamation of three angels in Revelation 14 has a special importance. Those three angels appear just before the Second Coming of Jesus Christ. They relate to God's last great appeal to this planet, God's last great altar call.

Did you know that the gospel going to all the world is both a command and a promise?

Just before Christ ascended to heaven he said:

> "Go therefore and make disciples of all the

> nations. . . teaching them to observe all things that I have commanded you" (Matthew 28:19, 20).

This is the Great Commission given to all followers of Christ. But it is also a promise. Jesus declared:

> "And this gospel of the kingdom will be preached in all the world as a witness to all the nations, and then the end will come" (Matthew 24:14).

The gospel *will* be preached all over the world. And *then* the end will come. That promise is echoed at the beginning of the three angel's messages. The first angel has the "everlasting gospel to preach to those who dwell on the earth—to every nation, tribe, tongue, and people" (Revelation 14:6).

Now when we look at places like America and Europe, it's not too hard to believe that the gospel can indeed reach every person.

But what about the remote corners of the earth? What about those isolated tribes and stone-age cultures? Can the gospel of Jesus Christ really reach every tribe, tongue, and people?

Let me share with you some of the ways God is finishing His work. Irian Jaya is one of the most isolated areas on earth. Half of the island used to be called New Guinea. Many of the tribes living in these mountains in the interior have only had contact with outsiders in the last few decades.

The Gospel of Jesus Christ *is* going to the remotest corners of the earth. It's building momentum. And it's doing so for only one reason: the power of God. The gospel is, after all, the story of the power of God. It's not just human strategy or human skill. It's His hand that is moving people's hearts—in every part of the earth.

Recently a team of four Adventists made a trek through the rocky hills and rivers of the central Philippines. They entered a completely isolated area inaccessible by motor vehicle. The people were animists who worshipped objects of nature.

After hiking through the jungle for eight hours they came to a village. And what did they find? They found a building already erected for the worship of God.

A villager had dreamed of a man dressed in white linen with shining shoes who said, "Build a big house for God and worship Him" He also said some people would be arriving who would teach "Bible truth." Another villager dreamed of a man telling her that the coming visitors were good people.

So these four Adventists began teaching about Jesus Christ and His gospel. The villagers accepted the message warmly. Soon there were twenty-four baptized believers to fill that "big house for God." Deep into the jungles of the island of Mindoro in the Philippines. The Olangan tribe has been untouchable but today they are accepting the gospel.

Can God's hand reach into the most inaccessible places of the earth? Beyond any doubt! We're seeing the fulfillment of that promise to the disciples:

> "you shall be witnesses to Me . . . to the end of the earth." Acts 1:8.

There's another reason the gospel is gathering tremendous momentum. Besides reaching remote, primitive areas, the gospel is doing something else that's remarkable. It's breaking down barriers that have stood for half a century. The iron curtain that closed off the communist world from Christian witness for so long has been shredded. And the gospel is rushing in to fill an enormous spiritual vacuum in the lives of millions.

Albania was long known as the most rigid and repressive of all the communist states. The bunkers built through the land, and the militant slogans proclaimed everywhere, seemed to completely isolate the Albanian people from the rest of the world. It was difficult to fathom how the gospel could ever penetrate the country. But now the gospel is reaching hearts in Albania.

After a recent Adventist evangelistic series, over 30 people made commitments to Christ. Christ's body is being built up. I have personally conducted evangelistic meetings in the former Communist countries of Poland, Hungary, Yugoslavia, Romania and Russia.

Russian army trucks delivered over 20,000 Bibles to the former Kremlin Palace of Communism for the many thousands who gathered there for our It Is Written Bible Prophecy presentations. Tens of thousands gathered at Moscow's Olympic Stadium to hear God's word.

In September of 1999, I spoke to over 4,000 people each evening in the former Congress of Communication Hall in Bucharest, Romania. Nicolae Ceausescu, one of the most ruthless dictators of all time, once used this auditorium to preach Communist propaganda to the masses. Now, God's power penetrates Communism's inner chambers. Our meetings were satellited using the most sophisticated equipment to all of Eastern and Western Europe.

Mongolia is another area of the world that has been almost completely cut off from the gospel. The land is frozen much of the year. The people have traditionally been suspicious of outsiders.

But that didn't stop a courageous young Adventist

couple, Brad and Cathie Jolly. In October of 1991 they began work trying to break down barriers in the city of Ulan Bator. They learned the language and adopted local customs. Brad and Cathie began meeting privately in their small flat with groups of young people. They had to keep a very low profile in order not to arouse the suspicions of authorities.

Two years later, their efforts culminated in one of the first baptisms in Mongolia in many decades. Brad Jolly became tragically sick and paid for his commitment with his own life. But the door is now open in Mongolia. During their first baptism, about 40 young people stood by as three individuals were lowered into the water and raised to newness of life, sealing their commitment to Jesus Christ.

But there's another reason that I'm very confident— even in the face of the world's growing population. That's because of what God has been doing through radio and television.

In January of 1994, Adventist World Radio began a powerful broadcast, from two 250-kilowatt transmitters in the new Republic of Slovakia. That station began regular 24-hour broadcasts of Christian programming in Arabic, Czech, English, French, German and in India's four major languages. That means we are now covering all of central and eastern Africa, all of India, and all of the Middle East with the good news of Jesus Christ.

Another powerful Adventist transmitter on the island of Guam sends radio programming over much of the Orient, including much of China. Then there's the newly-built Adventist Media Center in Tula, Russia. Gospel radio programs are sent out from there in 16 languages every day. These programs cover Southern Europe, much of Asia, and extend in China. They are transmitted through five of the Russian government's most powerful stations. Transmitters once used to jam radio signals coming in from the West, are now used to proclaim the gospel of Jesus Christ!

Yes, Jesus *is* coming again very soon. How do we know? Because the Gospel of Jesus Christ going to all the world is building momentum.

God wants you to be part of His mighty movement as we approach the end-times. He wants you to be caught up in the momentum of the Gospel of Jesus Christ.

We can accomplish so much more together than apart. Please don't settle for a merely private religion. Allegiance to Christ can't grow in a closet. Make your commitment open and public.

If we are to become a part of God's great end-time movement, we need to make a serious commitment of our whole lives, to Jesus Christ. And the way the New Testament says we do that is through baptism. Being immersed in Christ is how we start experiencing the fullness of Christ.

In baptism each of us may point our lives toward a new beginning. We are buried with Christ in order to rise up with Him to a new life, a life that includes complete forgiveness and real transformation.

We are given a new title, child of God, and counted as righteous in Christ. We receive all the rights and privileges of the our Elder Brother, Jesus, who marched confidently into heaven and into God's throne room after a triumphal life on earth.

Why not take that step and join Him one day soon! Make your commitment public. You can begin to enjoy the fullness of companionship with Jesus Christ. ❏